The Principle of Mutual Recognition in the European Integration Process

Also by Fiorella Kostoris Padoa Schioppa

REPORT ON THE STATE OF THE EUROPEAN UNION
(*with Jean-Paul Fitoussi*)

The Principle of Mutual Recognition in the European Integration Process

Edited by

Fiorella Kostoris Padoa Schioppa

palgrave
macmillan

First published in 2005 by
PALGRAVE MACMILLAN
Houndmills, Basingstoke, Hampshire RG21 6XS and
175 Fifth Avenue, New York, N.Y. 10010
Companies and representatives throughout the world.

PALGRAVE MACMILLAN is the global academic imprint of the Palgrave Macmillan division of St. Martin's Press, LLC and of Palgrave Macmillan Ltd. Macmillan® is a registered trademark in the United States, United Kingdom and other countries. Palgrave is a registered trademark in the European Union and other countries.

ISBN 13: 978–1–4039–3489–5
ISBN 10: 1–4039–3489–4

This book is printed on paper suitable for recycling and made from fully managed and sustained forest sources.

A catalogue record for this book is available from the British Library.

Library of Congress Cataloging-in-Publication Data
The principle of mutual recognition in the European integration process / edited by Fiorella Kostoris Padoa Schioppa.
p. cm.
Includes bibliographical references and index.
ISBN 1–4039–3489–4 (cloth)
1. Europe—Economic integration. 2. Mutualism—European Union countries. 3. European Union. 4. European Union countries—Relations. 5. European Union countries—International cooperation. I. Padoa Schioppa, Fiorella, 1945–
HC241.P75 2005
337.1′42—dc22 2004061948

10 9 8 7 6 5 4 3 2 1
14 13 12 11 10 09 08 07 06 05

Printed and bound in Great Britain by
Antony Rowe Ltd, Chippenham and Eastbourne

Contents

Notes on the Contributors

Alfonso Mattera is a Special Adviser to the President of European Commission, former Deputy Director-General for the Internal Market, European Commission, and Professor at the European Colleges of Bruges and Parma, and at the University 'LUISS – Guido Carli' of Rome.

Kalypso Nicolaïdis is a University Lecturer in International Relations, at Oxford University, UK.

Fiorella Kostoris Padoa Schioppa is a Professor at the University of Rome 'La Sapienza', Faculty of Economics, Department of Public Economics.

Jacques Pelkmans holds the Jan Tinbergen Chair and is director of the economics department at the College of Europe, Bruges; he is a Council Member at the WRR, The Hague.

Joseph H.H. Weiler is University Professor and Director of the Global Law School Program at NYU School of Law.

List of Abbreviations

ASEAN	Association of South East Asian Nations
APEC	Asia-Pacific Economic Co-operation
CEN	Comité Européen de Normalization
CENELEC	Comité Européen de Coordination des Normes Electriques
EC	European Community
ECJ	European Court of Justice
FDI	Foreign Direct Investment
GATS	General Agreement on Trade in Services
GATT	General Agreement on Tariffs and Trade
MFN	Most Favoured Nation
NAFTA	North American Free Trade Association
OECD	Organisation for Economic Co-operation and Development
QMV	Qualified Majority Voting
SMEs	Small and Medium Enterprises
UNCTAD	United Nations Conference on Trade and Development
UNESCO	United Nations Educational, Scientific, and Cultural Organization
WTO	World Trade Organization

Preface

> Thou shalt neither vex a stranger, nor oppress him: for ye were strangers in the land of Egypt.
>
> *Exodus* 22, 21

> HERALD OF AEGYPTUS
> The prey is mine, unless force rend it from me. ...
>
> THE KING OF ARGOS
> Know that if words unstained by violence
> Can change these maidens' choice, then mayest thou,
> With full consent of theirs, conduct them hence.
> But thus the city with one voice ordained-
> No force shall bear away the maiden band...
>
> DANAUS
> Ye, to the many words of wariness
> Spoken by me your father, add this word,
> That, tried by time, our unknown company
> Be held for honest: over-swift are tongues
> To slander strangers, over-light is speech
> To bring pollution on a stranger's name.
>
> Aeschylus (VI b.c.), *The Suppliants*

'The man who finds his country sweet is only a raw beginner; the man for whom each country is as his own is already strong; but only the man for whom the whole world is as a foreign country is perfect' (myself, a Bulgarian living in France, borrow this quotation from Edward Said, a Palestinian living in the United States, who himself found it in Erich Auerbach, a German exiled in Turkey).

T. Todorov (1992), *The Conquest of America*

[And in turn myself, the daughter of a Greek-speaking mother, a German-speaking father and four grandparents of different nationalities, none of which is Italian, borrow the quotation.]

From an historical, logical and cultural point of view – as Chapter 6 of this volume shows – there are three forms of integration of the 'alien' into an 'homogeneous' Community of nationals, who have been residing in a country 'for ever':

- *Ghettoization* or *apartheid*, where diversity is recognized but not valued and is therefore even marginalized to the point of segregating it completely from the core society.
- *Assimilation* (in the forms of *closed* or *open*), where diversity is not accepted, it has no value (in the closed form), or has a limited value (in its open form); therefore it is completely (or partially) unrecognized or even eliminated to the point that the minority is fully assimilated into the identity of the triumphant majority (or in a process of osmosis and transformation the minority adopts the manners of the majority, but the latter changes to a limited extent when in contact with the minority).
- *Mutual recognition*, accepting and valuing diversity without segregating it; this is a more significant phenomenon than tolerance, because tolerance implies asymmetry between the tolerator and the tolerated, while in mutual recognition there is a reciprocal respect.

In the postwar process of its economic and social construction, the European Union has been following different paths ranging between open assimilation to mutual recognition. The former arises in the attempts, either negotiated between partners or proposed by Community institutions, to attain harmonization, coordination, convergence or strengthened cooperation, through peer pressures or moral suasion, looking at benchmarks or at best practices.[1] These are all forms of mediation, compromise and variable geometry between Member States, which show a certain degree of success, but also many failures, mainly because they are unable to accept unity in diversity making the large and existing heterogeneity in Europe a form not of weakness but of wealth. Yet on philosophical – though not on historical-grounds, it has been clear in Europe at least in the last 2,500 years that 'from the strain of binding opposites comes harmony', as the Greek Heraclitus was saying. Few centuries later, the Latin poet Horace was using the oxymoron '*concordia discors*' to convey a similar message. This is indeed the very gist of the principle of mutual recognition: its symbolic value can be easily perceived simply by thinking that, if the American currency bears the caption '*ex pluribus unum*', the euro motto becomes 'unity in diversity', as stated in her 4 May 2000 speech by Mme. Nicole Fontaine, Chairperson of the European Parliament; and, more generally, in the European Constitutional Treaty, approved by the Brussels Intergovernmental

Conference of 18 June 2004, it is written that the Union motto is '*unity in diversity*'.

Mutual recognition has irreversibly entered the European Union markets since the 1979 famous European Court of Justice (ECJ) ruling, *Cassis de Dijon*. Up to then, the sale of *Cassis* was forbidden in Germany, as German law envisaged a mandatory minimum alcohol content for alcoholic beverages to be marketed, while the *Cassis* had a lower alcohol content: strangely enough, the proliferation of low alcohol percentages was thought to induce an addiction towards alcohol more than highly alcoholic beverages. This provision, hampering the import of *Cassis de Dijon* originating in France, was alleged to protect German consumers, but in fact was likely to protect the interest of beer producers. Since 1979, one cannot state that, if *Cassis de Dijon* is not damaging French citizens, it could damage German people. Each State of the Union is free in choosing its own regulation, but in a system based on mutual recognition, when importing a good, it has to acknowledge the rules adopted by others and, if national standards are different from foreigners', the sending (home) country and not the receiving (host) country rules have to be applied within Europe. The presumption has to be that goods, services and capital produced by each of the Member States with a different regulation can and must have access to all Union countries, provided that in their home country they do not damage the consumers' health, do not cause irreversible harm to the natural and artistic environment, and protect ownership and economic agents in incomplete and asymmetric information. A new approach based on the respect of different national regulations is, therefore, emerging: each legislation has its own (same and different) ways to protect public interests. Thus, harmonization is not always necessary for European construction and in any case must limit itself to minimum, often optional, elements concerning only fundamental aspects. Moreover, mutual recognition, being an instrument of competition in regulation, in the end leads to regulation convergence within the European Union without any top-down harmonization process.

The ECJ 1979 ruling on *Cassis de Dijon* has prompted an innovative and effective convergence process in the commodity, service and capital sectors: the latter derives from the elimination of barriers to entry, from the competition of different standards and country-systems, with consequent enhancing of the goods' quality and quantity, cost-reduction and knowledge enlargement. Thus, mutual recognition helps the Union in finding its original spirit; namely, making competition an harmonious instrument for economic, social and civil development, where efficiency and equity grow together. Such a principle is therefore perfectly consistent with the traditional instruments and objectives as well as with the new challenges of the European construction. It helps to promote the completion of the internal market and to approach the 2010 targets established by the Lisbon (2000) agenda, in order to transform Europe in the 'most competitive and dynamic knowledge-based economy in the world capable of sustainable economic growth with more and better jobs and greater social cohesion'.[2]

The principle of mutual recognition, by revealing the acceptance of the sovereignty of European Member States and of their rules on a perfectly equal basis, is not only already operational in many fields, but it is also potentially applicable in various others, from economics to law, from private markets to welfare states. Indeed, we share the idea of Delors' White Paper on the internal market (European Commission, 1985) that 'mutual recognition of national provisions, according to agreed procedures, should be the fundamental principle' on European markets.[3] It is no coincidence that, as stressed in the Presidency Conclusions of the European Council in Tampere (European Council, 1999), the Union is widening its scope, even going towards 'enhanced mutual recognition of judicial decisions ... The European Council therefore endorses the principle of mutual recognition which, in its view, should become the cornerstone of judicial co-operation in both civil and criminal matters within the Union. The principle should apply both to judgments and to other decisions of judicial authorities' (Point. 33 of the 'Concluding Remarks').[4]

The principle of mutual recognition could have an even larger potential utilization in the European future, after the enlargement of the Union to 25 countries since 1 May 2004. It could provide a decisive support to establishing an area truly without frontiers between and within Western and Central-Eastern Europe, where the free movement of goods, services, people and capital would be ensured. From this viewpoint it is really a pity that mutual recognition has not been included in the new European Constitutional Treaty, in particular in one of the first 59 articles of Part 1, addressed to basic principles with far-reaching consequences.

This book is mainly focused on law- and economic matters. It includes six chapters, four of which were presented in a preliminary form in a Conference in Rome I organized at ISAE in 2002.[5] The first two chapters illustrate the most important European norms on mutual recognition, the third and the fourth describe the actual adoption of that principle in the European commodity and service markets, including professional services of the highly qualified self-employed, the fifth chapter is dedicated to the proposal of an innovative utilization of that principle in European labour markets and welfare states, so as to reduce unemployment and raise the well-being of people.

The historical foundations of mutual recognition are sketched by Mattera in Chapter 1 and, to some extent, by myself in Chapter 6, together with the philosophical foundations. In his opinion the old Roman model imposing 'unity not uniformity' paves the way to mutual recognition in Europe. Mattera then illustrates the most important articles of the European Treaty indirectly referring to that principle, reminding that mutual recognition as such 'was never spelt out in any of the European Treaties signed to date'. He considers that one could hardly overemphasize the relevance of mutual recognition for Europe not only to safeguard its national, regional and local identities and traditions, but also to establish and complete the internal market and to implement the major other policy-interventions including those for 'the creation of an internal justice and security area'.

As a certain degree of mutual recognition appears to characterize all the five authors contributing to this volume in their different opinions regarding the whole issue under examination, no wonder that Weiler in Chapter 2 is critical in various respects relative to Mattera. First he explains why he prefers another lexicon where the formula of 'functional equivalence' is a substitute for the traditional wording of mutual recognition. He then summarizes the complete European jurisprudence on mutual recognition according to a five-generation history of ECJ cases, from the mid-60s to the late 90s, indicating the changing attitude of the Court over this time from a more radical market integration approach to one more respectful of national regulatory autonomy. He argues that in the ECJ decisions the switching is observed from an attitude consisting in opposing discrimination and protectionism to a more pro-active concern tending to eliminate unjustified obstacles to free trade. Consequently Weiler states that 'mutual recognition or parallel functionalism was perhaps an intellectual breakthrough but a colossal market failure ... goods which do not meet the technical standards of the importing country may not be marketed ... There are genuine differences ... where there is no functional parallelism. In this case harmonization is simply required.'

Pelkmans examines in Chapter 3 costs and benefits of the mutual recognition application to European commodity and service markets. After noticing that there are 'three ways of realizing free movements of goods in the internal market: liberalization, approximation and mutual recognition', he remarks that the latter has strategic advantages and facilitates economic intercourse across borders without sacrificing essential regulatory objectives such as health, safety, environment and consumer protection. According to Pelkmans' analysis, 'mutual recognition in homogeneous goods markets tends to be strongly pro-competitive whereas in differentiated goods markets there are likely to be forceful incentives for trading up, the opposite of a race-to-the-bottom'. In the service sector, however, he believes that the adoption of mutual recognition is more rare, as competitive pressures are lower for example for non-tradables, some services such as transport are highly regulated, information costs are higher. In general Pelkmans remarks that there exists a curious paradox: despite the almost universal acclaim of mutual recognition merits, the applications in the European internal market for goods and services have not been an unambiguous success story, because information, transaction and compliance costs are not negligible. Thus, 25 years after the *Cassis de Dijon* ruling 'mutual recognition covers about half of intra-EC industrial trade, but it only matters for the 30 per cent of intra-EC trade for which national regulations exist'.

Another paradox is outlined in Chapter 4 by Nicolaïdis, relative to productive factors: while capital flows freely move across borders not only within Europe but more generally in the global economy, the international movement of people appears to be 'managed'. Even persons with professional training (doctors, engineers, accountants, architects etc.), able to supply cheaper but equally qualified self-employed labour relative to that existing in receiving countries face numerous obstacles if not binding constraints, even though host member states would benefit from their professional services. This is because the mutual recognition of qualifications, licensing, certification requirements, necessary to enhance the capacity of foreign highly skilled independent workers to exercise their activities across borders is far from being completed. Nicolaïdis draws the historical sequence of alternative paradigms on professional services which have been emerging in the European experience. She indicates that the first step was the 1957 Directive on the mutual recognition of diplomas, certificates and other evidence of formal qualification both for the purpose of freedom of establishment and the free movement of services, erroneously interpreted until the mid-70s as if it required the full harmonization of professional training standards as a prerequisite for the mutual recognition of diplomas. A second paradigm has followed since the mid-70s, replacing the above-mentioned quantitative with a qualitative harmonization: equivalence of diplomas were then based not on their similarity but on their comparability. A third paradigm started in the early 80s delinking mutual recognition from harmonization: without entering into the complexities of each particular profession, in 1984 European heads of states and governments declared to be in favour of a general system 'ensuring the equivalence of university diplomas, in order to bring about the effective freedom of establishment within the Community'. Nicolaïdis thinks that in order to fully promote a managed mutual recognition of professional self-employed in Europe, four dimensions should be fulfilled: 'prior conditions for equivalence, automaticity, scope, and ex-post guarantees'.

But perhaps the most worrying paradox concerning this whole subject is mentioned in my Chapter 5. Unlike what happens in the commodity, capital, service markets – including professional services – where mutual recognition is at least to a certain extent adopted, in the European labour markets precisely the opposite principle holds true, so-named 'equal treatment', and mutual recognition is on the contrary labelled 'social dumping'. Thus, the host and not the home country principle is always enforced. A concrete example of the negative consequences of such an attitude for the well-being of Europeans refers to the implications of inhibiting Eastern German job-seekers after the Berlin wall fell to work in the Western Germany building sector at lower wages and less privileged conditions than the Western resident workers, as they would have liked, therefore reducing the demand for their unskilled labour, their employment and income, at the same time increasing the price of Western houses. On logical grounds Chapter 5 shows how questionable it is that 'a German firm today can import the *Cassis* from Dijon, but if it asks Dijon workers to emigrate to Germany and produce the *Cassis* in the Rhine valley, it cannot pay them the French wage, granting the French national holiday of 14 July and promising the French pension ... This almost absurd situation stems from a peculiar interpretation of the principle of equal treatment ... the factual result is to protect national workers from other European workers' potential competition.' Without denying and indeed pledging for non-discrimination in European welfare states and labour markets, Chapter 5 not only indicates that, according to the so-called equal treatment, current legislation denies the right of diversity in the receiving country, assimilation remaining the only feasible solution for workers, but more importantly it proves that if mutual recognition were adopted in the European labour markets, mobility would rise and unemployment would decline in the Union, increasing the level of equity and efficiency of all our societies.

FIORELLA KOSTORIS PADOA SCHIOPPA

Notes

1 On this issue, see Padoa Schioppa, F. Kostoris (ed.), *Rapporto sullo stato dell'-Unione Europea*, ISAE, Roma, 2001 and 2002.
2 European Council, *Presidency Conclusions*, Lisbon, 23 and 24 March 2000.
3 Commission of the European Communities, *Completing the Internal Market: White Paper from the Commission to the European Council*, COM(85) 310 final, 1985.
4 European Council, *Presidency Conclusions*, Tampere, 15 and 16 October 1999.
5 I gratefully acknowledge the great collaboration I received on occasion and immediately after by Doctor Beatrice Mariani.

4. [illegible]

1
The Principle of Mutual Recognition and Respect for National, Regional and Local Identities and Traditions

Alfonso Mattera

A European Union obsessed with standardization?

The European Commission: a scapegoat *par excellence*

Politicians, journalists, writers and sometimes even representatives of trade unions and economists accuse the European Union of creating a 'superstate', a sort of centralized and spendthrift 'welfare state' whose rules and actions tend to merge and homogenize identities, traditions and national, regional and local features.

Indeed, some journalists have provided examples – sometimes distorted or even invented – accusing Brussels officials of being pedantic, vaudeville-like interventionists. Legions of Eurocrats would produce mountains of useless and complicated rules and regulations born of a 'regulatory madness', with the sole aim of tormenting European citizens and firms. In this way, the European Commission in particular has become a scapegoat *par excellence* and the favourite target of policy-makers and journalists who accuse it of being the main cause of all problems affecting present-day society. The harm done by the European Commission is sometimes even paradoxical or has become a caricature.

As Commission President Romano Prodi recently indicated in an article published in the *Corriere della Sera* on 15 March 2002, 'nothing could be more wrong than this artificial image of an invasive and tyrannical Europe that too many people disseminate out of personal interest, comfort or simply ignorance'.

Euromyths and tales

The European Union and in particular the Commission have recently been accused of imposing the use of English to the detriment of other languages, and one writer has asked the following question: 'Will we continue to teach in French in France (and in Italian in Italy, in Danish in Denmark, in Greek in Greece)?' We shall come back to this question later.

With regard to languages, some years ago one of the most prestigious Spanish newspapers devoted its front page to a sensational piece of news: the European Commission was about to launch a campaign to standardize keyboards and intended to do away with the Spanish 'ñ'. As a result – *horribile dictu* – even the very name 'España' would become 'Espagna'. The reaction of Spanish readers was one of surprise, indignation and revolt. This was a fine scoop worthy of mention.

Another report that made a stir was that an Italian politician who had been harshly criticized by his fellow countrymen for having transformed national car registration plates into 'anonymous' plates bearing just a few letters and numbers (they used to carry the first two letters of the city of origin followed by numbers) accused the 'Brussels administration' of undermining local identity and the feeling of attachment to one's place of origin, a deceptive ploy attributable to his desperate search for an alibi.

Recently, the European Commission was accused of rejecting the proposal from a national government to reduce VAT on catering services from 19.6 per cent to 5.5 per cent. It pointed out that it was a decision taken unanimously by the 15 European Finance Ministers which set the tax at 19.6 per cent and that the decision had to be complied with until amended by the EU Council of Ministers. Indeed, in its original proposal the Commission had proposed that it be left to Member States to decide whether or not to apply the reduced tax, but the then Minister of the country concerned had opposed that proposal because the reduced tax rates would benefit the rich.[1]

An eminent Italian journalist recently wrote in one of the most respected Italian newspapers that the European Commission was drafting a directive that would standardize the colour of taxis throughout Europe. In the past, that same Commission had allegedly posed a similar threat to the ingredients of pasta and certain types of cheese and was also intent on laying down a uniform shape for bananas and a specific colour for watermelons ...

Recently, a politician in a Member State denounced the move towards a European technocratic superpower that would lead to the disappearance of national sovereignty, revealing at the same time the existence of a 'mysterious plot paving the way for a future Constitution and not dissimilar to intrigue of the kind described in Umberto Eco's *The Name of the Rose*'. Fortunately, another eminent member of the same government contradicted him.

The examples are so numerous that they could be assembled in a report ... for the pleasure of those who like to read fairy tales or who wish to profit most from Voltaire's warning 'Lie, lie, something will remain.'

The opinion of a wise observer

With regard to the ideas and lies circulating about 'Brussels Eurocrats', it is interesting to note a neutral comment by Yann de l'Ecotais, a well-known writer and journalist and a wise observer of European matters. In his book,[2] he decries the situation in which:

> many policymakers become accomplices to an enormous fraud: namely, they let public opinion believe that 'Europe' is a frightening bureaucratic mechanism and that there, in Brussels, cohorts of irresponsible officials regulate, hamper, impose, destroy. When they work in Paris or in Perpignan, they are simply 'directors' or 'managers' but, as soon as they cross frontiers and move 300 kilometers away from the headquarters of the French administration, they become 'Eurocrats' and immediately lose their sense of reality ...
>
> As for the excessive number of European officials, the French complaint simply sounds paradoxical: the entire Community civil service comprises 20,000 people. The French customs alone have more employees than all the Commission departments in Brussels put together ...
>
> Do those Eurocrats govern us? Clearly, they don't. They only have the authority conferred on them by Member State governments under a political agreement ... European bureaucracy does not govern Europe. National bureaucracies are trying to impede Europe because they feel – and rightly so as far as they are concerned – that, for them, it will be the beginning of the end ... There is a suffocating bureaucracy in Europe, but it is not in Brussels, it is in national capitals.

On the question of the 'cohorts of European officials', let me add that one-third of the 20,000 European officials are employed in the translation and interpreting departments because all official acts are translated into all the Community languages, and Member States' representatives may express themselves in their own language. This means that the Community is helping to safeguard one of the fundamental features of national identity, namely language. Indeed, when quoting the figure of 20,000 officials, one has to take account of these aspects and the real number of officials should be made known.

In responding to one of the stories circulating for some time (that is, 'the European Commission is an expensive and useless bureaucracy', as denounced by Franco Tatò in the *Corriere della Sera,* 9 July 2002), the President of the European Commission Romano Prodi (*Corriere della Sera,* 10 July 2002), referring to the number of officials working for the institution he heads, stressed that:

> the number of officials at the Commission corresponds to that of the municipal administration of any medium-sized European town. Indeed, 20,000 European officials look after – among other things – on behalf of 300 million European citizens the control of public budgets, the management and smooth functioning of the European Single Market, of fair competition, of international trade relations, of the common agricultural policy, of regional development, of policies to assist developing countries, and of many other European policies conducive to EU enlargement, the creation of a European area of security and justice, of a common foreign and security policy, of a common justice policy, etc. Do you know the size of the Community budget allocated to all those policies? It corresponds to 1.2% of the GDP of Member States. Yes, 1.2%!

While these examples clearly show that 'the Brussels administration' provides a first-class alibi for politicians and managers and becomes a favourite target for journalists, we feel that it would be expedient to bring a number of observations and certain data to the attention of readers less familiar with these phenomena.

It must not be forgotten that, within the framework of the Community legislative procedure, the Commission has only a right of initiative. The legislative power belongs to the Council and to the European Parliament, which may reject proposals. Indeed, most proposals do not emanate from creative initiatives but are in response to specific matters raised by Member States, the Council and the European Parliament. Member states sometimes ask the Commission to draw up draft legislation even though there is no pressing need to do so.

A study carried out by the Commission – the results of which were published in 1996 – found that in the period 1960–95 the Community approved 415 pieces of legislation on products, whereas in the period 1992–94 Member States placed 1,136 laws on the statute book (excluding national laws transposing Community directives). The three Member States which joined the Community most recently (Austria, Sweden and Finland) and are far from being addicted to rules and regulations adopted in 1994 alone more rules (475) than the Community did in the previous 35 years.

To label this approach as 'regulatory madness' is perhaps no more than the Freudian manifestation of regulatory overload in some Member States.[3]

From the Europe of the Roman Empire to the European Community: some common principles

The principle of 'unity but not uniformity' inherited from the Roman Empire

The Europe of the Roman Empire embodied a model of civilization which we define as Graeco-Roman and which was based on values that permeated the very nature of the European peoples to such an extent they are still clearly distinguishable today. Those values were embodied in certain principles, namely:

- A '*civitas romana*' (Roman citizenship) granted in the year AD 212 by the Emperor Caracalla to all the citizens of the Roman Empire. The granting of Roman citizenship implied full and equal treatment in terms of freedoms, rights and obligations for all citizens of the Empire.
- A common language (Latin), which is the historical memory of the Europeans and which lies at the heart of all European languages. Latin did not replace the local languages, which remained alive.
- For some two hundred years, the Roman Empire guaranteed its peoples an unprecedented period of peace (the *pax romana*), prosperity and security.
- The most remarkable characteristic of ancient Rome is respect for the identities and diversity of its conquered peoples. The Roman Empire was a sort of federation of autonomous cities. The control and tutelage exercised by Rome were not oppressive. The Roman model was based on the principle of 'unity but not uniformity', which paves the way for the principle of mutual recognition.

The capitularies of Carolingian Europe

The concept of 'Europe' which stems from the culture of the Middle Ages has an eminently geographical meaning. With Charlemagne, it acquired a political meaning to such an extent that some historians see in the Carolingian Emperor the first European. The poet Angilbert called him the 'King and Father of Europe'.

Charlemagne enforced the first 'European policies' by adopting a series of ordinances called 'capitularies' in the political, economic, cultural and even ecclesiastic spheres. Those ordinances applied to all citizens of Europe regardless. They did not replace the rules and regulations which were already enforced in the conquered countries, but adapted to them in the light of local practices and traditions. This was the Carolingian principle of mutual recognition.

The European Community

Those who know (even roughly) the history of the European Union cannot be unaware that, since 1980, the Commission and the other European institutions have pursued a new political and legislative approach based on respect for diversity, for traditions and for specific national, regional and local characteristics. This new approach is based on the implementation of the principle of mutual recognition, derived from the Court of Justice ruling in the *Cassis de Dijon* case. As some authoritative studies – particularly American – have demonstrated, enforcement of that principle has profoundly altered the European Union and the legislation, policies and model of society which it advocates.

The principle of mutual recognition as such was never spelt out in any of the European Treaties signed to date (Treaty of Rome, Single European Act, Treaty of Maastricht, Treaty of Amsterdam and Treaty of Nice). It derives from two articles of the EC Treaty, namely:

- Article 47 (ex Article 57), whereby 'in order to make it easier for persons to take up and pursue activities as self-employed persons, the Council shall, acting in accordance with the procedure referred to in Article 251, issue directives for the mutual recognition of diplomas, certificates and other evidence of formal qualifications'.
- Article 293 (ex Article 220), whereby 'Member States shall, so far as is necessary, enter into negotiations with each other with a view to securing for the benefit of their nationals ... the mutual recognition of companies or firms within the meaning of the second Paragraph of Article 48, the retention of legal personality in the event of transfer of their seat from one country to another, and the possibility of mergers between companies or firms governed by the laws of different countries'.

Admittedly, these provisions merely identify objectives which policy-makers have to attain. They are not rules stating a general principle.

The principle of mutual recognition stemmed from the judgment given by the Court of Justice on 20 February 1979 in Case 120/78 (*Cassis de Dijon*) and then confirmed and developed by the ensuing legislation. We shall briefly describe the approach that was followed before that judgment, its content and importance and the policies adopted by the EU institutions to implement that principle.

The judgment in *Cassis de Dijon*

The traditional approach

According to the traditional approach adopted by the Commission and by other European institutions before the judgment in *Cassis de Dijon*, directives were aimed at harmonizing and standardizing different national laws, regulations and administrative provisions of Member States pursuant to Article 94 (ex Article 100) of the EU Treaty. This also extended to the freedom to provide services and the right of establishment, particularly where the regulated professions were concerned.

Directives unanimously approved by the Council on the basis of that article in the 1960s and the 1970s followed that approach. They were known as 'vertical' directives and defined the technical or qualitative characteristics of products or the content or duration of vocational training courses. With regard to products, it was a fully fledged strategy of approximation and harmonization that led to the creation of a group of 'Europroducts', namely Eurojam, Eurochocolate, Eurojuice, Eurocristals, Eurothermometers and the like. At the same time, the Single Market towards which that approach was leading became a sort of melting pot in which the traditional and typical products of each member state were submerged.

In turn, the Commission attempted to bring about a radical change in terms of the options and methodology for adapting Directive 70/50/CEE of December 1969, and in particular Article 3, which had anticipated the principle adopted by the Court in *Cassis de Dijon*. A close reading of that Directive and of points 8, 9, 10 and 11, which clarify it, reveals the profound similarity between its provisions and the principles laid down by the Court of Justice in its 1979 judgment. Indeed, a judge of the Court of Justice reached the same conclusion in an article on this subject.[4]

It needs to be recognized that, while adopting this new approach, the Commission had not drawn all the necessary conclusions, even though the traditional approach continued to be applied up to 1980.

The sources

The fundamental principle stemming from the case law in *Cassis de Dijon*, which is a benchmark for the Commission's action with regard both to the elimination and prevention of obstacles to free trade and to the establishment of the Single Market in general, is the acceptance on the part of each Member State of any product which has been lawfully produced and marketed in another Member State, even if it has been produced according to different technical or quality standards, in so far as it meets the legitimate objective which the legislation is designed to achieve.

The Commission spelt out and explained this principle in its interpretative communication on the consequences of the judgment given by the Court of Justice in *Cassis de Dijon*. In particular, the Commission reiterated that, following the *Cassis de Dijon* judgment, the principle of acceptance of any product lawfully produced and marketed in one Member State implies that:

> Member States, when drawing up commercial or technical rules liable to affect the free movement of goods, may not take an exclusively national viewpoint and take account only of requirements confined to domestic products. The proper functioning of the common market demands that each Member State also give consideration to the legitimate requirements of the other Member States.

The Commission also stresses that the 'acceptance of products lawfully produced' within the Community implies the 'mutual recognition' of technical rules, procedures and certificates imposed by other Member States to guarantee a level of protection equivalent to the one set by the importing country:

> The principle deduced by the Court implies that a Member State may not in principle prohibit the sale in its territory of a product lawfully produced and marketed in another Member State even if the product is produced according to technical or quality requirements which differ from those imposed on its domestic products. Where a product 'suitably and satisfactorily' fulfils the legitimate objective of a Member State's own rules (public safety, protection of the consumer or the environment, etc.), the importing country cannot justify prohibiting

its sale in its territory by claiming that the way it fulfils the objective is different from that imposed on domestic products.

In such a case, an absolute prohibition of sale could not be considered 'necessary' to satisfy a 'mandatory requirement' because it would not be an 'essential guarantee' in the sense defined in the Court's judgment.

This is the core of the problem and of the legislation on *Cassis de Dijon* and the innovative principles stemming from it, including the principle of 'mutual recognition of rules and processes of manufacturing, of equivalent controls and certifications of products'. While stating this principle bravely and clearly since 1980, the Commission has underlined its importance for the establishment of the common market.

The principle of mutual recognition stems from the *Cassis de Dijon* jurisprudence and, in particular, from some judgments of the Court of Justice concerning:

- the equivalence of technical rules and specifications (*Woodworking machines* judgment);
- the procedure which Member States have to follow (*Sandoz* and *Beer Purity Law* judgments) for the acceptance of products from other member states;
- the recognition of controls, tests and equivalent analyses already made in other Member States (*Biologische Produkten* judgment);
- acceptance of certificates provided by officially recognized laboratories in other Member States (*Bouchara* judgment).

Below are relevant extracts from these judgments.

In *Biologische Produkten* (judgment of 17 December 1981 in Case 272/80 Frans-Nederlandse Maatschappij voor Biologische Produkten [1981] ECR 3277), the Court underscores the fact that:

> Whilst a Member State is free to require a product ... which has already received approval in another Member State, to undergo a fresh procedure of examination and approval, the authorities of the Member States are nevertheless required to assist in bringing about a relaxation of the controls existing in intra-Community trade. It follows that they are not entitled unnecessarily to require ... laboratory tests where those ... tests have already been carried out in another Member State and their results are available to those authorities, or may at their request be placed at their disposal.

> For the same reasons, a Member State operating an approvals procedure must ensure that no unnecessary control expenses are incurred if the practical effects of the control carried out in the Member State of origin satisfy the requirements ... in the importing Member State. (Paragraphs 14 and 15)

In *Woodworking machines* (judgment of 28 January 1986 in Case 188/84 *Commission of the European Communities* v. *France* [1986] ECR 419), the Court stresses the principle that a Member State:

> is not entitled to prevent the marketing of a product originating in another Member State which provides a level of protection of the health and life of humans equivalent to that which the national rules are intended to ensure or establish. It is therefore contrary to the principle of proportionality for national rules to require such imported products to comply strictly and exactly with the provisions or technical requirements laid down for products manufactured in the Member State in question when those imported products afford users the same level of protection. (Paragraph 16)

In *Bouchara* (judgment of 11 May 1989 in Case 25/88), the Court states that:

> the authorities of the State of importation are however not entitled unnecessarily to require technical or chemical analyses when the same analyses or tests have already been carried out in another Member State and their results are available to those authorities. That rule is a particular application of a more general principle of mutual trust between the authorities of Member States and must therefore also apply when the verification is the responsibility of the importer himself. It follows that the latter must be able to discharge his responsibility by producing a certificate concerning the composition of the product issued by the authorities of the Member State of production or by a laboratory authorized to issue such certificates by those authorities. (Paragraph 18)
>
> ... or, if the legislation of that Member State [of origin] does not require the production of such certificates, on other attestations providing a like degree of assurance. (Paragraph 20)

In this last judgment, the Court underlines that the acceptance on the part of a Member State of the controls, laboratory tests and analyses carried out by other Member States is a specific expression of the principle of 'mutual confidence', which is the basis of the principle of 'mutual recognition'. The adoption of those principles constitutes an exceptional element of cohesion and integration between States which, in spite of their different traditions and legislations, have common cultural and scientific roots and belong to the same Community, which is held together by links stemming from a common-body legislation, common institutions and a supranational jurisdiction within which rulings apply to all states. Hence, the 'guarantees offered' are such that, even in the absence of common rules and regulations, they justify the need for each Member State to exhibit confidence in its 'neighbour' and in its legislation, administrative structures, control bodies and procedures.

In the absence of Community rules and regulations, Member States may require that imported products comply with those provisions, but within the limits mapped out by the Court and listed earlier. This means in particular that a Member State cannot require compliance with either a 'standard' not based on scientifically acceptable principles, or a standard not justified by attainment of the underlying objective.

Observance of the 'principle of proportionality', which is the basis of the philosophy pursued in this area, requires that the instruments adopted take into account the coexistence of two needs; namely, free movement of goods on the one hand, and protection of the health and life of individuals and other legitimate objectives on the other. Indeed, if a Member State adopts an instrument aimed at establishing an excessive level of protection to the detriment of the free movement of goods, there is *no equilibrium between 'instruments' and 'objectives'*.

Finally, enforcement of these principles means that Member States cannot require imported products to comply with a standard 'equivalent' to the one imposed on national products if this is excessive compared with the objective in mind or if it accords preference to one need (for example health protection) over another (for example free movement of goods).

In its interpretative communication of 3 October 1980, the Commission states that Member States cannot deny access to national markets for imported products produced on the basis of the technical provisions applicable in other Member States in so far as they are produced 'suitably and satisfactorily' and fulfill the legitimate objective. That translates into practice the need to respect both the 'principle of equivalence' and the 'principle of adjustment' (or 'proportionality') between national standards by fulfilling legitimate objectives and the fundamental principle of free movement of goods contained in the Treaty.

The new approach

In its above-mentioned interpretative communication, the Commission proposes a new approach based on respect for national diversity.

The opportunity to launch that initiative was provided by a debate held in September 1979 in the European Parliament on the Internal Market, the establishment of which was being hampered by legislation based on the approximation of national laws. M. Davignon, the then Commissioner responsible for the Internal Market, had underlined the pressing need to create a European open space which could help to bring an end to the vicious circle of 'protectionism and economic crisis' which the Community was experiencing. He had himself undertaken to devise a new policy which explored the scope for action afforded by the *Cassis de Dijon* ruling. That was the enormous challenge of establishing an Internal Market. The European Parliament overwhelmingly welcomed M. Davignon's undertaking and his new approach. During the debate, M. Davignon, whom I had the honour to assist and advise, charged me with the task of drafting a 'dynamic' interpretative document on the *Cassis de Dijon* ruling, spelling out some operational guidelines and bringing them together in a transparent instrument. That was the birth of the Commission's interpretative communication, which was drawn up one year later on the basis of my interpretative note.

When it issued that communication and then, some years later, the White Paper on establishing the Internal Market, the Commission clearly indicated that, within that market, national and regional features had to be safeguarded because they were a source of richness for the entire Community. Martin Bangemann, Vice-President of the Commission, who was responsible for implementation of the action programme for establishing the European Single Market by the deadline of 31 December 1992, stated that the *Cassis de Dijon* ruling and the principle of mutual recognition which stemmed from it would never have had the impact on trade liberalization and on the new approach towards establishing an Internal Market that it did have if the Commission had not taken the initiative of setting out and explaining in its interpretative communication the principles and guidelines it had in mind and the actions it wished to take. Mr Bangemann added that the 300 Directives contained in the White Paper 'should never make one forget the 3000 directives saved by the introduction of the new political approach based on mutual recognition'.[5]

The abundant legislation which followed that judgment confirmed the guidelines contained in the communication and the justified nature of the new approach towards establishing and ensuring the smooth functioning of the Internal Market.[6]

The instruments for implementing the principle of mutual recognition

There are four facets to the new policy adopted by the Commission and the action programme through which it was enforced.

Eliminating any feudal servitude belonging to an autarkic past

Since 1980 a gradual process has been underway, based on Article 28 (ex Article 30) of the Treaty, aimed at adapting many sectors of national legislation (the famous 'recipe laws' concerning foodstuffs and the 'type-approval' techniques in the industrial sector) to the new principles under the new politico-legal and cultural approach. The aim has been to safeguard the acceptance of national diversity. It is worth underlining that that approach did not imply the dismantling of national 'recipe laws', which all too often had become part of the traditions of a country (take, for instance, the laws on beer purity in Germany or pasta ingredients in Italy), or of 'type-approval' techniques. National legislation continued to regulate national products; traditional products were safeguarded. However, Member States were required to incorporate in their legislation a clause to the effect that they accepted products lawfully produced and marketed in other Member States, even if they had been produced according to different technical or quality standards.

It is the consumer who makes his or her own choice from among a wide range of products from different countries, regions and territories of the Community. This brought to an end all the trappings of feudal servitude and all the royal prerogatives of nation states, which had been designed to crystallize consumers' habits by imposing product types corresponding to a national recipe or technical standard with the sole aim of safeguarding the preferential positions occupied by national producers.

That approach, by dispensing with the need for legislative acts at European level, made it possible to preserve the traditions and special characteristics of both the country of origin (which can export its products without intrinsically altering them) and the country of destination (which can maintain its production, technical standards, recipe laws and cultural values). Take the situation of the two countries referred to above, where the producing country and the importing country today recognize the well-founded approach adopted by the Court and by the

Commission at the time. It was the solemn recognition of the right to diversity!

Abandoning the old harmonization-based approach

The assertion and enforcement of the principle of mutual recognition led to the abandoning of the harmonization-based approach that had held sway in the past and that had threatened to transform the Community into a sort of steamroller levelling everything in its path, or – even worse – into a sort of interventionist 'welfare state' spewing out rules and regulations which, for the sake of technical perfection, would end up harming European citizens.

The principle of mutual recognition has put into practice the values of subsidiarity by prompting national and Community institutions to rethink their policies and strategies, and has brought about a profound change in terms of options and methods. The idea of a Community set on approximating national legislation was abandoned in the 1980s, to be replaced by a Community wishing to safeguard national, regional and local characteristics. Under the new approach, which underlies the harmonization envisaged in the White Paper, directives will no longer contain detailed technical standards or specifications but will be confined to setting out essential needs in terms of health and safety, leaving technical solutions to European or national bodies. In other words, Community policy-makers will merely identify the objectives (for example guaranteed safety levels for cars) and leave the task of devising the necessary technical solutions to specialists, that is to technicians.

Prevention as an instrument for partnership and subsidiarity

As mentioned in our interpretative note and as announced in the interpretative communication of 2 October 1980, the Community had endowed itself with a new instrument to enforce the principle of mutual recognition, namely Directive 83/189 (subsequently Directive 98/34), which required Member States to notify all draft technical standards to the Commission in order that it could examine their conformity with Community law before they were approved.

Thanks to that instrument, the seed of the acceptance of diversity germinated in many (about 6,000 in all) new national rules and regulations covering many sectors and invariably based on the principle of mutual recognition. Indeed, the dialogue and partnership engendered by that instrument between the Commission and national authorities, as well as the educational values that spawned that very idea, led national authorities to act in a European perspective. This brought about a new culture based on decentralization and subsidiarity, which fostered the smooth functioning of the Community and relations between the institutions.

In its 'Foie gras' ruling of 22 October 1998, the Court of Justice – officially recognizing the principle of mutual recognition and identifying it as the basic principle of the legal system of the Community – confirmed the approach followed by the Commission since the late-1980s and calling on all Member States to include in national regulations and, in particular, in their draft technical regulations, which were notified to the Commission pursuant to Directive 98/34, the clause providing for mutual recognition of products lawfully produced in another Member State.

Thus, the Commission availed itself of Directive 98/34 to ensure the smooth functioning of the Single Market and safeguard the industrial competitiveness of European firms.

Mutual recognition of the systems of voluntary certification

These are agreements based on the accreditation of evaluation bodies. In the sectors not covered by Article 30 (ex Article 36) of the Treaty, since they concern private activities, such recognition cannot be imposed by law. Accordingly, in order to eliminate any obstacle to trade resulting from national systems of voluntary certification, it is necessary to promote voluntary agreements between evaluation bodies and laboratories.

Thanks to the instruments described so far, about 4,000 national trade rules and regulations judged incompatible with the rules on the free movement of goods have been amended, with the inclusion of the clause on mutual recognition. Similarly, about 6,000 draft technical regulations notified to the Commission pursuant to Directive 98/34 have been brought into line with the Single Market rules.

The free movement of goods thus became the most important Community achievement, mostly on account of the principle of mutual recognition. The results are self-evident. Economic protectionism, which in the late 1970s was poised to destroy the achievements of 20 years of free trade and to undermine the Internal Market, was vanquished and eventually eliminated. The share of intra-Community trade grew from 22 per cent 35 years ago to 68 per cent today. Member States are now enjoying the most prosperous period in their history, and European consumers are able to choose from a very wide array of products reflecting the different cultures and traditions of the Community.

The principle of mutual recognition in the areas of right of establishment and freedom to provide services

In the areas of right of establishment and freedom to provide services, the European Court of Justice has developed a body of case-law which is as rich and advanced as the one concerning the free movement of goods. The principle of mutual recognition in these areas has the same meaning and importance as it acquired in the wake of the *Cassis de Dijon* ruling. Let us take a look in particular at the judgments given in *Webb* in December 1981 and in *Vlassopoulou* in May 1991.

In *Webb*, the Court states that the freedom to provide services implies the following:

> The Member State in which the service is provided ... takes into account the evidence and guarantees already produced by the provider of the services for the pursuit of his activities in the Member State in which he is established.

In *Vlassopoulou*, the Court states that:

> even if applied without any discrimination on the basis of nationality, national requirements concerning qualifications may have the effect of hindering nationals of the other Member States in the exercise of their right of establishment guaranteed to them by Article 43 [ex Article 52] of the EEC Treaty. That could be the case if the national rules in question took no account of the knowledge and qualifications already acquired by the person concerned in another Member State.

The Member State of destination is required to recognize the professional and technical skills, as well as the knowledge and qualifications and the diplomas or any other certificates issued by another Member State to the extent that they correspond or are equivalent to the skills, knowledge, qualifications and diplomas possessed by nationals and required as conditions of access to an economic activity or its exercise.

For example, the Member State where the service is provided is held to accept the equivalent qualifications concerning the professional and technical skills and the financial requirements which the person providing the service has acquired in another member state. As regards firms, apart from the enforcement of the Directive on technical harmonization, the evidence of equivalence may be provided through agreements on the mutual recognition of the systems of voluntary certification. Those agreements may be based on an accreditation system demonstrating the competence of the evaluation bodies.

The *Vlassopoulou* judgment, while confirming these principles, specifies with considerable clarity and precision the procedures and arrangements which a Member State must apply in guaranteeing equivalence between the skills, knowledge, qualifications and diplomas of foreign citizens and nationals. It even indicates (although this may be considered a sort of restatement of previous legislation) the methods and instruments which Member States must adopt in order to ensure protection of the rights of Community citizens living abroad.

Meaning and importance of the principle of mutual recognition

It is crucial to dispel a misunderstanding within national administrations and at Community level whereby the principle of mutual recognition would imply that all products and services lawfully produced and provided on the market of one Member State must be *automatically* accepted as such by the other member states of the Community. That 'automatic acceptance' led some observers to propose renaming that principle the 'principle of equivalence' or 'the principle of functional parallelism'.

It is evident from the case law of the Court of Justice and from the Commission's interpretative communication that the principle of mutual recognition must not be interpreted in that way, as it does not imply an automatic recognition of products and services lawfully produced and provided by another Member State. As the Commission stated in its report of 23 July 2002 on the application of the principle of mutual recognition in the Single Market, which it sent to the European Parliament, the Council and the Economic and Social Committee, 'mutual recognition is not automatically applicable: the host Member State retains the possibility of requiring that the degree of protection afforded by a product from another Member State is equivalent to that provided for in its national regulations'.

In other words, the member state of destination is required to accept products and services that satisfy the rules of the member state of origin even though these differ from its own rules, provided that:

- the product or service guarantees a level of protection and meets a legitimate objective equivalent to the one required in the Member State of destination; and

- the level of protection must be 'reasonable and satisfactory' in so far as it complies with the results of scientific research in the sector (particularly for products affecting public health and security).

These considerations hold true until such time as full and definitive European rules are adopted in that sector, that is, until such time as specific Community harmonization is introduced.

The *minimum threshold* is the one required by the Member State of destination, provided that it is appropriate and reasonable. Thus, it is better to refer to the 'ranking of values' (the expression is taken from the case-law of the Court) of the Member State of destination when applying the principle of mutual recognition and identifying the minimum threshold to be met. This means that minimum thresholds may differ from one Member State to another, something which is not surprising since, for want of a Community regulation in the sector, member states retain the right to apply their own concept. Only Community harmonization will introduce a *common threshold* of protection for the legitimate objective being pursued.

In other words, adoption of the principle of mutual recognition concerns the production details, the characteristics of a particular product or service, the technical means adopted for planning, producing and marketing it, and so on, but it does not concern the acceptance of a level of protection for the legitimate objective equivalent to the one existing in the Member State of origin.

This interpretation of the principle of mutual recognition permits respect for the diversity, specific characteristics and traditions of each Member State (for example the national language, which is discussed below). Otherwise, it would be a one-way principle which would not take account of the features of each Member State and would not produce the promised outcome.

Multilingual information: an essential component of the cultural diversity safeguarded by the Union

Should it be *'foie gras'* or 'fat liver'?

The French press recently gave wide coverage to the reactions of the public, politicians and writers who denounced the alleged 'diktat of Eurocrats to introduce English for the labelling of foodstuffs sold in France'. It is not our intention here to enter into the details of the case which triggered those reactions and in which the European Commission intervened, but the principles are important.

The case concerns the problem of 'labelling', and the issue may be summarized as follows: can a product be presented on the market of a Member State (for example France) with its label written in the language of the producing country (in our case, English), accompanied by all indications concerning its content and composition (for example the list of ingredients) in French, or is it necessary to translate the entire label into French? And, if the second option is chosen, will French producers accept that the Member States to which they export their products label them in another language, so that labels such as '*foie gras*', 'pâte', 'croissant' and so on are translated into the languages of those states? Will this not be tantamount to a sort of 'depreciation' of specialties in the eyes of consumers? Can we be sure that the indications provided in the national language and carefully explaining the meaning of a label written in its original language and the composition of the product provide consumers with sufficient information or do foreign labels undermine the purity of national languages?

We wonder whether that debate was launched with the aim of mobilizing the non-English-speaking population against a sort of hegemony of 'English-American', which is felt to be invasive and programmed and to be growing all the time, a hegemony which is neither favoured nor 'discretely imposed (as was alleged) by the European Commission and by its President as the sole language of European communication'.

French is and remains an official language of the Community, alongside other languages. With regard to the internal workings of the Commission, there are three working languages, viz. French (which, in our opinion, is still *de facto* the prevailing language), English and German. As an emeritus French professor said, 'the official coexistence of three languages is the practical attempt to reconcile three different sensitivities which have affected and express the European genius, namely Latin, German and Anglo-Saxon'.[7]

Community law and use of national languages

The European Commission has always taken the view that rules and regulations on the use of national languages are a matter for Member States. As was stated in its communication to the Council and to the European Parliament concerning language use in the information to consumers in the Community:

> Consumers have a right to information on the qualities and characteristics of products and services on the market. In practice this means that basic information must be readily available to consumers. The question as to the language chosen to disseminate the information is a crucial one.

> ... the Commission considers that rules concerning languages naturally fall within the competence of the Member States, notably in application of the principle of subsidiarity.[8]

Admittedly, that position has not changed since and will not change in the future, as national languages are a fundamental component of a country's identity and the Community has to respect and safeguard them as important components of the European heritage. Europe has no imperialist target of uniformization. Its model of society is made up of different social and cultural diversities – and this is what distinguishes it from the United States – and Europe aims to defend this standpoint and to propose it to the countries which wish to conclude a 'marriage contract' (to quote Jacques Delors) or to establish ever-closer links with it.

From a legal point of view, the Commission has clearly spelt out this standpoint, which follows the same operational approach. We are referring to its interpretative communication in this field, published on 23 December 1993 (*Official Journal* C 345/93). The Commission clearly states that the obligation imposed by some national legislations that 'certain particulars appearing on a foodstuff be drafted in, or at least translated into, the official language(s) of the country of marketing ... is nonetheless justified where intended to protect the ultimate consumer by informing him of the nature, composition, conditions of use and guarantees of the product.'

The French-language version contains the expression '*en principe*' (not translated in the English-language version), meaning that only in exceptional cases; that is, when the measure taken is clearly illegal and its aim is not to protect and inform consumers but to mask protectionist intentions, does that requirement run counter to Community rules. This holds true, for example, if national legislation requires the translation of terms used more or less everywhere ('on', 'off', etc.).

Some people have mentioned the provisions of Article 16 of Directive 2000/13/EC of 20 March 2000 adopted by the European Parliament and the Council of Ministers (that is, national ministers) – and not by the European Commission – on the approximation of the laws of member states relating to the labelling, presentation and advertising of foodstuffs,[9] which states that 'Member States shall ensure that the sale is prohibited within their own territories of foodstuffs for which the particulars provided for in Articles ... do not appear in a language easily understood by the consumer.' That provision is also found in a Directive of 18 December 1978 (Directive 79/112/EEC).

Admittedly, the expression 'language easily understood' is far from being easily understandable itself. Indeed, the Commission explained it in its above-mentioned interpretative communication, adding that 'the concept of a language easily understood by purchasers must obviously be left to the discretion of Member States' and that 'an official language of the Member State of marketing will in principle be a language allowing consumers a good understanding of the labelling'.

Let me conclude with a beautiful expression by Dominique Noguez,[10] who writes that the European Union and its institutions, among them the Commission, would all like to see Europe grow and assert itself 'so that we may be happier, surer and more proud of our cultures'. The European institutions are working to this end, as confirmed by those who follow the process of European integration and the great achievements to date, without claiming to know everything of the major events unfolding in our society and without further stoking up the stories pedalled by some popular tabloid newspapers.

Concluding remarks

For more than two decades the European Union has based its policies on the principle of mutual recognition. That principle has translated into practical terms the values of subsidiarity and has made it possible to safeguard national, regional and local identities and traditions, which are an inestimable heritage bequeathed to us by centuries of history. This holds true not only for policies aimed at establishing and completing the Internal Market but also for other policies, for instance those concerning the creation of an internal justice and security area. Isn't the European arrest warrant the first step towards the mutual recognition of penal judgments?[11]

Subsidiarity and mutual recognition are two benchmarks which must guide Europe in its long march towards a 'federation of Nation States' (to quote Jacques Delors again). Those values embody the European model as conceived by the founders of the Community and subsequently elaborated upon by those that have followed in their footsteps. It is a model consisting of historical, cultural, spiritual, economic and social differences. No European citizen, not even the most radical federalist, has ever dreamed of blurring those differences and renouncing his identity and native country.

So, why do so many politicians, writers, journalists and actors in society and economic life continue to denounce this European 'superstate' which we are constructing and which is supposed to suffocate our national identities? After Romano Prodi (whom we quoted at the beginning of this chapter), let us now listen to what a passionate federalist, one of the first promoters of the European ideal, Henri Brugmans, has to say:

> National homelands are rooted in the collective conscience. It is impossible to eradicate them. And yet, why should we? That diversity is at the same time our strength, our richness and our main problem. That is why even the most radical federalists have never thought of doing so and, when nationalists accuse them of trying to do so, either they do not know what they are saying or they are demagogic.[12]

So, advocates of the principles of national sovereignty, nationalism and Euroscepticism know little, if anything, about the process of European unification or are demagogic or rather – as indicated at the outset – they lie knowing that 'something will remain', to quote Voltaire's famous warning.

With regard to the attacks on the European Commission, the favourite target of the detractors of European unification, their objective is crystal-clear: to strike at the heart of the European Union and its process of integration. The Commission is indeed the engine of that process and the core of Jean Monnet's European project. It is at the same time the institution independent of the Member States that is responsible for bringing that project to fruition by exercising the executive powers it enjoys under the formative act of the European Community of 9 May 1950; moreover, it is the 'defender' of the common interests within the Community. Without the Commission, this process of European unification set in train by the Community's founders is bound to be one of those sterile forms of intergovernmental cooperation which, according to Jean Monnet, 'have never solved anything' and which 'have never prevented some Europeans taking up arms against other Europeans every twenty years'.[13]

Indeed, British voices have been raised against those practical jokers. The British Foreign Minister Jack Straw stated in 2001 that 'we need to re-think our attitude to concepts like independence and sovereignty ... By sharing sovereignty, a people may end up with more, not less, independence ... The EU does not threaten our independence, our sovereignty or our identity. Rather, in today's world, the EU provides the surest guarantee that our voice will be heard in the world.'[14]

Such declarations alone, even though voiced by eminent figures, cannot counter deliberate aggression comprising lies and fantasies; nor can they prevent that section of public opinion from being so shamefully manipulated. More thorough interventions are needed. We are in favour of initiatives aimed at informing European citizens and enabling them to directly contribute to the construction of Europe. We feel that two messages, one aimed at European public opinion and the other at the countries which are about to join the Union, should be launched and widely disseminated.

Europe will never stifle our identities and native countries. As underscored by Henri Brugmans, 'They will be maintained. Perhaps they will be strengthened as against other peoples. But they are not enough. To survive in modern times it is necessary to combine efforts.' In the face of disruptive globalization, the countries of Europe viewed in isolation will not be able to retain their identities and their cultural, social and economic diversity as they are unable to tackle the great problems of the twenty-first century, such as terrorism, environmental degradation, unemployment, and so on. Only a European Union will be able to take up those challenges and safeguard our identities; that is, will allow us to remain what we are, with our own ways of thinking and acting, our traditions and our specific characteristics.

The forthcoming enlargement will provide the Union with the opportunity to find a solution to a tragedy for which our countries are partly responsible; namely, the condemnation of the peoples of Central and Eastern Europe to 50 years of Soviet domination, during which their national identities and dignity were violated. Freed from Stalin's tyranny, those peoples have not hesitated in opting for our model of society rather than be attracted by the American model. Some of those peoples (the Hungarians, for example) will regain within the Union their unity which was shattered by 'congresses and peace treaties' (what an insulting expression!) that legitimized the booty of war.

Adoption of the principles of subsidiarity and mutual recognition will give the many countries which are about to join the Union the guarantee that their traditions and specific characteristics will not be harmonized or diluted in a 'common melting pot'. They can be assured of entering a Community which will respect their identities, a 'larger homeland' which will not suffocate smaller homelands but, quite the reverse, will defend their values, cultures, languages and religions; that is, their models of civilization.

Let me end with the prophetic words pronounced in 1932 by a philosopher belonging to 'European culture':

> Seventy years ago a Neapolitan from the Kingdom of the Two Sicilies and a citizen of Piedmont from the Kingdom of Savoy became Italian without renouncing their previous identities but by retaining them and adding this new Italian dimension. Similarly, French, Germans

and Italians and all other peoples of Europe will become European citizens and will address their thoughts to Europe: their hearts will beat for Europe as they used to do for their smaller motherlands, which will not be forgotten but will be loved in a better way.[15]

Notes

1 Cf. the editorial by Riccardi, F., *European Agency*, 29 June 2002, p. 3, and the Commission's press release.
2 De l'Ecotais, Y., *Naissance d'une Nation*, Paris, Grasset, p. 60 ff.
3 See Bangemann, M., *Revue du Marché Unique Européen*, no. 4, 1992.
4 Joliet, R., 'La Libre Circulation des Marchandises, l'Arret Keck et Mithouard et les Nouvelles Orientations de la Jurisprdence', *Journal des Tribunaux du Droit Européen*, no. 12, 1994.
5 *Revue du Marché Unique Européen*, no. 4, 1992, p. 7.
6 See the article 'L'Arrêt de Dijon, une Nouvelle Approche pour la Réalisation et le Bon Fonctionnement du Marché Intérieur', *RMC*, no. 241, November 1980.
7 Defraigne, P., 'Langues Pour Penser l'Europe', *Conference Débat sur la Langue Française et l'Élargissement – Représentation Permanente de la France*, Brussels, 28 June 2001.
8 See COM(93)456 final, 10 November 1993.
9 *Official Journal of the European Communities*, L 109 of 6 May 2000, p. 29.
10 *Le Monde*, 7 August 2002.
11 See Salazar, L., *Diritto penale e processo penale*, no. 2, 2002.
12 Brugmans, H., *Europe – Rêve – Aventure – Réalité*, Brussels, Elsevier.
13 Riccardi, F., *Au-delà de l'Information*, Agence Europe, 5–6 February 2001.
14 Article by the British Foreign Secretary, Jack Straw, dated 22 November 2001.
15 Croce, B., *Histoire de l'Europe du XIXeme Siècle*, 1932.

2
Mutual Recognition, Functional Equivalence and Harmonization in the Evolution of the European Common Market and the WTO*

Joseph H.H. Weiler

Prologue

The creation of a Common Market Place, indeed all trade liberalization regimes, produces an inevitable tension; a tension between the discipline of free trade and the regulatory autonomy of states. This tension is as true for the EU as it is true for the WTO, the NAFTA and all other similar trade regimes. It is structural. One way to reconcile this tension is by harmonization, but that is a heavy handed approach, which is politically difficult and might unnecessarily obliterate legitimate differences between states. The principle of mutual recognition (or as I shall eventually call it, functional equivalence) is an intermediate device

* The origins of this essay are in a series of internal lectures given at Harvard and Bruges in the early 1990s followed by a first public lecture at Edinburgh in 1996 and then, more formally, as the 1998 Ledingham Chalmers Annual Lecture in European Law, at the University of Aberdeen which was published as 'The Constitution of the Common Market Place: Text and Context in the Evolution of the Free Movement of Goods' in P. Craig and G. de Burca (eds), *The Evolution of EU Law*, pp. 349–76, 1999. This version is revised in some significant ways. I am very grateful to Miguel Poiares who commented critically and helpfully on some aspects of the thesis presented here, to Gráinne de Burca who made numerous helpful comments and suggestions on the first version, and to Sungjoon Cho who provided valuable research assistance. Christoph Feddersen, Imola Streho and Martina Kocjan provided very valuable research assistance to the current version.

which may help in reconciling the basic tension created by regulatory diversity in a single or liberalized marketplace. It cannot, however, be understood outside the general practice of free movement.

The focus of this essay will be on the European Community, indeed on the heart of the Community, the common market in goods (which over the years has been closely synchronized with the common market in the other factors of production, notably services) and the place of mutual recognition within this market. I will try and show how (and why), over time, an early radical approach to market integration has been replaced by a more mature approach far more respectful or national regulatory autonomy. I will further argue that within one generation the doctrinal foundation of the law of the common market has shifted from a sweeping insistence on removal of obstacles to an approach which, at its heart, interdicts discrimination and attacks obstacles only when these bar access to the marketplace.

My method will be simple enough. I will present snapshots of some of the most significant cases in the area of free movement of goods, cases so well-known as to obviate the necessity of any detailed description, and then attempt to transform these discrete snapshots into a cinematographic whole, a narrative over time in which the evolutionary nature of the jurisprudence will receive most attention. I regard this jurisprudence as suggestive of five 'generations': first, a foundational period stretching from the mid-1960s and culminating in *Dassonville* in the early 1970s; followed by a second generation in the late 1970s and early 1980s (*Cassis; Regenerated Oil*); a third generation in the mid- to late 1980s (a non-judicial phase of legal evolution consisting, *inter alia*, of the White Paper, the New Approach to Harmonization and the Single European Act); followed in turn by a fourth generation in the early 1990s (*Keck*). The present and near future will constitute the fifth generation for the purposes of this essay.

The metaphor of generations is used not simply to underline change from one period to another, but also to underline continuity – the new and different is, in this account, an outgrowth or reaction to that which preceded it. And in describing this change and continuity I will be at pains to suggest some ways in which material constitutionalism can be seen as situated in and conditioned by the structural constitutional evolution of the Community.

The shortcomings of my approach are self-evident: first, it is a story in which only landmarks feature. Much detail, important detail, is thus lost, though this might be a virtue, too, if the purpose of the essay is to provoke those who are already familiar with the field. The focus on court decisions and jurisprudence is another major limitation. Overall political economy, the dynamics and permutations of regulatory competition and the race to the bottom syndrome, economic analysis of various options adopted by the Court, and the true saga of implementing the White Paper are, at best, 'context' against which the jurisprudence takes place. Doctrine also suffers and not only where my positions or representations of doctrine will be challenged by many for which no apology is made, but also in eschewing whole areas such as price-fixing, intellectual property and the like for which I do make the proverbial apology of time and space.

The foundational period: constructing a common marketplace

On 24 November 1966, the Commission opened Art. 169 legal proceedings against Italy which led eventually to the Decision of the Court in the so-called *Statistical Levy* Case.[1] At issue was a charge levied at an equal rate on imported and exported goods the purpose of which was to finance the collection of statistical data on Italy's foreign trade. By coupling the levy on imports and exports the charge was, arguably, neither discriminatory nor protectionist. Even if a marginal discrimination did exist (after all, on the Italian market, domestic products competing with imports would not have had to pay that levy) it was, for the most part, infinitesimal: 10 lire on every 100 kilograms or every metric ton of goods or on every animal or vehicle. If ever *de minimis* had a meaning this would seem to be the place to apply it.[2] In addition, and this was argued by the Italian government, the charge could be regarded as financing a service for which the beneficiaries, importers and exporters, could be made to pay.[3] Moreover, the service which it financed was wholly beneficial to the overall design of creating a common market.[4] Knowledge is power in the marketplace too; and the knowledge gained by the trade statistics would enhance transparency and, thus, further the project of transnational market construction.

Why then bring the case at all?

The real motivation of the Commission is difficult to reconstruct. It seems as if they considered that the Italian charge contradicted some recently passed Regulations[5] – maybe it was their power which was at issue. But the thrust of the case was that the Italian charges violated the prohibition of Articles 9, 12, 13 and 16 EEC on customs duties and charges having equivalent effect. Perhaps the Commission sensed that this was a good case in which to invite the Court to pronounce for the first time on the definition of a charge having an effect equivalent to a customs duty. That was important as transitional periods came to an end. Though official customs duties had been abolished, a plethora of other 'charges' remained in place. Perhaps it was just fortuitous.

But maybe Commission ambition went even further – thereby providing the reason to select *Statistical Levy* as a convenient starting point for this disquisition on the evolution of the law (primarily judge-made) governing the free movement of goods in the Community legal order. For this important, principled and, somewhat unexpected, prosecution resulted not only in the still extant definition of charges having an effect equivalent to customs duties, but also in a conceptual and rhetorical construct – a true canon – which was, in time, to become the bedrock principle of the Court's understanding of intra-Community free movement of goods (and other factors of production) in its most celebrated jurisprudence from *Dassonville*[6] through *Cassis*[7] and beyond. Indeed, the huge flap attendant on the Court's more recent *Keck*'s jurisprudence[8] is precisely because the time-honoured canon consecrated in *Statistical Levy* and cases like it was violated.

At the centre of the *Statistical Levy* case was a dispute which seemed then (and, for very different and hugely important reasons, seems to many today) to cut to the heart of international trade regimes liberalizing transnational movement of goods, service, investment and the like, whether within the framework of the WTO-GATT or other free trade areas.

Did the legal commitment to free trade (and we must, here, make a supreme effort to reconstruct and reimagine the legal culture and political sensibilities of the mid-1960s) entail a regime which was directed at the elimination of discrimination and protectionism but no more (in which case Italy would stand on relatively strong grounds in defending the statistical levy), or did it go further and was directed at prohibiting any unjustified obstacle to trade – whether or not it was discriminatory or protectionist (in which case the Commission would be perched to win its case)? Camouflaged with many masks and disguises this question remains the single most potent underlying source of legal and political tension in all free trade regimes of which the Community is but one.

The Court, rejecting the benefits of the charge as too general to be characterized as a service for which a fee may be imposed and also differentiating the charge in question from a tax, gave its answer to the principal issue in Recital 9:[9]

> [A]ny pecuniary charge, however small and whatever its designation and mode of application, which is imposed unilaterally on domestic or

> foreign goods by reason of the fact that they cross a frontier, and which is not a customs duty in the strict sense, constitutes a charge having equivalent effect within the meaning of Articles 9, 12, 13 and 16 of the Treaty, even if it is not imposed for the benefit of the State, is not discriminatory or protective in effect and if the product on which the charge is imposed is not in competition with any domestic product.[10]

Five years later (1974), and this is where we begin to approach the territory of 'mutual recognition' almost to the day, in *Dassonville*, the Court made its most famous pronouncement ever, this time defining not a charge having an effect equivalent to a customs duty, but the similar concept of a measure having an effect equivalent to quantitative restrictions prohibited under Articles 30 and 34: 'All trading rules enacted by Member States which are capable of hindering, directly or indirectly, actually or potentially, intra-Community trade are to be considered as measures having an effect equivalent to quantitative restrictions.'[11]

Both cases seem to share the same logic of an obstacle rather than discrimination-based regime as well as the same sweeping, formulaic, all-encompassing rhetoric. What seemed to be constructed by this twin-like definition of charges and measures having an effect equivalent, respectively, to customs duties and quantitative restrictions was not a mere legal regime of 'fair' trade but a regime which was, in principle, designed to remove all unjustified obstacles to trade and not merely discriminatory and protectionist measures – a veritable common marketplace.[12] This construct and this philosophy[13] became the driving force of an entire jurisprudence which slowly seemed to harmonize the same set of rules for the free movement of all other factors of production and also define the fundamental way in which the Community was different from other regimes – principally the GATT. The GATT, to an entire generation of Community lawyers, was driven by the more 'old-fashioned' and primitive notion of a commitment to national treatment, that is non-discrimination – but no more. The move from *Statistical Levy* to *Dassonville* typified (and typifies to many) the very canon of the economic constitution of Europe: removing obstacles, not merely discrimination and protectionism is the hallmark of the true common or single marketplace.

The (apparent) similarity of logic and rhetoric between the two cases may also suggest, with no proof, that they sprang from the same mind-set, that they were associated with an identical or similar judicial world view of the Community and its *telos* as well as from an hermeneutic sensibility which regarded the interpretation of Articles 9, 12, 13 and 16 which led to *Statistical Levy* as involving the same 'moves' which would lead to the *Dassonville* formula. After all, the prohibition in the Treaty on charges having an effect equivalent to customs duties and of measures having an effect equivalent to quantitative restrictions seem equally opaque and equally open textured. With eyes clouded by the 'heroic period' in the Court's jurisprudence at that time, the text seems to invite a teleological interpretation conditioned by an overarching vision of the Community as a single marketplace in which, presumptively, goods can move freely and any obstacle must have an objective justification sanctioned by Community law and supervised by the Community Court. In this sense *Statistical Levy* and *Dassonville* stand to the material constitution as cases like *Van Gend en Loos*[14] or *ERTA*[15] stand to the structural constitution.

This canonical view is implicit in many text books – since the issues are rarely addressed explicitly – and I have observed in years of teaching thousands of students that once *Statistical Levy* is (superficially) internalized, *Dassonville* seems predictable and even unexceptional. That this view has become canonical is also evident by the cries of woe by certain writers when the Court has adopted decisions running against this orthodoxy – cries of woe as shrill as when the Court hands down decisions which run against the structural canon (such as refusing horizontal direct effect to directives).

And yet, placed in context – the context (*economie*) of the actual text as well as political and economic context – the two cases were and are fundamentally different and the seemingly easy move from the obstacle-oriented construct in *Statistical Levy* to that of *Dassonville* is nothing less than fateful.

For all its rhetorical sweep, the legal holding in *Statistical Levy* is based on conventional reasoning which would satisfy the most conservative canons of legal construction. It also forms part of a conventional and conservative view of a liberal trade regime which differentiates between rules governing market access and rules governing market regulation and considers that the former should, indeed, be obstacle-based and the latter be discrimination-based.[16] By contrast, *Dassonville* – at least the *Dassonville* formula – is another matter: an important departure based on a more complicated set of interpretative considerations.

Hermeneutically, *Statistical Levy* is a conservative case since it takes seriously the notion of equivalency in the text of the Treaty: 'Customs duties on imports and exports and charges having equivalent effect shall be prohibited between Member States.'

Customs duties usually are, though not necessarily so, protectionist or discriminatory: After all, they can, and often do, cover products for which there may be no identical, similar, substitutable or competing domestic items. And even so, they are prohibited. Likewise, customs duties can be very small – *de minimis* – and this alone does not save them from the prohibition.[17] So, charges having *equivalent effect* to customs duties also need not be discriminatory or protectionist in order to fall within the prohibition and may be very negligible too.[18] There is no teleology in this interpretation. This hermeneutic fact does not give the interpretation a necessarily higher order of legitimacy; it simply means that the Court did not need to stretch itself to arrive at this result; that *Statistical Levy* was hardly 'heroic' stuff.

Consider another hugely important aspect to *Statistical Levy*: the Court, in Recital 11, necessarily had to differentiate between a pecuniary charge imposed by reason of the fact that a good crosses a frontier – which would thereby be classified as a prohibited customs duty or charge having an effect equivalent to a customs duty – and internal taxes:

> [I]t follows from Articles 95 et seq. that the concept of a charge having equivalent effect does not include taxation which is imposed in the same way within a State on similar or comparable domestic products, or at least falls, in the absence of such products, within the framework of general internal taxation, or which is intended to compensate for such internal taxation within the limits laid down by the Treaty.[19]

The distinction, not always easy to apply,[20] is important for practical and conceptual reasons.[21] The practical consequences, at least to litigators, are self-evident. A pecuniary imposition classified as a charge having an effect equivalent to a customs duty would be *per se* prohibited. A pecuniary imposition classified as falling within the general system of taxation would be prohibited only if discriminatory and protectionist – since Article 95 so decreed.[22] This is a far more difficult and challenging (though also lucrative) task for the litigator.

The conceptual significance cannot be overestimated. *Statistical Levy* seems to articulate a distinction, resulting from the economy of the Treaty, in relation to pecuniary burdens on imports: A pecuniary imposition may occur at, and be part of, a market-access regime such as a customs duty or a charge having an equivalent effect: In that case it is viewed as an obstacle which, in principle, is *per se* prohibited. By contrast, a pecuniary imposition may be part of an internal regulatory regime – a tax. In this case it will not be prohibited unless discriminatory and protectionist.[23]

For reasons which will shortly emerge it is worth digressing at this point to paint, with the broadest of brush strokes, the equivalent provisions of the GATT.

In the area of pecuniary impositions the EC and the GATT have parallel regimes. True, unlike a free trade area or a common market, the GATT did not prohibit, outright, customs duties and charges having an effect equivalent to customs duties.[24] But this should not obscure the fact that in its regime of progressive reduction of tariffs, in relation to both customs duties and charges having an equivalent effect, the GATT regime, too, is obstacle-based.[25] Any tariff imposed on an import in deviation from the agreed schedule of tariff reductions cannot be excused on the basis that it is non-discriminatory, that there is no competing product or that it is *de minimis*.[26] Thus, the GATT prohibition of new customs duties and equivalent charges is, in principle, a regime of rigorous (not *de minimis*) and strict (discrimination or protectionism need not be proved) liability. By contrast the GATT regime on taxes, ex Article III, is limited to the principle of national treatment, that is to a discrimination-based test.[27]

We already noted in discussing *Statistical Levy* that this distinction is replicated in the Treaty of Rome when it comes to pecuniary impositions: Pecuniary impediments to market access – whether customs duties or charges having an effect equivalent – are, like the GATT, strictly and rigorously prohibited. By contrast, market regulation through pecuniary means – taxes – is subject only to the duty of non-discrimination and non-protectionism.[28] Article 95 EC is remarkably similar to the tax provisions in Article III GATT.[29]

What, then, of non-pecuniary measures affecting trade? Let us first examine the GATT with an excerpt from Article XI:

> Article XI: General Elimination of Quantitative Restrictions
>
> 1. No prohibitions or restrictions other than duties, taxes or other charges, whether made effective through quotas, import or export licenses or other measures, shall be instituted or maintained by any contracting party on the importation of any product of the territory of any other contracting party or on the exportation or sale for export of any product destined for the territory of any other contracting party.

The text is peremptory. Unlike Article III GATT, it does not refer to the hallowed 'national treatment' principle. The prohibition is, on its face, of an obstacle-based nature rather than a discrimination-based nature,[30] though it is, of course, subject to the GATT's overall derogation clause and played a nominal role in international economic law until recently.

On this reading, in principle (the practice was to be quite different for a long time),[31] not only are quotas as such prohibited, but also measures the effect of which is to prevent, like a quota, access to the market could be prohibited[32] unless justified under one of the GATT's derogations.[33] But in an Ad note to Article III it was specified:

> Ad Article III
> Any internal tax or other internal charge, or any law, regulation or requirement of the kind referred to in Paragraph 1 which applies to an imported product and to the like domestic product and is collected or enforced in the case of the imported product at the time or point of importation, is nevertheless to be regarded as an internal tax or other internal charge, or a law, regulation or requirement of the kind referred to in Paragraph 1, and is accordingly subject to the provisions of Article III.

Measures equivalent to quantitative restrictions seemed to be restricted to border measures. It could have been that the reason for Ad III was to make sure that *discriminatory* internal measures applied at the border were not equated to quotas and excluded under the original grandfathering agreement of the GATT. Even if this were the motive, the reasoning has persisted and Article XI has been confined to border measures.

As a result, border measures which act as quotas are prohibited,[34] unless they can be justified under one of the recognized public policy justifications in, say, Article XX GATT.[35] By contrast, under the GATT, state regulation which, like a tax, does not bar access of the imported product to the marketplace but simply impedes or hinders its marketing through regulation of, say, use or conditions of sale, is dealt with like a tax: such state regulation is not caught by the GATT and is not prohibited unless it violates the principle of national treatment, that is it discriminates in law or in fact.[36] Indeed, It is caught by the same Article III GATT which deals equally with both dimensions of state internal regulation through pecuniary (tax) and non-pecuniary measures:[37]

> Article III: National Treatment on Internal Taxation and Regulation
> 1. The contracting parties recognize that internal taxes and other internal charges, and laws, regulations and requirements affecting

> the internal sale, offering for sale, purchase, transportation, distribution or use of products, and internal quantitative regulations requiring the mixture, processing or use of products in specified amounts or proportions, should not be applied to imported or domestic products so as to afford protection to domestic production.

Put differently, the principle of national treatment extends not only to regulation through taxes but to regulation through legislative and administrative measures.[38]

I will make two preliminary comments on the GATT regime which seems in principle to differentiate between state regulation barring market access at the border which is *prima facie* a violation unless coming within a GATT derogation, and other state regulation, whether by tax or all other regulatory measures which is not a violation unless discrimination against imported goods is practiced.[39]

First, it is self-evident but worth recalling that whilst the prohibition on discrimination and protectionism imposes an important restriction on the state *vis-à-vis* imported products,[40] it also grants them an important liberty: the liberty of social and economic regulatory choice.[41] Let us put it differently. Whilst you may not use, say, your tax regime in a discriminatory or protectionist manner, you may use it, freely, to further your statal social and economic agenda. You may not, for example, use taxation to afford protection to your local cognac against imported whiskey, but you may, in the words of the European Court of Justice in *Hansen and Balle,* create tax distinctions and apply differentiated tax rates so as to 'serve legitimate economic or social purposes, such as the use of certain raw materials by the distilling industry, the continued production of particular spirits of high quality, or the continued production of particular spirits of high quality, or the continuance of certain classes of undertakings such as agricultural distilleries'.[42]

We know, of course, that sometimes, in 'hard cases', the duty of non-discrimination will impede full regulatory freedom. That a lot will turn on the definition of the product market (must all fruit, domestic and imported, be taxed at the same rate, or may we differentiate between, say, soft fruits such as bananas and hard fruits even if it turns out that the hard fruit is mostly local and the soft fruit is imported?)[43] or even more delicately, on the protectionist purpose of the state. But, for the most part, the principle of national treatment which prohibits discrimination and protectionism is intended to create a balance between free trade and very broad national regulatory autonomy.[44]

The second comment is equally obvious but also worth making. There is a very powerful logic to the manner in which the GATT 'lumps' together tax and other legislative and administrative regulatory instruments in Article III. Imagine that the state, for reasons of public health, wants to discourage smoking. It may do so in one of two ways: it may impose very high taxes on cigarettes which, experience has shown, does lead to a reduction in cigarette consumption. Or it may use its non-pecuniary regulatory instruments and, for example, ban smoking in public spaces which may have the same reductive impact. Or in combating alcoholism, it may impose high excise taxes on alcohol which leads to reduction in consumption and may, too, finance rehabilitation projects, or it may bar public drinking to certain licensed establishments, to certain hours of the day and the like which could have similar effects to the excise tax.

Does it make sense to apply the principle of non-discrimination and thereby give the state near total freedom to regulate through tax (so long as the tax does not favour domestic cigarettes or alcoholic beverages over imported ones), but to apply the principle of obstacles to any non-pecuniary regulation (even if non discriminatory) and require the state to justify its regulatory choice such as the smoking ban by reference to some authorized list of exceptions each and every time its non-pecuniary regulation hinders the marketing of imported products?

When the choices between the two methods of regulation are fungible, a distinction between the two methods of statal regulation simply would not make sense: why treat them differently? And sometimes the choices are not fungible: regulation through product-oriented taxes is typically regressive – a high tax on cigarettes has greater impact on the poor than the rich. In that case the trade regime which maintained such a distinction would be providing an incentive for socially regressive state policies.

Be that as it may, the overall architecture of the GATT regime appears as follows:

- An obstacle-oriented prohibition on point of entry, whether instituted through unauthorized pecuniary charges (duties and charges of equivalent effect) or unauthorized quantitative restrictions and measures having equivalent effect.
- A discrimination-oriented prohibition on internal market regulation, whether instituted by pecuniary means (taxes) or legislative and administrative measures.

- An overarching Derogation Clause – the General Exceptions of Article XX GATT[45] – which applies to all aspects of the agreement, i.e. equally to the provisions on market access and market regulation.

It is against this legal context that we can understand the sense in which *Dassonville* does not represent the natural, seamless extension of *Statistical Levy*, but represents instead an important departure.

The canonical statement in *Dassonville* referred to all 'trading rules'. This could have been interpreted, conservatively, as referring only to border measures which blocked entry to the market and, as such, equivalent to Article XI of the GATT. This may well have been the original intention of the Commission in advocating for this rule.[46] But with the passage of time, in the hands of the Court of Justice, and with a complicit Commission[47] the *Dassonville* canon came to be read as a blanket prohibition on any rule – trading or otherwise – which had the effect of not only barring access to the market but of merely hindering trade.

Though seemingly sharing the same logic and a similar rhetoric, *Dassonville* does the very opposite of *Statistical Levy*. Instead of affirming the GATT-oriented distinction between regulation which bars point of entry access on the one hand and regulation *within* the market which, however, allows market access to imported products, *Dassonville* did two things: first, it extended the notion of trading rules to all rules, internal and border, and then it conflated the two tests into one and applied the same obstacle-based, hindering rule both at the border and to internal regulation whether or not discriminatory and/or protectionist.

We should not jump to conclusions that this is our familiar 'heroic' Court privileging telos over text. Textually, the Treaty itself placed the Court in a difficult position. Whereas in relation to pecuniary charges the Treaty differentiated between point of entry regulation (customs duties and charges having an equivalent effect) and internal market regulation (taxation), and also, in the footsteps of the GATT, designated a different regime to each, no such explicit differentiation exists in relation to non-pecuniary state measures affecting imports. Conspicuously Article 95 EC which is so similar to Article III GATT[48] is restricted to taxation and does *not* cover 'laws, regulations and requirements affecting the internal sale, offering for sale, purchase, transportation, distribution or use of products'. In the EC Treaty regime of negative integration the latter are left in limbo.[49] The Article 30 conundrum for the Court was, thus, as follows: how does one treat non-pecuniary state regulation which affects trade in imported products. Surely, on any reading, the measures having an equivalent effect to quantitative restrictions ex Article 30 would catch those state instruments which bar access to the market, in which case they should be prohibited and subject to justification ex Article 36 whether discriminatory or not. A quota, including a zero quota, is like a customs duty: it is prohibited whether or not there exists identical, similar, substitutable or competing domestic items.[50]

But do you, following the logic of Article 95 and the GATT, exclude from the reach of Article 30 all those state measures which do not bar access to the market even if they appreciably affect the sales of and hinder the trade in imported products within the market and subject such measures only to the general EC Treaty prohibition on discrimination on grounds of nationality? Or do you include such measures within the definition of measures having an effect equivalent to quantitative restrictions ex Article 30 EC on the benign assumption that if 'innocent' they can also be exculpated by a public policy reason ex Article 36?

Hermeneutically, the fact that the Treaty did not draw a distinction between market access and market regulation in the non-pecuniary area could, in and of itself, be regarded as an invitation to conflate the two. Maybe it was even the intention of the drafters in deliberately deviating from the GATT model in this respect. The theory of intentional deviation from the GATT is weakened because of the Ad note to Article III and because for so long in the history of the GATT the principle of Article XI was whittled away by exceptions, derogations, lack of commitment to enforce and failure to grasp its potential implication. It is doubtful whether in the 1950s one really thought of the GATT prohibition in Article XI as being able to catch, *á la* Hormones, non-discriminatory state regulation which had the effect of excluding imported products from the market. Just as the EC became, somewhat artificially, dominated by the ethos of obstacles to trade, so did the GATT, also artificially, become dominated by the ethos of national treatment.

So, in constituting and Constituting a meaning for Article 30, it would make equal interpretative sense to have taken the opposite cue from the economy of the Treaty and argue that the model established in the pecuniary field should also be applied in the regulatory field; that it made no sense to create a distinction between regulation and access in relation to pecuniary imposition but not to have such a distinction as regards non-pecuniary state regulation.

What about the actual language of equivalence in Article 30 which was the key to the interpretation in *Statistical Levy*? We have similar hermeneutic ambivalence here. What measures can be said to be truly equivalent to straightforward quantitative restrictions (quotas)? On one reading it is perhaps more of a stretch to claim, as the Court does in *Dassonville* and its progeny, that any internal measure regulating the marketplace (such as a prohibition on smoking in public places) by the mere fact that it 'hinders' trade (and it surely does in the sense that if cigarette smoking is to fall, so will the consumption of imported cigarettes) is equivalent to a formal quantitative restriction. Is a ban on smoking in a public place really equivalent to a quota on imported cigarettes? A total ban on smoking would be equivalent – to a zero quota. It would, exactly as a quota does, bar access to the market. But is a regulatory measure which merely hinders even if appreciably, though without the ability to gauge with precision the exact effect on imports, really equivalent to a quota restricting with precision the number of allowable cigarette imports? Is not the essence of the quota, even the non-zero quota – the preemptory and sharp bar to access into the market of imported products which do not fall within the quota? On this reading, a measure merely hindering the marketing of a product which had free access to that market is not equivalent to a quantitative restriction. On the other hand it could be argued that just as quotas larger than zero are prohibited, so should other trading rules which have the equivalent effect of merely restricting the quantity of a product which may be sold on the market. I find this last textual argument less persuasive not simply because the non-zero quota is the exception rather than the rule, but also because even non-zero quotas have a sharp, definable edge which bars access of all imports outside the quota to the market. A regulation which appreciably affects sales but does not differentiate between imports and domestic products is really not equivalent in this sense to a quota larger than zero. This is not simply a formal distinction, but one with great substance. Even when a state regulation affects the volume of sale, the imported product can compete on the domestic market and, if better in quality and price, can displace all its domestic competitors. A non-zero quota does not allow such market competition and it is very rare to have a non-zero quota imposed on imports and domestic products alike.

The purpose of this analysis is not to decide whether *Dassonville* was right or wrong, but to indicate that the Court had (and retained) hermeneutic leeway in construing Article 30 and that the route it took represented a definite teleological choice.

That leeway means that the Court could have followed the Article 95 EC and the GATT logic in interpreting Article 30 and holding that it was a Treaty provision designed to prohibit any trading rules which effectively denied access to the market to imported products, but was not designed to catch regulatory measures which merely hindered marketing of products. Such regulatory measures would be caught by the general Treaty prohibition on discrimination on grounds of nationality. It would avoid the peculiar situation that social outcomes freely obtainable by taxation, would be prohibited unless specifically authorized, by regulation.

How, then, can one explain the choice in *Dassonville*? What was its teleology? Could it be said that this very choice defined the difference between a regime committed merely to free trade (GATT) and to the creation of a veritable Common Market? Had the Court constituted and Constituted Article 30 to catch only measures barring access to the market, would the face of the Community as it evolved be fundamentally different? Would it materially be a different constitutional order?

Our answer must, I fear, be nuanced: As a matter of principle – I do not think so. As a matter of fact – quite possibly. As a matter of legal and general culture – decidedly so. As a matter of principle one must, first, remember that a vast area of state market regulation does have the impact of barring access – primarily all regulation which concerns the quality of the product in the health and safety fields.[51] All these regulations would be caught by Article 30 even if the Court had taken the less-expansive approach. Now that the GATT is finally beginning to take *its* prohibition on quantitative restrictions seriously, interesting and contentious days lie ahead even within its more restrictive approach. One must also remember that, unlike the GATT, the Treaty did have Article 100 and a project of harmonization.[52] This, in my view, is the critical principled difference between the GATT and the Common Market, not the nature of the negative integration prohibition. Under the GATT if a measure is justified as a legitimate pursuance of a public policy recognized in, say, Article XX,[53] the matter, in principle, ends there even if the justified measure totally excludes an imported product which would have to be modified to meet the justified safety requirements in different markets. Market fragmentation is in-built. In the Community, the matter begins there, for when justified measures fragment the market, legislative harmonization is available.[54] So one could have, after all, taken the more restrictive approach to Article 30 and, in principle, still end up with a Common Market very different from the GATT.

So why not? What explains the Court's alternative choice in its *Dassonville* formula which barred both measures which barred and hindered the marketing of imports?

I have already suggested one possibility, a certain Jacobean conception of the common marketplace which regards *Statistical Levy* and *Dassonville* as one of a kind, and explicitly or implicitly rejects the GATT philosophy of trying to find an uneasy balance between transnational free trade and broad choice of national social and economic options exercised by states enjoying wide regulatory autonomy, which really has as its implicit ideal-type a transnational marketplace which is identical to a national marketplace.

There is another more benign reading. After all, the *Dassonville* formula *does not mean* that all obstacles resulting from the activities of the regulatory state are actually going to be struck down.[55] Article 30 is subject to the discipline of Article 36. It is not as if regulatory autonomy is truly removed. The state is left with plenty of social choice under the various rubrics of Article 36.[56] It does, however, mean that such measures would be illegal on their face unless scrutinized and found permissible by reference to the authorized exceptions in Article 36.[57] *Dassonville* restricts the autonomy, not the choice.[58] Why, in turn, would the Court, consciously or unconsciously, wish to keep the choice but restrict the autonomy? Recall in the narrative of Exodus the fateful turn on the way to the Promised Land, a turn that ushered several decades of hardship and travel through the desert. It was a detour necessary to create a new consciousness purged of all elements of slavery prior to entering the Promised Land. *Dassonville*'s departure from the GATT symmetry may be regarded as a similar fateful turn necessary, perhaps, to create a new consciousness purged of the habits and instincts of protectionism which are sometimes so deeply embedded in a Continent with a long history of protectionism. A mechanism which would enable the Court to scrutinize even those measures which on their face seem non-discriminatory and non-protectionist but which, in fact, may be found to be so on deeper scrutiny, especially a scrutiny one part of which included the test of proportionality in the sense of least-restrictive-measure. The importance of *Dassonville* is thus pragmatic (avoiding the much more difficult need of proving discrimination before a state has to come in and justify its measures which impact trade) and symbolic: an all-out rallying cry against the ethos of protectionism.

On this reading *Dassonville* important as it may be – revelation happened after all during the detour in the desert – must be regarded as a transitory device.[59] *Keck* will be seen as a welcome return to normalcy in the Promised Land of the Single Market and a major move, matched on its part by *Hormones*, of reconvergence of the EC and the GATT as regards the basic concepts of transnational free-trade legal regimes.

To judge, however, from the reactions to *Keck* there are many a Moses in our profession who prefer the desert to the Promised Land.

There is one final important legal consideration to complete the description of the foundational period in the evolution of the material constitution of Europe. It is not only Article 36 which complements Article 30; there are also, as mentioned, Articles 100 and 100a.[60] The precise legal circumstances which must prevail for the Community legislator to enact legislation on the basis of Article 100, and 100a, are not fully explored. The very logic of the triangle 30, 36, and 100 (or 100a) produces, however, the following legal result: When a state measure violates on its face the *Dassonville* formula, the member state is required to justify it by reference to European law criteria – ex Article 36 or as a Mandatory Requirement ex *Cassis de Dijon* often before the European Court of Justice. If the measure cannot be justified it is inapplicable or must be modified appropriately. Critically, when it is justified and can, thus, be upheld, Article 100 or 100a come into play.[61] For unless this were so, a common market could never be achieved if each Member State could keep its own different regime for, say, consumer safety, even if each state measure was legally justified.[62] We can call that the problem of the legally fragmented marketplace. It can only be resolved by harmonizing the varying legal state measures.[63] Put differently, the Community legislative competence ex Articles 100 or 100a is triggered each time there is a finding of a *prima facie* transgression by a state measure of the *Dassonville* formula, even when, necessarily, the state measure in question is justified.[64] This may not be the exclusive ground for using Article 100 or 100a, but it is certainly a sufficient ground.[65]

Evaluating the foundational period

We can now evaluate certain aspects of the heritage of the foundational period as outlined above. The Court's choice to conflate in the non-pecuniary area market access and market regulation and subject both to an obstacle-based test is understandable politically and defensible hermeneutically. When establishing a common market you may want to lean on the side of rigour. But one should not hide the anomalies and other consequences of this basic choice:

1 We have already pointed out the anomaly which differentiates between regulation through taxes and regulation through norms, a differentiation which might seem to favour state regulation through tax even if, socially, taxing goods is almost invariably regressive.

2 Another anomaly which I shall not elaborate in this essay is the divergence between the Court's *Dassonville* obstacle-based jurisprudence on imports and its discrimination-based jurisprudence ex Article 34 on exports. This anomaly was prompted by two factors: a more relaxed attitude by the Court to restrictions on exports which are rarely motivated by protectionist impulses, and a clearer vision – antedating *Keck* by a generation, of the constitutional implications of *Dassonville*.
3 A third consequence of the *Dassonville* jurisprudence is that it dramatically expands the number and type of cases in which a member state is required to justify its social choices in regulating the marketplace and its public sphere.[66] Consequently the pressure on the derogation clause – (Article 36) becomes enormous.[67] It comes, thus, as no surprise that the Court had to enshrine another important principle; namely, that the derogation has to be construed narrowly.[68] In symbolic terms[69] this meant, of course, an inbuilt conservative bias, or at least presumption, in favour of free trade,[70] creating an ethos that *any* obstacle to free trade is in some ways improper and has to be 'justified'.
4 Institutionally, *Dassonville* thrust the Court to the centre of substantive policy dilemmas. The Court, as a Community institution, had to become the arbiter of delicate social choices, reconciling trade with competing social policies.
5 Constitutionally, as mentioned, *Dassonville* represented a massive expansion in the legislative competence of the Community ex Article 100 and 100a.

How does one explain the relative equanimity of reaction to these significant constitutional, institutional and substantive consequences. There are several, non-mutually exclusive, possible explanations.

Consider first the issue of legislative competences. Who paid much attention to legislative competences in an era governed by the Luxembourg Compromise and in an area governed by the unanimous voting requirement of Article 100. It was neither noticed and, if noticed, not considered of great political significance. Explaining the positioning of the Court is more delicate. On the one hand the *Dassonville* move is even more consequential than its constitutional structural counterparts. For all the drama of direct effect and supremacy, these concepts represented a rather exquisite balance between an emerging constitutional law and Community governance: the balance struck by the Court was to allow the political institutions and the governments of Member

States considerable freedom in making their policy choices, in negotiating and in striking their eventual bargains. But once a substantive bargain was struck, the structural constitutional new order achieved through doctrines such as direct effect and supremacy meant that bargains could not be abandoned, that they would be upheld and enforced. Free bargaining but no free-riders sums up that part of the constitutional interplay. It is not surprising that, despite all, direct effect and supremacy were, for the most part, embraced and not rejected by the governments of the Member States. *Dassonville* and its progeny is different since here the Court itself was making substantive and material policy determinations and not simply enforcing the bargains of others. It should be easy to agree that in the relationship between the Court and its interlocutors, this is at least a different ball-game, though whether it is as different as ice hockey and field hockey or baseball and cricket is something that we can wait to be illuminated by those political scientists who think they can answer this question. But, on the whole, if we look at the overall climate rather than the case to case weather, the Court's *Dassonville* jurisprudence could be construed as flushing out free-riders trying to enjoy the benefits of the expanded export market, but attempting to restrict imports. For the empirical fact remains that although the Court insisted that a mere obstacle would snap the Article 30 trap, in most cases even apparently innocuous state measures were found to be either discriminatory or, at a minimum, to fail one critical aspect of the proportionality test – in that their declared objectives could be achieved by means less burdensome on imports.

The second generation: towards judicial mutual recognition

The second generation in this evolutionary narrative is perceived as occurring round the late 1970s and early 1980s. *Cassis* is the central second-generation case as regards Article 30 and must be understood as a response to two major unresolved problems from the foundational period:

1 We have already noted the need to construe the derogations to Article 30 as narrowly as possible. But Article 36 does represent, after all, the important areas where social policy could be allowed to trump the interest in free trade, a foundation of the modern mixed economy and interventionist state. It was, however, written with the sensibilities of the 1950s: consumer protection, for example, is focused mostly on

physical safety and not on fairness and transparency; ecological concerns are minimal and would require true textual stretch to be acknowledged. What happens, and this is the first second-generation problem, when public sensibilities change and Member States wish to introduce for legitimate social reasons measures protecting the interests of, say, consumers which are not recognized in Article 36? It is one thing to construe existing derogations narrowly to avoid their abuse as a means for disguised restriction to trade.[71] It is quite another thing to freeze the Community and its Member States in defining the balance between free trade and other competing values in a time capsule sealed in 1957.[72] The Court could, of course, give a broad meaning to the public policy exception, but that would militate not only against, say, the original French version of the Treaty where this provision seemed far narrower, but would compromise the policy of construing derogations narrowly.[73]

2 We noted, too, the problem of market fragmentation which results from differing standards adopted by Member States, each one in full compliance with Articles 30 and 36 but cumulatively fragmenting the marketplace. In theory, as we noted too, Article 100 was to provide the answer, but in practice the unanimity requirement rendered that article useless. The record of harmonization as we enter the second generation is poor:[74] there are, apparently, always one or more Member States able to block harmonization proposals. How then, and this was the second second-generation problem, could one address market fragmentation given the *blockage* of decision-making ex Article 100.

A third second-generation problem I shall briefly mention rested in the area of taxation. Strangely, the Treaty did not provide a social policy derogation clause to Article 95 – an equivalent to Article XX GATT or Article 36 EEC. If Britain or Ireland were to impose vaccination and quarantine requirements on imported animals susceptible to rabies, the two countries would be able to rely on Article 36 to justify such a measure. By contrast, if, say, in an attempt to preserve natural resources Italy were to tax natural alcohol at a rate lower than synthetic alcohol, which would become a burden which fell disproportionately on imported products, there would be no Treaty provision with which to defend such a policy preference. Did Article 95 mean that any taxation scheme which resulted in a heavier burden on imported products, even if imposed for non-protectionist reasons, was outside the scope of member state regulatory competences?

Cassis responded to the first two problems. The doctrine of mandatory requirements was an obvious and welcome response to the first problem since, subject to its various doctrinal hoops, it allowed member states to plead non-economic policies which were not mentioned in Article 36.[75] Fairness of commercial transactions, public health, cultural policy and other 'ways-of-life' justifications could now be proffered.[76]

The second great doctrine in *Cassis*, misleadingly called by some the doctrine of mutual recognition and more accurately described by Alan Dashwood as functional parallelism or, perhaps even better, as functional equivalence, was a valiant attempt to respond to the second problem.[77] After all, in principle, the need for harmonization would appear far less pressing if goods complying with the technical standards required in one Member State could be marketed freely in another Member State provided the standards of the first state were functionally parallel to those of the second.[78] Why would one need to harmonize a common standard at all?

Finally, cases such as *Vinal* v. *Orbat*[79] and *Commission* v. *Italy (Regenerated Oil)*[80] introduced a *de facto* derogation clause to the field of taxation. Whether one reads these cases as permitting origin-neutral taxes instituted with a legitimate social policy to result in tax brackets that would otherwise be considered discriminatory and protectionist, or whether one simply reads them as introducing an unwritten derogation clause which would redeem otherwise discriminatory tax distinctions is irrelevant. The end result of this jurisprudence was to allow Member States to defend tax distinctions within the EC (which does not contain a written derogation clause) even more effectively than one can in the GATT (which has such a written derogation).

Despite the familiarity of these cases and the doctrines they introduced it is worth highlighting some features important for this evolutionary perspective:

1 There is language in some Court decisions which suggests (and it is a thesis favoured by several notable commentators) that the doctrine of mandatory requirements differs in at least one fundamental respect from the derogation plea under Article 36.[81] According to this thesis, mandatory requirements are part of what qualifies a measure for the purpose of deciding whether or not it violates Article 30 in the first place.[82] Thus, according to this thesis, if a state is successful in defending a measure under the doctrine of mandatory requirements,

Article 30 will be considered not to have been violated at all. One can have sympathy for the Court in not wishing to acknowledge that with mandatory requirements it simply had written into the Treaty a new open-ended derogation clause complementing Article 36.[83] One can have less sympathy for those judicial decisions which try to camouflage this fact by pretending that mandatory requirements simply qualify what is or is not a violation of Article 30, as distinct from Article 36 which 'redeems' or justifies a *prima facie* violation.

It is respectfully submitted that this is no more than formalist sophistry driven by the embarrassment of the Court (and perhaps some observers of the Court) to admit what is really happening. You extend (with good reason in my view) the Law of Justification extensively by allowing the Member States to plead justifications nowhere mentioned in Article 36 but you pretend that this is all part of what 'qualifies' a violation of Article 30.[84] Who do they[85] think they are fooling? The material test of a violation of Article 30 is the need of a Member State to come into Court and defend its actions as justified in accordance with the doctrinal hoops of *Cassis*: legitimate policy, absence of extant harmonization, proportionality, and so on. If a Member State is required to justify in this manner – Article 30 has been violated on its face. It is also clear, and the Court as much as says that in *Cassis* and cases like it, that even when a state measure is justified under mandatory requirements, Community harmonization would be indicated in precisely the same way as would be the case if a measure were justified under Article 36. The only meaningful doctrinal difference between Article 36 and mandatory requirements is the puzzling stipulation that the Court itself imposed as one of the conditions for its successful invocation; namely, that the state measure in question must be indistinctly applicable. I say puzzling since if a state has a good reason to impose a distinctly applicable measure (such as in our rabies example), why should it be able to rely on justifications listed in Article 36 but not those deriving from *Cassis* and its progeny?

2 But for this anomaly, the first cumulative effect of the first doctrine in *Cassis* coupled with the tax cases represent in my view the emergence of a general principle of justification operating parallel to the general principle of non-discrimination on grounds of nationality according to which it is always possible to plead any social policy – other than protectionism of course – as a justification for violating fundamental economic freedoms provided it could be shown that the importance of such policy and its specific implementation in the particular case overrides

the interest in the free movement of goods and cannot be achieved by measures lesser burdensome to trade.

3 As regards the second doctrine in *Cassis*, the Court famously preaches the rhetoric of mutual recognition: 'There is therefore no valid reason why, provided that they have been lawfully produced and marketed in one of the Member States, [products] should not be introduced into any other Member State.'[86]

This statement would be alarming if it represented legal reality. After all, different Member States may have different standards of protecting their consumers. Why should the fact that a product is lawfully produced and marketed in one Member State allow that product to be introduced into another Member State if the standards of protection in the two jurisdictions are different?

In fact, the Court may have used the language of mutual recognition but employs the practice of functional parallelism.[87] After all, even in *Cassis* itself, it allowed Germany to insist that a product lawfully marketed in France be labelled differently as a requirement for accessing the German market. Only with a label indicating its (lower) alcoholic content does French *Cassis* become functionally parallel to the German regulation of fairness of commercial transactions.[88]

This is a welcome precision and very important for the marketplace for, indeed, if the standards of two Member States are functionally equivalent, there is no reason to exclude the products. It should also be noted that for all the attention *Cassis* received, 'mutual recognition' or functional equivalence is not a radical hermeneutic departure, but in fact a very conservative and fully justified application of the principle of proportionality.[89] For a Member State to insist on a specific technical standard even if a different standard is functionally parallel in achieving the desired result, is to have adopted a measure which is not the least restrictive possible.[90]

I cannot overstate the importance of this doctrinal point since, in my view, it foreshadows that which will, inevitably, happen in the WTO. Under the GATT, proportionality, under the appellation of the doctrine of necessity, is well-established in broad terms. Thus, if the logic of *Cassis*-style 'mutual recognition' or functional parallelism is rooted in the requirement that a restriction will be 'necessary', it becomes inevitable that a similar doctrine will emerge in the GATT too.[91] How can a State justify excluding an imported product which meets functionally parallel regulation? Why would it be necessary under Article XX GATT to do so? This is already mandated in the regime set up by SPS, advocated in the TBT and argued in the GATT[92] and their equivalents in the NAFTA.

Evaluating the second generation

We may now turn to evaluating the second generation.

1 The doctrine of mandatory requirements was a successful doctrine giving an effective answer to the first second-generation problem. But it had the effect of even deepening the enmeshment of the Court in the evaluation and sanctioning of Member State social policies in conflict with free movement and this in ever more delicate areas. It is one thing, and never an easy thing, for the Court to pronounce on, say, matters of health of animals or humans; it is altogether more difficult and delicate to pronounce on the policies behind Sunday trading bans and the like. As the endless material reach of the *Dassonville* formula began to sink in and the justifications that may be pleaded by member states became wider and wider, and as it was, ultimately, for the Court to decide whether a specific policy and its application were so important as to override the interest of free movement of goods, the improbability of its adjudicatory role became more and more acute.

2 This became particularly so in relation to the proportionality test and mutual recognition and equivalence. As noted, a central feature of the proportionality test is whether a policy objective could be achieved by a less-restrictive measure or, whether the policy of another member state is functionally equivalent. Very often, functional equivalence is established by the method of labelling: if the consumer is informed of the content of a product, the dangers associated with the product etc., one can more easily recognize the functional equivalence of different regulatory standards.

Supposedly this is a technical, value-free, determination which the Court could make on the basis of evidence submitted to it or review when made, as a matter of mixed law and fact, by a Member State court. Is the insulating requirement of Member State A on a washing machine excessive? Can the safety of the user be guaranteed by a more modest insulating requirement applied by Member State B on its washing machines? Call in the experts, weigh the evidence and make a determination – it is quite amusing to note how these hot potatoes are tossed between the national judiciary and the Court; it often appears that member state courts would much rather the ECJ took those decisions on proportionality. When it works it is very beneficial and has been appropriately received with accolades.[93] But there is a dark side to this moon too. Reality is far more complex and involves, in countless cases, the European Court imposing its values on the level of tolerable risk allocation in society.

Take, by way of example, the least probable case of all, *Cassis* itself. The Court found that the objective of the German government of ensuring that the consumer should not be misled into buying a liqueur believing it to have a higher alcoholic content was legitimate. But it also found that that objective could be achieved by a measure less restrictive than the German outright ban; namely, by requiring the product to carry a label displaying its alcoholic content. What is involved in this banal and intuitively correct decision? It is clear that even if Cassis and other French liqueurs were to carry that label, some consumers would still be misled: some cannot read, others do not read. The communicative effect of labels is notoriously quite limited. What, in effect, the Court decides in *Cassis* is that the German policy of zero-tolerance to any consumer confusion does not override the societal interest in free movement of goods. Instead, the Court imposes its risk assessment reflected in the label requirement which, in effect, decides that in this area allowing a certain percentage of consumers to be misled (because of the limited communicative effect of a label) is acceptable. In other words, proportionality and functional equivalence (mutual recognition) are not doctrines which leave the Member State in question regulatory autonomy to decide on their own tolerance to risk. Surreptitiously they represent an encroachment on that very freedom.

Who cares? Well, one does care when one moves to the area of automobile safety, of food and beverage additives and the like in which such risk determination can decide, for example, the number of persons who will die on the road each year, the number of persons whose health will be put at risk by certain nutritional substances and the like. And certainly the Court itself feels uneasy in having to take these types of decisions. In these respects, then, the success of mandatory requirements is also a ticking time-bomb.

3 'mutual recognition' or parallel functionalism was, perhaps, an intellectual breakthrough but a colossal market failure. It simply did not, in practice, solve the second second-generation problem. There are several reasons for this. The most important is infinitely banal: goods which do not meet the technical standards of the importing country may not be marketed. Litigation may, of course, ensue; victory may even be achieved. But from a commercial point of view this is a nonsense.[94] One cannot plan, produce and market product lines hoping that eventually a court decision will vindicate a claim of mutual recognition or functional parallelism.

4 There are other reasons which explain the practical failure of the doctrine. In many instances there are product lines where there are genuine differences in regulatory regimes, where there is no functional parallelism. In this case harmonization is simply required and cannot be achieved by judicial means. In some cases, the nature of the product requires a single pan-European standard.

Cassis in this respect is a lesson on the potential and limits of judicial impact: There is only so much that can be achieved by the courts.

The third generation: from judicial to political mutual recognition

The third generation of free movement which took place in the late 1980s moved away from the Courts and was characterized by the New Approach to Harmonization (NAH) by the White Paper[95] and the Single Market 1992 project, by the Single European Act[96] and the very important modifications introduced by Article 100a and by the adoption, in the legislative arena, of the ideas explored *inter alia* in *Cassis*.[97]

This is not the place to describe in detail the NAH and it will be sufficient to highlight its key features. They form an important part of the convergence paradigm since in a fundamental sense the NAH is about a greater respect for national regulatory autonomy.

The first feature of the NAH is encapsulated in the regime of the information directives.[98] These require Member States to notify the Community (and other Member States) of any new proposed measures which would constitute an obstacle to free movement of goods. This regime allows the Commission and other Member States to react before the national measures come into force and if necessary 'communauterize' them or challenge them. On its face this looks like part and parcel of the harmonization discipline of the *Dassonville* genus. But in fact at a deeper level it is a recognition that in the setting of socio-economic values and the mix of regulation and market, it is the Member States and the organic societies they represent which are the long-term repositories of wisdom and legitimacy.

The central feature of the NAH – as reflected initially in the Low Voltage Directive[99] and then in the establishment of bodies like CEN and CENELEC[100] – is adoption at the *legislative* level of the *Cassis* rationale. Two features characterize the new system: first, a minimalist approach to harmonization, meaning that the Community will seek to harmonize only that which is truly necessary to ensure a common marketplace in goods allowing otherwise a fare share of regulatory competition.[101] Second, in the setting of Community standards, where possible, the Community will only set overall standards and allow standard-setting bodies within member states to establish their own specifications which would meet the overall Community standards.[102] Here the deference to regulatory autonomy is clear long before subsidiarity came into vogue. The key to the success of the NAH was the shift in the presumption: Goods certified by a national body as complying with specifications established pursuant to a Community standard would be allowed to circulate freely without having to prove on a case by case basis their equivalence.[103] Simply, but with profound market implications. This coupled with the shift to majority voting which made it possible to set standards at the Community level meant a veritable sea change in the evolution of the marketplace.

It is also a reminder to the limits of judicial power. Functional parallelism may have been a brilliant legal construct but it could not have major market impact without the intervention of the legislator.

The fourth generation

The early 1990s see a new departure in the famous or infamous[104] 1993 *Keck* decision and its subsequent line of cases. Advocate General Gordon Slynn in *Cinéthèque*[105] jolted the prevailing legal culture. The Court intermittently issued the odd case, such as *Oebel*,[106] seemingly at odds with its normal jurisprudence which was a sign of subterranean cracks appearing in the *Dassonville* construct. Walter van Gerven became the Prophet standing at this gate, the intellectual hero of a new phase in the writing and rewriting of the economic constitution of Europe. Already in the late 1980s in, say, the Sunday-trading cases,[107] he made a powerful plea for a change of direction.[108] Sunday-trading well represents the 'end-game' of the *Dassonville* rationale, arguably a pathological end-game. Since a ban on Sunday trading, instituted for deep historical, cultural and social reasons, affects the volume of trade, notably in some sectors such as the DIY industry, and since that volume reduction would also affect imports, the *Dassonville* formula is triggered and a member state would have to justify such a rule by reference to the criteria of Article 36 and/or mandatory requirements. Let us assume that the member state would be successful in mounting its justification. For the Advocate General this was no solution. It was the methodology that he attacked, not the result. His plea was that Sunday-trading-type cases would not be considered as having violated Article 30 at all. When the

Court in, say, *Torfaen* holds 'that Article 30 of the Treaty must be interpreted as meaning that the prohibition which it lays down does not apply to national rules prohibiting retailers from opening their premises on Sunday where the restrictive effects on Community trade which may result therefrom do not exceed the effects intrinsic to rules of that kind',[109] it may appear that the Advocate General had already won his battle in that case. But we should not be misled. These conclusory Recitals in the Court's decisions are just another instance of the formalist sophistry mentioned above. In the Sunday-trading cases, the Member States were duly put through their hoops, the measure duly had to be justified by reference to legitimate policies and the test of proportionality was duly applied and, indeed, conditioned the results. What the Advocate General had in mind was a veritable reversal of *Dassonville* to exclude Sunday-trading-type cases from the very catch of Article 30 so that they would not even have to be justified.

The change comes in *Keck* where the Court famously held:

> contrary to what has previously been decided, the application to products from other Member States of national provisions restricting or prohibiting certain selling arrangements is not such as to hinder directly or indirectly, actually or potentially, trade between Member States within the meaning of the Dassonville judgment (case 8/74 [1974] ECR 837), so long as those provisions apply to all relevant traders operating within the national territory and so long as they affect in the same manner, in law and in fact, the marketing of domestic products and of those from other Member States.[110]

From the evolutionary perspective I am first interested in the possible motives, articulated or otherwise, which can explain this change of direction.[111] The Court itself, uncharacteristically, addresses in Recital 14 of its decision the question of motive as distinct from legal reasoning:

> in view of the increasing tendency of traders to invoke Article 30 of the Treaty as a means of challenging any rules whose effect is to limit their commercial freedom even where such rules are not aimed at products from other Member States, the Court considers it necessary to re-examine and clarify its case-law on this matter.[112]

One may read this statement as a simple concern for docket control, a worry by the Court that it is being swamped by limitless cases. But we should, I think, give more credit to the Court. If the doctrine is justified on its merits, your alarm at an increase in case load should be directed at the phenomena that give rise to the increase, not to the doctrine. You do not address a growing flood of murder cases by changing the definition of murder. Recital 14 must, thus, be taken as a rethinking of the very merits of the *Dassonville* doctrine as it developed in the jurisprudence of the Court almost 20 years after its inception.[113] A willingness on the part of the Court to openly acknowledge that its judicial doctrines are rooted in a socio-political and economic reality which changes with time and which call for revision even of the most hallowed canons.[114]

What, then, are the conditions which had changed since *Dassonville* which could explain the new approach by the Court? Speculating, of course, the following come to mind:

1 1993 is a symbolic date – the first year of the post-Single Market 31 December 1992 deadline (in France it was always 1 January 1993). Twenty years after *Dassonville* things had truly changed. In large measure the commitment to a Single Market was internalized by national administrations and the reflexive habits of intra-Community protectionism had not disappeared perhaps but were certainly not presumptive. This was, after all, post-Maastricht, a Union committed to EMU and all that. There was, too, a maturing of economic thinking as evident in the New Approach to Harmonization which was much more tolerant to regulatory diversity if it did not have major impact on access to the market, and even the virtues of some regulatory competition became apparent. Unlike twenty years earlier, the harmonization programme had, by comparison, become hugely successful and the need for judicial activism as a means of driving the common market agenda had considerably lessened. Conditions existed for a more relaxed, more mature, doctrinal framework.

2 The Court will have had its own 'self-preservation' agenda. As noted, the Sunday-trading-type case puts the Court increasingly into 'no-win' conundrums in which it has to engage in balancing public interest concerns of a delicate and extremely intrusive nature.[115] The hot-potato saga of who will decide proportionality – national courts or the European Court – is a veritable sign of the Court's unease at the situation it found itself in, an unease that was not apparent in earlier generations of jurisprudence.

3 In its human-rights jurisprudence the Court had held in cases such as *ERT*[116] that member state measures in derogation of, *inter alia*, the Article 30 prohibition would be subject to judicial scrutiny not simply

for, say, proportionality but also for human rights – a very controversial and delicate, even if fully justified, position. From this perspective *Dassonville* was a disaster: For even if the Court was to give a clean bill of health to member state measures, it would find itself in a position which it finds particularly inimical: having to stand as a *de facto* appeal instance *vis-à-vis* national courts. For, after all, national courts will happily refer to the ECJ questions on the correct interpretation of, say, Article 30, but they feel perfectly competent to decide themselves if a member state measure (!) violates fundamental human rights.

4 The issue of competences is, in my view, one of the most important issues which explain *Keck*. There are two linked dimensions to it. The first is the general Maastricht attention to limiting competences – through the concept of subsidiarity,[117] through the legislative restrictions imposed, say, in the public health or cultural field. But, even more critical is the fact that since the late 1980s and the entry into force of the Single European Act, the entire issue of limits to Community competences took on a new urgency. The force behind this urgency was the shift to majority voting. Hitherto, the delicacy of Community jurisdictional limits was attenuated by the political fact of unanimity. The governments of the member states could block any measure that they did not like. Jurisdictional overreach of, say, the Commission could be checked by an outraged member state at the negotiating table. Since July 1987 this was no longer so. Suddenly, constitutional limits rather than political power became very important in the competences game. *Dassonville* is also a disaster from this perspective: the broader the catch of Article 30, the broader the legislative competences of the Community. If Sunday-trading rules are held to violate Article 30 ex *Dassonville* even if justified by reference to mandatory requirements, they become 'prey' to the Community legislative process ex Article 100a operating by majority vote. If they are excluded from the catch, they are beyond the reach of the Community legislator, unless some other independent Treaty legislative legal basis could be found. In *Keck*, knowingly or otherwise, the Court made a major contribution to a more limited form of Community governance, very much in the *geist* of the times.

Be the motives for *Keck* as they may, there is a second central issue concerning this decision: its precise catch. The Court's formulation restricting the new departure to 'certain selling arrangements' is surely inadequate. The Court, after all, was intent on excluding from the catch of Article 30 'Such legislation [which] may ... restrict the volume of sales, and hence the volume of sales of products from other Member

States'.[118] But without barring their access and without discriminating against them. Why then restrict the formula to selling arrangements? Why should, say, a ban on the selling of cigarettes in machines or in candy stores frequented by children come under the *Keck* formula and be excluded from Article 30 (even thought it will restrict the volume of sales and hence the volume of sales of products from other member states), and a ban on smoking in public places which will have precisely the same effect of restricting the volume of sales and so on but since not a 'selling arrangement' not be caught by *Keck* and thus come under the old reach of *Dassonville* and constitute a violation of Article 30 with all the attendant consequences?

The test, surely, should be the following: rules that bar market access are caught by Article 30 and must be justified; market regulation rules – whether selling arrangements or otherwise – that do not bar access should not be caught unless discriminatory in law or in fact. There is in fact, in Recital 17 of *Keck*, language to support this reading:

> Provided that those conditions are fulfilled, the application of such rules to the sale of products from another Member State meeting the requirements laid down by that State is not by nature *such as to prevent their access to the market* or to impede access any more than it impedes the access of domestic products. Such rules therefore fall outside the scope of Article 30 of the Treaty. (Emphasis added)

If access is prevented, the need for justification is triggered. If access is merely impeded, the need for justification is triggered only if it is discriminatory, that is when the access of imports to the marketplace is impeded 'more than it impedes the access of domestic products'. It is a pity that the Court has in subsequent cases stuck with the selling-arrangement terminology of Recital 16, instead of the market-access terminology of 17.

If one could rid oneself of the selling-arrangements formula, *Keck* would come to represent a departure even greater than it appears at first sight. For it would allow us to reformulate a new 'universal field theory' of Free Movement of Goods and reduce it to a couple of simple propositions:

> The General Rule of Free Movement: National provisions which do not affect in the same manner, in law and in fact, the marketing of domestic products and of those from other Member States, must be justified by a public interest taking precedence over the free movement of goods.

This first proposition could be seen as based on general principles of Community law which derive from, but stand independently of, any specific Treaty provision. Note that it catches both pecuniary and non-pecuniary measures and is, in effect, a National Treatment overarching principle for the Community:

> The Special Rule of Free Movement (Article 30): National provisions which prevent access to the market of imported goods must also be so justified.

This represents a redimensioning of Article 30 and its repositioning not as the fount from which the field derives, but as a special rule designed to catch a specific (and diminishing) category of Member State measures, those which totally exclude a good from the market – even when such exclusion is not discriminatory or overtly protectionist. It is a reading of Article 30 which regards quantitative restrictions as measures which bar access to the market and, thus, insists that measure having an effect equivalent should also be so construed.

The combined effect of the above General and Special Rules is to make the combat against discrimination the key premise of the field and to downsize the old law of obstacles to those cases where the obstacles result in effective exclusion of products from the market. Obviously in operationalizing these rules one would have recourse to the myriad analytical tools developed in the previous generations of free movement such as proportionality, such as the various notions of what constitutes discrimination, such as onus and burden of proof. But, nonetheless, this new 'field theory' would have two virtues: first, it signifies a change, a maturation, to a system which is based on the substantial accomplishment of a Single Market rather than on the need to accomplish it, an accomplishment which permits a greater tolerance of national and local regulatory diversity; and, secondly, it does away with the artificiality of having different doctrinal regimes for pecuniary regulation and legislative and administrative regulation as well as subdivisions within this last category. Above all it represents what seems to me the right balance between the exigencies of a single market and the regulatory autonomy of member states.

If a product trading lawfully in another Member State is excluded from your market – even in a non-discriminatory fashion, you 'owe' your trading partners a justification, and you should accept the discipline of harmonization as part of the common market compact. But if you allow the products of your partners to enter into your marketplace, provided you do not discriminate against them, they should not seek justification, nor should the Union have the right to harmonize away your specific regulatory choice.

The fifth generation

The Court, judges as well as Advocates General, are still ambivalent about their *Keck* jurisprudence, uneasy about its extension to other areas of free movement such as services and still working out its permutations. In the literature it is still contested with the usual strategies of such cases: one tries either to claim that it is wrong, or that it is unimportant, or that it does not change much since we were already there. I have staked my position clearly: it is a good decision and in that sense it is 'right' though it does not go far enough by sticking to the selling arrangements formula; it is very important; it does represent a change. Time will tell whether it becomes the new foundation as suggested in my presumptuously titled universal field theory – which, of course, is hardly a theory at all, but a way to cap the culmination of a new constitutional settlement; or whether it is marginalized.

By way of conclusion I want to suggest what in my view will be the critical jurisprudence of the 'next generation'. Here, too, I detect a strong convergence between disparate trade regimes including the GATT and the EC. This convergence is manifest in many areas and I shall mention but a few:

1 The GATT until recently never took seriously its own Article XI and the prohibition contained therein. For complex reasons which I shall explain elsewhere, it was rare to challenge non-discriminatory quantitative restrictions even where those totally barred access of imported products to a domestic market. The *Hormones* Panel Decision represents the GATT attempt to take Obstacle seriously. *Keck* represents a 'bending' of the EC towards the National Treatment rationale of the GATT. *Hormones* represents the 'bending' of the GATT towards the Obstacles rationale of the EC.

2 I have already mentioned my prediction that 'mutual recognition' or, more accurately, functional parallelism, will inevitably find its way into GATT jurisprudence. Likewise one is going to find, increasingly, attempts at the transnational level to find equivalents to Article 100 and 100a-type harmonization as a means of addressing in-built fragmentation. TBT, SPS and various transnational codes are the visible signs of this.[119]

3 As the convergence process progresses, the simplistic dream of 'constitutionalizing' the GATT in the structural terms and in some ways using the EU as a 'model' for the WTO (and other transnational regimes) through the advocacy of Article 234 (former 177) type of court referral procedures will become far more nuanced. European constitutionalism is undergoing a certain crisis and Reformation conditioned by the tension and gap between its legal imperatives and its social and political reality. The Appellate body decision in *Hormones,* which clawed back some of the more audacious aspects of the Panel, was apparently mindful of the problems of giving binding constitutional force to standards adopted by faceless officials and enforced by adjudicatory bodies whose legitimacy is a matter of some considerable delicacy.[120] Sounds familiar.

4 Finally, in a convergence story of which much more could and should be told, there is a new set of cases in which the WTO and EC seem to be facing a similar and new type of problem. The harbingers are cases like *Hedley Lomas*[121] in the EU context and *Dolphins*[122] and *Turtles*[123] in the context of the WTO–GATT. Cases such as these are bound to become more prevalent and more difficult. They concern the ability of the importing state to place restrictions based not on the characteristics of the product, but in terms of the methods of production in the exporting state. The classical premises of extant jurisprudence are reluctant to acknowledge such concerns as legitimate justification for excluding products. International trade theory is also ambivalent, especially since place of production concerns can extend to factors of production which are part of the comparative advantage of the exporting state.[124] Political economists are ambivalent since these concerns are often no more than a form of cultural imperialism. On the other hand, the very success of open markets and free trade drives home to people that their own consumption habits and practices are inevitably complicit in practices that would be banned in the country of consumption.

One should not leave this story with the impression that the convergence trend is more than just a trend. Even if the WTO moves increasingly to a regime which is willing to challenge non-discriminatory barriers to access, reality will surely be that in many cases such barriers will be justified and the problem of WTO-fragmented markets will remain. The EU harmonization philosophy, even if attenuated by the New Approach still represents a major difference between the two. But I will repeat two predictions which, I believe, will be part of the next stages in the convergence process. It will not be long before a WTO Panel and/or the Appellate Body will pronounce a WTO version of the Doctrine of

Parallel Functionalism (or mutual recognition). One can restate the simple reason. Mutual recognition may seem to some the highlight of Community particularism,[125] a result of its very cohesive nature and unsuited to the broader Community. But in fact it is but a banal doctrinal manifestation of the principle of necessity which is also a pillar of GATT jurisprudence. If an imported product meets the safety or other *objectives* of the importing state regulatory regime but does so by adopting a different set of technical standards which are not authorized by the importing state regulation – how could they ever claim that it is *necessary* to exclude that import from the national market? And if they cannot so claim, how could they justify the exclusion under the Justification regime of Article XX GATT? We already find a legislative expression of this in the TBT[126] and SPS Agreements.[127]

We will also see an increase in the pressure on WTO bodies or WTO-approved bodies to adopt international standards which private operators in the global marketplace could adopt as a way to ensure the access of their products to national markets. The WTO may not call this harmonization, but it will be the functional equivalent. Indeed, the most intriguing development in this respect will be the convergence of national regulatory regimes among the large trading blocs (the USA, the EU, Canada and so on) as a means of ensuring smooth operation of 'their' corporations and then the internationalization of such harmonized standards.

Notes

1 Case C-24/68, *Commission of European Communities* v. *Italian Republic* [1969] ECR 193.

2 In fact, the Italian government tried to argue that the statistical levy was 'too insignificant in amount to disturb the market', see Case C-24/68, *Commission of European Communities* v. *Italian Republic* [1969] ECR 193, 197.

3 Case C-24/68, *Commission of European Communities* v. *Italian Republic* [1969] ECR 193, Par. 15: 'The Italian Government further maintains that the disputed charge constitutes the consideration for a service rendered and as such cannot be designated as a charge having equivalent effect. According to the Italian Government the object of the statistics in questions is to determine precisely the actual movement of goods, and, consequently, changes of the state of the market. It claims that the exactness of the information thus supplied affords importers a better competitive position in the Italian market whilst exporters enjoy a similar advantage abroad and that the special advantages which dealers obtain from the survey justifies their paying for this public service and moreover demonstrates that the disputed charge is in the nature of a qui pro quo.'

The Court has held in the past that a charge to be interpreted as a compensation for administrative or governmental services must be of direct effect to the goods or traders and must not exceed the actual cost of the service rendered. See Joined Cases C-52/65 and C-55/65, *Federal Republic of Germany* v. *Commission of the European Economic Community* [1966] ECR 159, 170: '... In this case the disputed charges are charges levied by the Federal Republic of Germany on the actual importation of goods and specifically on certain products originating in the other Member States. They may therefore have the effect of increasing to some extent the price of the imported products on which they are levied. The applicant Government submits however that they do not have the same effect as a customs duty, because, since they represent the consideration for a specific service provided by the administration for the benefit of and at the request of importers, they do not have a discriminatory effect on the products imported. The service provided by the administration consists of the various investigations and tasks necessary to alleviate the effects of the quantitative restrictions which the Federal Republic of Germany, acting within its powers, has established on the free importation of the products in question. The benefit which the importer obtains from the operations of the administration in respect of which the disputed charges are levied is the permission to market the products in question in the Federal Republic of Germany. The imported products themselves enjoy no direct or indirect advantage on the German market. For this reason the disputed charges have a discriminatory effect on the imported products, which, however small it may be, is equivalent to that of a customs duty ...'.

Case C-39/73, *Rewe-Zentralfinanz eGmbH* v. *Direktor der Landwirtschaftskammer Westfalen-Lippe* [1973] ECR 1039, 1044 Recital 4: 'Although it is not ruled out that there may be certain circumstances in which particular service rendered may possibly give rise to some consideration, which should not exceed either the value or the cost of the service, they can only be special cases which cannot lead to the provisions of Article 13 of the Treaty being circumvented. The activity of the administration of the State intended to maintain a phytosanitary system imposed in the general interest cannot be regarded as a service rendered to the importer such as to justify the imposition of a pecuniary charge.'

Joined Cases C-2/69 and C-3/69, *Sociaal Fonds voor de Diamantarbeiders* v. *S.A. Ch. Brachfeld & Sons and Chougol Diamond Co.* [1969] ECR 211, Recital 19/21: 'Although it is not impossible that in certain circumstances a specific service actually rendered may from the consideration for a possible proportional payment for the service in question, this may only apply in specific cases which cannot lead to the circumvention of the provisions of Articles 9 and 12 of the Treaty.'

C-132/82, *Commission* v. *Belgium* [1983] ECR 1649, Recitals 10–14: '10. ... It should therefore be noted, in the first place, that the placing of imported goods in temporary storage in the special stores of public warehouses clearly represents a service rendered to traders. A decision to deposit the goods there can indeed be taken only at the request of the trader concerned and then ensures their storage without payment of duties, until the trader has decided how they are to be dealt with ... 11. However it appears ... that the storage charges are payable equally when the goods are presented at the public warehouse solely for the completion of customs formalities, even though they have been exempted from storage and the importer has not requested that they be put in temporary storage ... 13. ... Whilst it is true that the use of a public warehouse in the interior of the country offers certain advantaged to importers it seems clear first of all that such advantages are linked solely with the completion of customs formalities which, whatever the place, is always compulsory ... 14. ... when payment of storage charges is demanded solely in connection with the completion of customs formalities, it cannot be regarded as the consideration for a service actually rendered to the importer.'

4 Case C-24/68, *Commission of European Communities* v. *Italian Republic* [1969] ECR 193, 197, Recital 16: 'The statistical information in question is beneficial to the economy as a whole and inter alia to the relevant administrative authorities. Even if the competitive position of importers and exporters were to be particularly improved as a result, the statistics still constitute an advantage so general, and so difficult to assess, that the disputed charge cannot be regarded as the consideration for a specific benefit actually conferred.'

5 The Commission's opinion was that the statistical levy was originally incompatible with Regulations of the Council nos. 19 (13/64/EEC), 20 (14/64/EEC), 21 (16/64/EEC) – all of which were repealed and replaced by Regulations of the Council nos 120/67, 121/67, 123/67, 804/68, 805/68, and 359/67, and 22 (136/66/EEC), see Case C-24/68, *Commission of European Communities* v. *Italian Republic* [1969] ECR 193, 195.

6 Case C-8/74, *Procureur du Roi* v. *Benoît and Gustave Dassonville* [1974] ECR 837.

7 Case C-120/78, *Rewe-Zentral AG* v. *Bundesmonopolverwaltung für Branntwein* [1979] ECR 649.

8 Joint Cases C-267/91 and C-268/91, *Criminal Proceedings against Keck and Mithouard* [1993] ECR-I, 6079.

9 Case C-24/68, *Commission of European Communities* v. *Italian Republic* [1969] ECR 193, 201.

10 The same wording of Recital 9 can be found in Recital 2 of another decision handed down on the same day, see Joined Cases C-2 and C-3/69, *Sociaal Fonds voor de Diamantarbeiders* v. *SA Ch. Brachfeld & Sons and Chougol Diamond Co.* [1969] ECR 211, Recital 2: 'Consequently, any pecuniary charge, however small and whatever its designation and mode of application, which is imposed unilaterally on domestic or foreign goods by reason of the fact that they cross a frontier, and which is not a customs duty in the strict sense, constitutes a charge having equivalent effect within the meaning of Articles 9 and 12 of the Treaty, even if it is not imposed for the benefit of the State, is not discriminatory or protective in effect or if the product on which the charge is imposed is not in competition with any domestic product.'

In this decision the Court struck down a charge which was levied on imported diamonds to the benefit of the *Sociaal Fonds voor de Diamantarbeiders*, the Social Fund for workers engaged in the diamond industry.

11 Case C-8/74, *Procureur du Roi* v. *Benoît and Gustave Dassonville* [1974] ECR 837, 852 (Recital 5).

12 René Barents, 'Charges of Equivalent Effect to Customs Duties', *Common Market Law Review*, 415, 418 [1978].

Case C-132/82, *Commission* v. *Belgium* [1983] ECR 1649, Par. 9: 'The prohibition of charges having an effect equivalent to customs duties, laid down in provisions of the Treaty, is justified on the grounds that pecuniary charges imposed by reason or on the occasion of the crossing of the frontier represent an obstacle to the free movement of good.'

13 Rabe, H.J., 'Garantien und Sicherungen des freien Warenverkehrs im Lichte der Neuesten Rechtsprechung des EuGH – Cassis de Dijon und die Folgerechtsprechung', in J. Schwarze (ed.), *Das Wirtschaftsrecht des Gemeinsamen Marktes in der Aktuellen Rechtsentwicklung*, 41–2, Baden-Baden: Nomos, 1983.
14 Case C-26/62, *Van Gend en Loos* v. *Nederlandse Administratie der Belastingen* [1963] ECR 1.
15 Case C-22/70, *EC Commission* v. *EC Council: ERTA* [1971] ECR 263.
16 Kohler, J., *Abgaben Zollgleicher Wirkung*, 68–71, Berlin: Duncker & Humblot, 1978.
17 Oppermann, T., *Europarecht*, 513, Munich: Auflage, 1999 [mentioning that it is sufficient that they could be deemed appropriate to form obstacles].
18 Barents, R., 'Charges of Equivalent Effect to Customs Duties', *Common Market Law Review* vol. 15, 415–21, Den Haag: Kluwer Law [1978].
19 Case C-24/68, *Commission of European Communities* v. *Italian Republic* [1969] ECR 193, 201.
20 Voß, R., 'Commentary on Article 95 EC', in E. Grabitz and M. Hilf (eds), *Kommentar zur Europäischen Union*, Supp. 12, May 1998, Par. 63–4.
21 The Court has thus decided that the scope of Art. 12 and 95 is mutually exclusive, see C-35/76, *Simmenthal Spa* v. *Ministere des Finances Italien* [1976] ECR 1294, Recitals 6 and 7: '6. Pecuniary Charges imposed by reason of veterinary or public health inspections of products on the occasion of their crossing the frontier are to be regarded as charges having an effect equivalent to customs duties. 7. Charges imposed by the Various Public Authorities on the occasion of veterinary and public health inspections carried out within Member States on both domestic and imported products constitute internal taxation to which the prohibition of discrimination in Article 95 of the Treaty apply.'

Case C-90/79, *Commission of the European Communities* v. *French Republic, Levy on the Use of Reprography* [1981] ECR 1446, Recital 1: 'The prohibition of charges having an effect equivalent to customs duties covers any charge exacted at the time of or on account of importation which, being borne specifically by an imported product to the exclusion of the similar domestic product, has the result of altering the cost price of the imported product thereby producing the same restrictive effect on the free movement of goods as a customs duty. The essential feature of a charge having an effect equivalent to a customs duty which distinguishes it from an internal tax therefore resides in the fact that the former is borne solely by an imported product as such whilst the latter is borne both by imported and domestic products.'
22 Voß, R., 'Commentary on Article 95 EC', in E. Grabitz and M. Hilf (eds), *Kommentar zur Europäischen Union*, Supp. 12, May, 1998, Par. 62.
23 Kohler, J., *Abgaben Zollgleicher Wirkung* 71, Berlin: Duncker & Humblot (1978); Barents, R., 'Charges of Equivalent Effect to Customs Duties', *Common Market Law Review*, vol. 15, 415–24, Den Haag: Kluwer Law (1978); Oppermann, T., *Europarecht*, 46, Munich: Auflage, 1999; Beschel, M. and N. Vaulont, 'Commentary on Article 12 EC', in H. von der Groeben, J. Thiesing and C.D. Ehlermann (eds), *Kommentar zum EU-/EG-Vertrag*, 5th ed. Baden-Baden: Nomos, 1997, p. 476.
24 Beschel M. and N. Vaulont, 'Commentary on Article 12 EC', in H. von der Groeben, J. Thiesing and C.D. Ehlermann (eds), *Kommentar zum EU-/EG-Vertrag*, 5th ed., Baden-Baden: Nomos, 1997, p. 462.

25 Tietje, C., Normative Grundstrukturen der Behandlung Nichttarifärer Handelshemmnisse in der WTO/GATT-Rechtsordnung, Berlin: Duncker und Humblot, 1998, p. 203.

26 Stoll, P.T., 'Freihandel und Verfassung. Einzelstaatliche Gewährleistung und die Konstitutionelle Funktion der Welthandelsordnung (GATT/WTO)', 57 Zeitschrift für Ausländisches und Öffentliches Recht und Völkerrecht, 83, 121–2, 1997. But see Langer, S., Grundlagen einer Internationalen Wirtschaftsverfassung, 86–92, 1997, who interprets GATT's Art. I as (only) resulting from 'negotiations on a reciprocal and mutually advantageous basis'.

27 Tietje, C., Normative Grundstrukturen der Behandlung Nichttarifärer Handelshemmnisse in der WTO/GATT-Rechtsordnung, Berlin: Duncker und Humblot, 1998, p. 225; Epiney, A., 'Welthandel und Umwelt, Ein Beitrag zur Dogmatik der Art. III, IX, XX GATT', 115 Deutsches verwaltungsblatt 77, 79, 2000; Barents, R., 'Charges of Equivalent Effect to Customs Duties', 15 Common Market Law Review, 415–24, Den Haag: Kluwer Law, 1978 ('... [This is based on the concept of] GATT that fiscal competitive benefits may be compensated in international trade. ... [W]hen a domestic product is subject to taxation, a charge may also be imposed on a similar imported product in order to compensate for the competitive benefit that has thus arisen ...').

Joined Cases 2/62 and 3/62, *Commission of the European Economic Community* v. *Grand Duchy of Luxembourg and Kingdom of Belgium* [1962] ECR 425, 431: 'The substance of the case the applications are brought for the purpose of obtaining a declaration of illegality in respect of the increase of the special import duty on gingerbread imposed after the Treaty entered into force, and, of the extension of that duty to other similar products considered as a charge having equivalent as a charge having equivalent effect to a customs duty prohibited by Articles 9 and 12. A charge having equivalent effect to a customs duty according to the terms of Article 9, the Community is based on a customs union founded on the prohibition of customs duties and of "all charges having equivalent effect". By Article 12 it is prohibited to introduce any "new customs duties on imports ... or charges having equivalent effect" and to increase those already in force. The Positions of these Articles towards the beginning of that part of the Treaty dealing with the "foundations of the Community" – Article 9 being placed at the beginning of the title relating to "free movement of goods", and Article 12 at the beginning of the Section dealing with the "elimination of customs duties" – is sufficient to emphasize the essential nature of the prohibitions which they impose. The importance of these prohibitions is such that, in order to prevent their evasion by different customs or fiscal practices, the Treaty sought to forestall any possible breakdown in their application. Thus it is specified (Article 17) that the prohibitions contained in Article 9 shall be applied even if the customs duties are fiscal in nature. Article 95, which is to be found both in that part of the Treaty dealing with the "policy of the Community" and in the Chapter relating to "tax provisions", seeks to fill in any loop-hole which taxation procedures might find in the prescribed prohibitions. This concern is taken so far as to forbid a State either to impose in any manner higher taxation on the products of other Member States than on its own or to impose on the products of those States any internal taxation of such a nature as to afford indirect "protection" to its domestic products.'

28 Voß, R., 'Commentary on Article 95 EC', in E. Grabitz and M. Hilf (eds), *Kommentar zur Europäischen Union*, Munich: Beck, Supp. 12, May 1998, Par. 2.

29 This reasoning is also resembled in the (slightly) different statements of the US and the EC with regard to possible justification of a different treatment of 'like' products under Art. III:2 GATT in the Panel Report on 'Japan – Taxes on Alcoholic Beverages', WT/DS8/R; WT/DS10/R; WT/DS11/R (11.7.1996). Whereas the US explained in this context that Art. 95 EC is more or less similar to Art. III GATT, the EC was of the opinion that one can infer from Art. XX GATT that a different treatment of 'like' products in the meaning of Art. III:2 GATT would only be possible for the reasons enumerated in Art. XX GATT. See Panel Report on 'Japan - Taxes on Alcoholic Beverages', WT/DS8/R; WT/DS10/R; WT/DS11/R (11.7.1996), Par. 4.26 (US statement) and 4.28 (EC statement):

'4.26 As a result, argued the United States, WTO Members are permitted to make regulatory distinctions among products that might otherwise be considered ... like ..., in pursuance of a legitimate objective other than trade protection. This is what the 1992 Malt Beverages report recognized in analyzing the regulatory regime for low alcohol and high alcohol beer. In the US view, that panel sought to avoid a result that would make even an unintentional coincidence between domestic regulation and the presence or absence of foreign competition in the market amount to a violation of Article III:2. Such a result would force policy harmonization and encroach on the policy options available to legislators and regulators to an extent unanticipated when GATT was drafted. The United States also pointed out that the European Court of Justice (ECJ) had reached similar conclusions in interpreting Article 95 of the EC Treaty.

4.28 On this comparison between the ECJ case law and GATT Article III, the Community argued that it is important to begin by pointing to a basic difference between GATT Article III:2 and the corresponding tax discrimination provision of the EC Treaty (Article 95). Article III:2 is covered by the general exception of GATT Article XX; Article 95 is not subject to any exception. 'The latter situation has certainly contributed to the ECJ's acceptance of the EC Treaty's regulatory distinctions for tax purposes of its own invention (but largely corresponding to treaty exceptions to Article 30, which prohibits quantitative restrictions). For the Community, the WTO legislator has provided a number of exceptions in Article XX, to which panels can refer, and, indeed, regulatory distinctions for tax purposes between products which would normally be considered like should not be made on grounds other than those included in GATT Article XX.'

30 Weiß, W., 'Gibt es eine EU-Inländerdiskriminierung?', 34 Europarecht, 499, 502–3, Munich: Auflage, 1999; Epiney, A., 'Welthandel und Umwelt, Ein Beitrag zur Dogmatik der Art. III, IX, XX GATT', 115 Deutsches Verwaltungsblatt, 77–9, footnote 12, Köln: Heymans, 2000.

31 Trebilcock, M.J. and R. Howse, The Regulation of International Trade, 30, 2nd ed., New York: Routledge, 1999.

32 Diem, A., Freihandel und Umweltschutz in GATT und WTO, 22, Baden-Baden: Nomos, 1996.

33 Weiß, W., 'Gibt es eine EU-Inländerdiskriminierung?', 34, Europarecht, 499, 503, Munich: Auflage, 1999.

34 Herdegen, M., Internationales Wirtschaftsrecht, 117, Munich: Beck, 1995.

35 It is well established in WTO practice – as it was under GATT '47 – that GATT's Article XX is a 'limited exception ... from obligations under certain other provisions of the GATT' and not a 'positive rule ... establishing obligations' in itself, see Appellate Body Report on 'United States – Measures Affecting Imports of Woven Shirts and Blouses from India', WT/DS33/AB/R (25.4.1997), p. 16; Panel Report on 'Brazil – Export Financing Program for Aircraft', WT/DS46/R (14.4.1999), Par. 7.55. Regarding the practice under GATT'47 see Panel Report on 'United States – Section 337 of the Tariff Act of 1930', GATT B.I.S.D. 36S/345 (adopted on 7.11.1989), Par. 5.9; Panel Report on 'United States – Prohibition on Imports of Tuna and Tuna Products from Canada', GATT B.I.S.D. 29S/91, Par. 4.8 (adopted on 22.2.1982); Panel Report on 'Canada – Administration of the Foreign Investment Review Act', GATT B.I.S.D. 30S/140, Par. 5.20 (adopted on 7.2.1984); Panel Report on 'Japan – Restrictions on Imports of Certain Agricultural Products', GATT B.I.S.D. 35S/163, Par. 5.1.3.7 (adopted on 2.2.1988).

36 Weiß, W., 'Gibt es eine EU-Inländerdiskriminierung?', 34, Europarecht, 499, 502, Munich: Auflage, 1999; Hahn, M.J., 'Eine Kulturelle Bereichsausnahme im Recht der WTO?', 56, Zeitschrift für Ausländisches Öffentliches Recht und Völkerrecht, 315–39, Heidelberg: Max-Planck-Institut, 1996; McGovern, E., 'Standards and Technical Regulations as Barriers to Trade', in A. Oureshi, H. Steiner and G. Parry (eds), *The Legal and Moral Aspects of International Trade*, 207, 208, 1998.

37 But see (in a wider context) Ruggiero, R., 'Whither the Trade System Next?', in J. Bhagwati and M. Hirsch (eds), *The Uruguay Round and Beyond*, 123, 135, 1998 [stating that the original GATT rules dealt with border measures as barriers to market access and starting with the Tokyo Round trade policy began to move inside the border by tackling issues such as subsidies, technical barriers to trade and Government procurement].

38 Tietje, C., Normative Grundstrukturen der Behandlung Nichttarifärer Handelshemmnisse in der WTO/GATT,-Rechtsordnung, 225–8, Berlin: Duncker und Humblot, 1998.

39 Thus, it has been argued that GATT's Art. III complements GATT's Art. I see Diem, A., Freihandel und Umweltschutz in GATT und WTO, 20, 1996; Langer, S., Grundlagen einer Internationalen Wirtschaftsverfassung, 108, 1997.

40 Sacerdoti, G., 'Standards of Treatment, Harmonization and Mutual Recognition: A Comparison between Regional Areas and the Global Trading System', in P. Demaret, J.F. Bellis and G. García Jiménez (eds), *Regionalism and Multilateralism after the Uruguay Round*, 613, 615–16, Brussels: European Interuniversity Press, 1997.

41 Diem, A., Freihandel und Umweltschutz in GATT und WTO, 98, 1996; but see Langer, S., Grundlagen einer Internationalen Wirtschaftsverfassung, 89, 1997, who assumes that the current international trade regime (which also includes trade in goods) acts as 'balancing the diverging social policy interests and goals between States'.

42 Case C-148/77, *H. Hansen and O.C. Balle GmbH and Co.* v. *Hauptzollamt Flensburg* [1978] ECR 1787.

43 Tietje, C., Normative Grundstrukturen der Behandlung nichttarifärer Handelshemmnisse in der WTO/GATT-Rechtsordnung, 211–13, Berlin: Duncker und Humblot, 1998.

44 But see Tietje, C., Normative Grundstrukturen der Behandlung nichttarifärer Handelshemmnisse in der WTO/GATT-Rechtsordnung, 240, 1998, who tries – from a different perspective – to infer Art. III's object and purpose exclusively from the theory of comparative advantage.

45 Art. XX GATT reads as follows:

'Art. XX General Exceptions. Subject to the requirement that such measures are not applied in a manner which would constitute a means of arbitrary or unjustifiable discrimination between countries where the same conditions prevail, or a disguised restriction on international trade, nothing in this Agreement shall be construed to prevent the adoption or enforcement by any contracting party of measures:

(a) necessary to protect public morals;
(b) necessary to protect human, animal or plant life or health;
(c) relating to the importation or exportation of gold or silver;
(d) necessary to secure compliance with laws or regulations which are not inconsistent with the provisions of this Agreement, including those relating to customs enforcement, the enforcement of monopolies operated under Paragraph 4 of Article II and Article XVII, the protection of patents, trade marks, and copyrights, and the prevention of deceptive practices;
(e) relating to the products of prison labour;
(f) imposed for the protection of national treasures of artistic, historic or archaeological value;
(g) relating to the conservation of exhaustible natural resources if such measures are made effective in conjunction with restrictions on domestic production or consumption;
(h) undertaken in pursuance of obligations under any intergovernmental commodity agreement which conforms to criteria submitted to the CONTRACTING PARTIES and not disapproved by them or which is itself so submitted and not so disapproved;*
(i) involving restrictions on exports of domestic materials necessary to ensure essential quantities of such materials to a domestic processing industry during periods when the domestic price of such materials is held below the world price as part of a governmental stabilization plan; Provided that such restrictions shall not operate to increase the exports of or the protection afforded to such domestic industry, and shall not depart from the provisions of this Agreement relating to non-discrimination;
(j) essential to the acquisition or distribution of products in general or local short supply; Provided that any such measures shall be consistent with the principle that all contracting parties are entitled to an equitable share of the international supply of such products, and that any such measures, which are inconsistent with the other provisions of this Agreement shall be discontinued as soon as the conditions giving rise to them have ceased to exist. The CONTRACTING PARTIES shall review the need for this sub-Paragraph not later than 30 June 1960.

Annex I;
Notes and Supplementary Provisions;
Ad Article XX
Sub-Paragraph (h)
The exception provided for in this sub-Paragraph extends to any commodity agreement which conforms to the principles approved by the Economic and Social Council in its resolution 30 (IV) of 28 March 1947.'

46 Cf. the excellent Mattera A., 'Les Barrières Frontalières à l'Intérieur de la CEE et l'Action Menée par la Commission pour Leur Démantelement', RMC, 1987, n. 307, pp. 264–76, spec. p. 266.

'L'acception ≪mesure d'effet équivalent≫ est une notion originale (aucun autre accord international n'avait auparavant eu recours à une telle expression); évolutive (comme le suggère l'acceptation textuelle elle-même, le terme ≪équivalent≫ de ≪aequus≫ et ≪valere≫ est une notion relative) et dans un certain sens ≪indéfinie≫ (nous avons pour preuve le fait que les définitions de l'expression ≪mesure d'effet équivalent≫ données par la Commission et la Cour sont à la limite de la ... tautologie)'. Cf. too Dona-Viscardini, W., 'Les Mesures d'Effet Équivalent à une Restriction Quantitative', RMC, 1973, pp. 224–33 et Béraud, R.C., 'Les Mesures d'Effet Équivalent au Sens des Articles 30 et Suivants du Traité de Rome', RTDE, 1968, pp. 265–92, spec. pp. 266, 267. Cfr. also Daniele, L., 'Réfléxions d'Ensemble sur la Notion de Mesures Ayant un Effet Équivalent à des Restrictions Quantitatives', RMC, 1984, n. 281, pp. 477–86, spec. p. 480.

47 The Commission may have at first intended the sweeping reach of Dassonville to be limited to border measures which prevented access and to challenge other cases (where products were allowed in) only in the case of discrimination. Whatever their intention, the Commission itself got swept with the extensive Dassonville interpretation and itself brought cases concerning internal regulation where there was no discrimination. See, e.g. Cases 216/84, 76/86, 255/86, 298/86, 169/87, 95/89, 210/89, 293/89, 375/90. The Commission has intervened in all other cases and is not noted for volubly rejecting the Court's approach to Dassonville.

48 Demaret, P. and R. Stewardson, 'Border Tax Adjustments under GATT and EC Law and General Implications for Environmental Taxes', 28, Journal of World Trade, 5, 41, 1994-IV.

49 Case C-29/87, *Dansk Denkavit ApS* v. *Danish Ministry of Agriculture* [1988] ECR 2965, Recitals 31–35:

'31. By its fifth question the national Court seeks essentially to ascertain whether an annual levy imposed in the same manner on importers of feeding stuffs containing additives and national manufacturers of such products and intended to cover the costs incurred by the State in checking samples taken pursuant to Directive 70/524 is compatible with Articles 9 and 95 of the Treaty and the provisions of Directive 70/524.

32. As has been stated above, Directive 70/524, as amended up to the adoption of Directive 84/587, does not prevent Member States from requiring traders to obtain an authorization. However, the exemption provided for in Article 36 of the Treaty with regard to measures of control in regard to traders

is solely concerned with restrictions on imports or exports and measures having an equivalent effect. It may not be extended to customs duties or charges having an equivalent effect which, for their part, fall outside the compass of Article 36. It follows that the question whether such charges are permissible must be appraised in relation to Article 9 or, as the case may be, Article 95 of the Treaty.

33. In that respect the Court has consistently held that the prohibition laid down in Article 9 of the Treaty of any customs duty and charge having an equivalent effect in relations between Member States covers any charge levied on the occasion or by reason of importation specifically affecting an imported product to the exclusion of a similar domestic product. Such a charge however does not fall within that classification if, as in the present case, it relates to a general system of internal dues applied systematically and in accordance with the same criteria to domestic products and imported products alike, in which case it does not come within the scope of Article 9 but within that of Article 95 of the Treaty.

34. With regard to Article 95 Denkavit alleges that in relation to the annual levy the discrimination to the detriment of importers consists in the fact that there may be several buyers from a domestic producer without this involving him in additional charges whereas if a foreign producer has several importers each importer must again pay the charge in question.

35. That argument cannot be accepted where the burden of the charge in question is borne by traders as such, irrespective of the quantity of products imported or manufactured. As the Court held in its judgment of 28 January 1981 in Case 32/80 Officier van Justitie vs Kortmann (1981) ECR 251, Article 95 is where an internal tax applies in accordance with the same criteria, objectively justified by the purpose for which the tax was introduced, to domestic products and imported products so that it does not result in the "imported products" bearing a heavier charge than that borne by the similar domestic product.'

See as well the opinion of Advocate General Darmon in Case C-29/87, *Dansk Denkavit ApS* v. *Danish Ministry of Agriculture* [1988] ECR 2965, Recitals 18–19:

18. The fifth question concerns the compatibility with Directive 70/524 and Articles 9 and 95 of the Treaty of an annual levy in the same amount on domestic producers and importers holding the aforementioned authorization and intended to cover the expenditure occasioned by the checks by random sampling carried out in accordance with Directive 70/524/EEC. The levy appears as connected with the system of authorization which, as we have just seen, is not covered by the Directive. Accordingly, it is not necessary to consider the levy' s lawfulness with regard to the Directive. It remains to consider it in the light of Articles 9 and 95 of the Treaty. Article 9, which prohibits customs duties and charges having equivalent effect, cannot preclude a system of taxation which, as in the present case, is imposed annually in the same amount on importers and domestic producers, of the quantities imported. The fixed and non-discriminatory nature of that taxation means, in my opinion, that it is not possible to see in it the characteristics of a 'pecuniary

charge ... imposed ... on goods by reason of the fact that they cross a frontier', referred in the judgment in Denkavit Loire vs French State.

19. I am similarly led to the view that the contested measure is not incompatible with Article 95 of the Treaty. The internal taxation in question seems to be identical as regards importers and domestic producers who are taxed according to the same criteria. In that respect the criteria set out in the Court' s judgment in Officier van Justitie vs Kortmann (13) may be recalled: 'It is sufficient that the internal tax applies in accordance with the same criteria, justified by the purpose for which the tax was introduced, to domestic products and imported products so that it does not result in the imported product' s bearing a charge than that borne by the similar domestic product'.

50 Regarding the relationship between Art. 30 and 95 EC the Court held that Art. 30 EC is not applicable if the dispute barriers to trade are of a fiscal nature, see Case C-252/86, Gabriel Bergandi v. Directeur Général des Impôts, [1988] ECR 1343, Recitals 31–4:

'31 As regards the progressive nature of the taxation as between the categories of products thus established, the court has held, most recently in its judgment of 17 September 1987 in Case 433/85 (Feldain v. Directeur des Services Fiscaux (1987) ECR 3521), that as Community law stands at present, the member states are in principle at liberty to subject products to a system of taxation which increases progressively in amount according to an objective criterion, provided that the system is free from any discriminatory or protective effect.

32 It must therefore be stated ... that a system of taxation graduated according to the various categories of automatic games machines, which is intended to achieve legitimate social objectives and which procures no fiscal advantage for domestic products to the detriment of similar or competing imported products, is not incompatible with Article 95.

33 ... [I]t need merely be borne in mind that Article 30 of the EEC Treaty covers in general all barriers to imports which are not already specifically covered by other provisions of the Treaty. Since the barriers ... are of a fiscal nature, their compatibility with the Treaty must be assessed only be reference to Article 95 of the treaty.

34 Consequently, it must be stated ... that Article 30 of the Treaty does not apply to the taxation of products originating in other Member States the compatibility of which with the Treaty falls under Article 95 thereof'.

See as well the opinion of Advocate General Mancini in Case C-252/86, *Gabriel Bergandi* v. *Directeur Général des Impôts* [1988] ECR 1343, Recital 9: 'The solution which I have proposed renders devoid of purpose the questions as to the compatibility of the contested tax with Articles 95 and 30 of the EEC Treaty; ... I shall merely make the following observations: a) as regards Article 95, the tax is not levied on goods but on the profitability of the service provided and, in the absence of proof of the non-existence of nationally manufactured automatic machines, it is impossible to identify discriminatory intent against the machines manufactured in other Member States; b) as regards Article 30, according to the decisions of this Court, obstacles of a fiscal nature to imports are not covered by that provision and in any event do not provide grounds for applying it in conjunction with Article 95 ...'.

51 Becker, U., Der Gestaltungsspielraum der EG-Mitgliedstaaten im Spannungsfeld Zwischen Umweltschutz und Freiem Warenverkehr, 13, Baden-Baden: Nomos, 1991; Everling, U., 'Zur Neueren EuGH-Rechtsprechung zum Wettbewerbsrecht', 17, Europarecht, 301, 303–4, 1982; Rabe, H.J., 'Garantien und Sicherungen des Freien Warenverkehrs im Lichte derNeuesten Rechtsprechung des EuGH – Cassis de Dijon und die Folgerechtsprechung', in J. Schwarze (ed.), *Das Wirtschaftsrecht des Gemeinsamen Marktes in der Aktuellen Rechtsentwicklung*, 41–3, Baden-Baden: Nomos-Verlagsgesellschaft, 1983.

52 Sacerdoti, G., 'Standards of Treatment, Harmonization and Mutual Recognition: A Comparison between Regional Areas and the Global Trading System', in P. Demaret, J.F. Bellis and G. García Jiménez (eds), *Regionalism and Multilateralism after the Uruguay Round*, 613, 622–5, Brussels: European Interuniversity Press, 1997; García Jiménez, G. and M. Gardeñes Santiago, 'Technical Standards in a Context of Regional Integration Agreements', in P. Demaret, J.F. Bellis and G. García Jiménez (eds), *Regionalism and Multilateralism after the Uruguay Round*, 631, 658, Brussels: European Interuniversity Press, 1997; Hahn, M.J., Die Einseitige Aussetzung von GATT-Verpflichtungen als Repressalie, 23–4, Berlin, New York: Springer, 1996.

53 Hahn, M.J., Die Einseitige Aussetzung von GATT-Verpflichtungen als Repressalie, 34, 1996; Gramlich, L., 'GATT und Umweltschutz – Konflikt oder Dialog? Ein Thema der Neunziger Jahre', 33, Archiv des Völkerrechts, 131, 153–4, Berlin, New York: Springer, 1995.

54 McGovern, E., 'Standards and Technical Regulations as Barriers to Trade', in A. Qureshi, H. Steiner and G. Parry (eds), *The Legal and Moral Aspects of International Trade*, 207, 213, New York: Routledge, 1998.

55 Müller-Graff, P.C., 'Commentary on Article 30 EC', in H. von der Groeben, J. Thiesing and C.D. Ehlermann (eds), *Kommentar zum EU-/EG-Vertrag*, Par. 43, 5th ed., Baden-Baden: Nomos, 1997.

56 Ehlermann, C.D., 'Die Bedeutung des Artikels 36 EWGV für die Freiheit des Warenverkehrs', 8, Europarecht, 1, 13, 1973.

57 Barents, R., 'New Developments in Measures Having Equivalent Effect', 18, Common Market Law Review, 271, 276, 1981.

58 Matthies, H. and R. von Borries, 'Commentary on Article 36 EC', in E. Grabitz and M. Hilf (eds), *Kommentar zur Europäischen Union*, Supp. 10, Par. 6, Munich: Beck, October 1996.

59 Veelken, W., 'Maßnahmen Gleicher Wirkung wie Mengenmäßige Beschränkunge' n. 12, Europarecht, 311, 338, 340, 1977.

60 Langer, S., Grundlagen einer Internationalen Wirtschaftsverfassung, 100–1, 1997.

61 Case C-5/77, *Carlo Tedeschi* v. *Denkavit Commerciale srl.* [1977] ECR 1555, Recitals 33–35:

'33 National measures regulating the composition of feeding-stuffs may in certain cases constitute measures having an effect equivalent to quantitative restrictions which are however capable, where they are justified by the protection of animal or human health, of coming within the application of Article 36 of the Treaty.

34 Article 36 is not designed to reserve certain matters to the exclusive jurisdiction of Member States but permits national laws to derogate from the principle of the free movement of goods to the extent to which such derogation is and continues to be justified for the attainment of the objectives referred to in that Article.

35 Where, in application of Article 100 of the Treaty, Community Directives provide for the harmonization of the measures necessary to ensure the protection of animal and human health and establish Community procedures to check that they are observed, recourse to Article 36 is no longer justified and the appropriate checks must be carried out and the measures of protection adopted within the framework outlined by the harmonizing Directive.'

62 Case C-5/94, *The Queen* v. *Ministry of Agriculture, Fisheries and Food, ex parte: Hedley Lomas (Ireland) Ltd.* [1996] ECR-I 2553, Recital 8: 'Article 36 of the Treaty allows the maintenance of restrictions on the free movement of goods, justified on grounds of the protection of the health and life of animals, which constitutes a fundamental requirement recognized by Community law. However, recourse to Article 36 is no longer possible where Community Directives provide for harmonization of the measures necessary to achieve the specific objective which would be furthered by reliance upon this provision.'

63 Matthies, H. and R. von Borries, 'Commentary on Article 36 EC', in E. Grabitz and M. Hilf (eds.), *Kommentar zur Europäischen Union*, Supp. 10, Par. 9, Munich: Beck, October 1996.

64 Recourse to Art. 36 EC is (only) derogated to the extent harmonization actually took place, see opinion of Advocate General Léger in Case C-5/94, *The Queen* v. *Ministry of Agriculture, Fisheries and Food, ex parte: Hedley Lomas (Ireland) Ltd.* [1996] ECR-I 2553, Recitals 14–16:

'14 Once a harmonizing Directive has been adopted, Member States can no longer impose requirements other than those provided for by the Directive, on condition that the harmonization introduced is complete.

15 If harmonization is only partial or if the Directive confers on Member States national powers to apply it or introduce measures of control, Articles 36 and 100 of the Treaty can apply at the same time.

16 Thus, as the Court ruled in its judgment in Van Bennekom: 'It is only when Community Directives, in pursuance of Article 100 of the Treaty, make provision for the full harmonization of all the measures needed to ensure the protection of human and animal life and institute Community procedures to monitor compliance therewith that recourse to Article 36 ceases to be justified. It is, however, not in dispute that such is not the case with the Directives dealing with pharmaceutical products. It is therefore necessary to consider whether measures which restrict the marketing of vitamins may be justified by Article 36 of the Treaty.'

65 Langeheine, B., 'Commentary on Article 100 EC', in E. Grabitz and M. Hilf (eds), *Kommentar zur Europäischen Union*, Supp. 7, Par. 76, Munich: Beck, September 1994; Müller-Graff, P.C., Binnenmarktziel und Rechtsordnung – Binnenmarktrecht, 42–3, Bergisch-Gladbach: J. Eul, 1989.

66 Steindorff, E., 'Unvollkommener Binnenmarkt', 158, Zeitschrift für das Gesamte Handels- und Wirtschaftsrecht, 149, 154, 1994.

67 Müller-Graff, P.C., 'Commentary on Article 30 EC', in H. von der Groeben, J. Thiesing and C.D. Ehlermann (eds), *Kommentar zum EU-/EG-Vertrag*, 5th ed. Par. 312, Bergisch-Gladbach: J. Eul, 1997.

68 McGovern E., 'Standards and Technical Regulations as Barriers to Trade', in A. Qureshi, H. Steiner and G. Parry (eds), *The Legal and Moral Aspects of International Trade*, 207, 208, New York: Routledge, 1998.

69 With regard to methodology, Müller interprets the (presumption of a) 'restrictive interpretation of exceptions clauses' as a petitio principii (Müller, F., Juristische Methodik, 211–12, 3rd ed., 1989).

70 Müller-Graff, P.C., 'Commentary on Article 30 EC', in H. von der Groeben, J. Thiesing and C.D. Ehlermann (eds), *Kommentar zum EU-/EG-Vertrag*, 5th ed., Par. 23, Bergisch-Gladbach: J. Eul, 1997, Veelken W., Maßnahmen Gleicher Wirkung wie Mengenmäßige Beschränkungen, 12, Europarecht, 311, 338, 1977.

71 Matthies, H. and R. von Borries, 'Commentary on Article 36 EC', in E. Grabitz and M. Hilf (eds), *Kommentar zur Europäischen Union*, Supp. 10, Par. 18, Munich: Beck, October 1996.

72 Ahlfeld, M., Zwingende Erfordernisse im Sinne der Cassis-Rechtsprechung des Europäischen Gerichtshofs zu Art. 30 EGV, 69, Baden-Baden: Nomos, 1997.

73 Schwintowski, H.P., 'Freier Warenverkehr im Europäischen Binnenmarkt, Eine Fundamentalkritik an der Rechtsprechung des EuGH zu Art. 28 EGV', 64, Rabels Zeitschrift für Ausländisches und Internationales Privatrecht, 38, 54, 55, 2000 [noting that the text of the Treaty did not include a 'mandatory requirement' and therefore concluding that it is incompatible with the Treaty].

74 Steindorff, E., 'Gemeinsamer Markt als Binnenmarkt', 150, Zeitschrift für das Gesamte Handels- und Wirtschaftsrecht, 687, 692, 1986; Rabe, H.J., 'Garantien und Sicherungen des Freien Warenverkehrs im Lichte der Neuesten Rechtsprechung des EuGH – Cassis de Dijon und die Folgerechtsprechung', in J. Schwarze (ed.), *Das Wirtschaftsrecht des Gemeinsamen Marktes in der Aktuellen Rechtsentwicklung*, 42–3, Baden-Baden: Nomos-Verlagsgesellschaft, 1983; Becker U., Der Gestaltungsspielraum der EG-Mitgliedstaaten im Spannungsfeld Zwischen Umweltschutz und Freiem Warenverkehr, 79, Baden-Baden: Nomos, 1991.

75 Steindorff, E., 'Gemeinsamer Markt als Binnenmarkt', 150, Zeitschrift für das Gesamte Handels- und Wirtschaftsrecht, 687, 691, 1986.

76 Müller-Graff P.C., 'Commentary on Article 30 EC', in H. von der Groeben, J. Thiesing and C.D. Ehlermann (eds), *Kommentar zum EU-/EG-Vertrag*, 5th ed., Par. 183, Baden-Baden: Nomos, 1997.

77 Becker, U., Der Gestaltungsspielraum der EG-Mitgliedstaaten im Spannungsfeld Zwischen Umweltschutz und Freiem Warenverkehr, 79, Baden-Baden: Nomos, 1991.

78 Schwintowski, H.P., 'Freier Warenverkehr im Europäischen Binnenmarkt, Eine Fundamentalkritik an der Rechtsprechung des EuGH zu Art. 28 EGV', 64, Rabels Zeitschrift für Ausländisches und Internationales Privatrecht, 38, 55, 2000.

79 Case C-46/80, *SpA Vinal* v. *SpA Orbat* [1981] ECR 77, Recitals 10–13:

'10 The plaintiff ... claims that the Italian system of taxes is compatible with the requirements of Article 95. It points out that Italy has a considerable production of ethylene, a petroleum derivative which is used in the manufacture of synthetic alcohol. It is accordingly impossible to accept that there is discrimination against imported synthetic alcohol when there is at least a potential for production of the same product in Italy. With regard to alcohol obtained by fermentation, Spa Vinal is concerned to show that there is no tax discrimination between alcohol produced in Italy and imported alcohol. Thus it appears that the Italian system of taxes is applied on the basis of objective conditions which are applicable without distinction to Italian products and to the products of other Member States. In this case there is a specific justification for these differing tax arrangements in that they are intended to promote types of production deserving of particular protection, namely the processing of a number of agricultural products, and to reduce correspondingly the consumption of petroleum products.

11 The argument ... was further developed by the Italian Government. It recalls that ... the court has recognized that the Member States may lay down differing tax arrangements, even for identical products, on the basis of objective criteria such as the conditions of production and the raw materials used ... According to the Court, such arrangements are compatible with the Treaty if they are laid down on the basis of objective factors and are not discriminatory or protective in their nature.

12 The arrangements challenged ... meet these requirements. In fact the different taxation of synthetic alcohol and of alcohol produced by fermentation in Italy is the result of an economic policy decision to favour the manufacture of alcohol from agricultural products and, correspondingly, to restrain the processing into alcohol of ethylene, a derivative of petroleum, in order to reserve that raw material for other more important economic uses. It accordingly constitutes a legitimate choice of economic policy to which effect is given by fiscal means. The implementation of that policy does not lead to any discrimination since although it results in discouraging imports of synthetic alcohol into Italy, it also has the consequence of hampering the development in Italy itself of production of alcohol from ethylene, that production being technically perfectly possible.

13 As the court has stated on many occasions ... in its present stage Community law does not restrict the freedom of each Member State to lay down tax arrangements which differentiate between certain products on the basis of objective criteria, such as the nature of the raw materials used or the production processes employed. Such differentiation is compatible with Community law if it pursues economic policy objectives which are themselves compatible with the requirements of the Treaty and its secondary law and if the detailed rules are such as to avoid any form of discrimination, direct or indirect, in regard to imports from other Member States or any form of protection of competing cosmetic products ...'.

80 Case C-21/79, *Commission* v. *Italy* [1980] ECR 1, Recitals 14–16:

'14 ... It is in fact clear from the judgment of the Court ... that at the present stage of development of Community law and in the absence of any unification or harmonization of the relevant provisions, Community law does not prohibit Member States from granting tax advantages, in the form of exemption from or reduction of duties, to certain products or to certain classes of producers. The Treaty does not therefore forbid, as far as domestic tax laws are concerned, the taxation at differential rates of products which may serve the same economic ends, especially if, as in the case of regenerated mineral oils, it appears that the cost of production, objectively speaking, differs considerably from that of oils of primary distillation.

15 ... Pursuant to the first Paragraph of Article 95 the tax advantages in question must also be granted without any discrimination to products from the other Member States which satisfy the same conditions as the domestic products which qualify for the exemption or reductions allowed by national law. The first Paragraph of Article 95 – the purpose of which is to ensure that the Treaty provisions relating to the abolition of customs duties and charges having equivalent effect cannot evaded or rendered nugatory by the introduction of internal taxation discriminating against imported products in comparison with domestic products – implements a fundamental principle of the common market. Consequently the disparities prohibited by it must be eliminated in spite of the difficult problems of comparison which may arise when assimilating the imported product to the various domestic products (which are subject to different taxes) and to which it may have some similarity.

16 Although the first Paragraph of Article 95 therefore places Member States under an obligation to extend the tax advantages accruing to domestic products to similar products imported from the other Member States as well provided that the latter products satisfy the conditions to which a reduced rate or an exemption have been made subject, it does not however impose upon the Member States the duty to abolish as regards internal taxes on domestic products differences which are objectively justified and which may be introduced by domestic legislation unless such abolition is the only way of avoiding direct or indirect discrimination against the imported products ...'.

81 See e.g. Case C-220/81, Criminal Proceedings Against Timothy Frederick Robertson and Others [1982] ECR 2349, Recital 9:

'9 Under Article 30 of the Treaty, quantitative restrictions on imports and all measures having equivalent effect are prohibited in trade between Member States. In accordance with the established case-law of the Court, any commercial legislation adopted by the Member States which is capable of hindering either directly or indirectly, potentially, intra-Community trade is to be regarded as a measure having an effect equivalent to quantitative restrictions. However, as the Court has repeatedly held ... in the absence of common rules relating to the marketing of the products concerned, obstacles to movement within the Community resulting from disparities between the national laws must be accepted in so far as such rules, applicable to domestic and to imported products without distinction, may be recognized as being necessary in order to satisfy mandatory requirements relating inter alia to consumer protection and fair trading.'

See also Case C-261/81, *Walter Rau Lebensmittelwerke* v. *De Smedt PVBA* [1982] ECR 3961, Recital 12: 'In this regard it must be recalled as the Court has repeatedly held ... that in the absence of common rules relating to the marketing of the products concerned, obstacles to free movement within the Community resulting from disparities between the national laws must be accepted in so far as such rules, applicable to domestic and to imported products without distinction, may be recognized as being necessary in order to satisfy mandatory requirements relating inter alia to consumer protection. It is also necessary for such rules to be proportionate to the aim in view. If a Member State has a choice between various measures to attain the same objective it should choose the means which least restricts the free movement of goods.'

82 See e.g. Mattera, A., 'Les Barrières Frontalières à l'Intérieur de la CEE et l'Action Menée par la Commission pour Leur Démantelement', RMC, 1987, n°307, pp. 264–76, spec. p. 267: 'La justification d'une réglementation nationale sur la base d'une exigence impérative constitue, dès lors, un critère de qualification d'une mesure au regard de l'Article 30 et non un principe de dérogation tel que celui résultant de l'Article 36/CEE'. See also Marenco, G., 'Pour une Interprétation Traditionnelle de la Notion de Mesure d'Effet Équivalant à une Restriction Quantitative', CDE, 1984, 3–4, pp. 291–364. Rabe H.J., 'Garantien und Sicherungen des Freien Warenverkehrs im Lichte der Neuesten Rechtsprechung des EuGH – Cassis de Dijon und die Folgerechtsprechung', in J. Schwarze (ed.), *Das Wirtschaftsrecht des Gemeinsamen Marktes in der Aktuellen Rechtsentwicklung*, 52, Baden-Baden: Nomos, 1983; Everling U., 'Zur Neueren EuGH-Rechtsprechung zum Wettbewerbsrecht', 17, Europarecht, 301, 305–6, 1982; Herdegen, M., Internationales Wirtschaftsrecht, 136, 1995.

83 Dörr, O., 'Die Warenverkehrsfreiheit nach Art. 30 EWG-Vertrag – Doch Bloß ein Diskriminierungsverbot?', 54, Rabels Zeitschrift für Ausländisches und Internationales Privatrecht, 677, 690, 1990 [stating that the 'inclusion' of mandatory requirements into the scope of Art. 30 EC is 'against the system of Art. 30 and 36'].

84 See Demaret, P., Droit Économique Européen, Cours de Bruges 1998–1999, Chapitre cinq, p.123: 'Depuis l'arrêt Cassis de Dijon, la démarche de la Cour de Justice est en effet parfois différente selon qu'elle examine la justification d'une mesure restrictive au regard de l'Article 36 ou au regard des exigences impératives au sens de Cassis de Dijon. Dans le premier cas, la Cour normalement qualifie la mesure jugée restrictive de mesure d'effet équivalent et examine ensuite la question de sa justification. Dans le second cas, il arrive que la Cour examine d'abord si la mesure restrictive est justifiée et ne qualifie celle-ci de mesure d'effet équivalent au sens de l'Article 30 que lorsqu'elle apparaît dénuée de justification. Alors que la qualification de mesure d'effet équivalent n'est pas synonyme d'interdiction dans le premier cas, elle est dans la second. Cette différence terminologique peut heurter un esprit cartésien, mais n'a pas de conséquence pratique. Dans les deux cas, la Cour se fonde sur le critère de proportionnalité pour déterminer si une mesure restrictive est justifiée et donc compatible avec le traité.

Dans un souci de clarté et de simplification, la Cour de Justice devrait abandonner cette différence de terminologie. Mais ceci supposerait qu'elle finisse par admettre que les exigences impératives au sens de Cassis de Dijon s'ajoutent aux causes de justification mentionnées à l'Article 36 et qu'elles doivent donc être traitées de la même façon, y compris du point de vue de leur champ d'application'.

Cf. too, Deringer, A., 'Zum Spannungsverhältnis Zwischen den Freiheiten des Gemeinsamen Marktes und den Nationalen Interessen der Mitgliedstaaten in Europäische Gerichtsbarkeit und Nationale Verfassungsgerichtsbarkeit', in W.G. Grewe, H. Rupp and H. Schneider (eds), *Festschrift zum 70. Geburtstag von Hans Kutscher*, 95, 96, 1981.

85 By 'they' I mean the Court (when it remembers to draw the distinction – since it is not always consistent) and the commentators peddling this line of reasoning.

86 Case C-120/78, *Rewe-Zentral AG* v. *Bundesmonopolverwaltung für Branntwein* [1979] ECR 649, 664 (Recital 14, Sub-paragraph 4).

87 It has been also argued that the term 'mutual recognition' is misleading since a formal (legal) act to mutually recognize standards is missing (see Matthies, H. and R. von Borries, 'Commentary on Article 36 EC', in E. Grabitz and M. Hilf (eds), *Kommentar zur Europäischen Union*, Supp. 10, October 1996, Par. 26).

88 However, the Court has held that such a provision must not be of a discriminatory nature, see Case C-59/82, *Schutzverband gegen Unwesen in der Wirtschaft* v. *Weinvertriebs-GmbH* [1983] ECR 1217, Recitals 7–11:

> '7 [I]t is apparent ... that a provision of the importing Member State fixing a minimum degree of alcohol only for imported Vermouth prevents the marketing of a product lawfully made in the exporting Member State, whereas it imposes no condition in relation to the minimum content of alcohol for the marketing of similar domestic products.
>
> 8 Since such a provision affects only imported products, it is of a discriminatory nature.
>
> 9 The fact that the law in issue refers to the rules governing production in the exporting Member State does not affect the aforesaid conclusion since the discriminatory nature must be determined solely on the basis of the law of the State where the marketing takes place, that is to say, the importing Member State.
>
> 10 The Schutzverband nevertheless maintained that the rule was justified on the ground that German consumers, in particular the very large number which visits Italy each year, expect Italian Vermouth marketed in the Federal Republic of Germany to be identical to the Vermouth marketed in Italy and that the would therefore be misled by Italian Vermouth the alcoholic content of which by volume is less that that of the same Vermouth drunk by them in Italy.
>
> 11 Although it is true that ... the court has repeatedly stated that protection of consumers, in particular, may justify obstacle to the free movement of goods resulting from disparities in national rules, the discriminatory nature of the rule in issue excludes application of that criterion, which concerns only legislation governing the marketing of national and imported products uniformly. Therefore in the present case it is not possible to pleas consumer protection to exclude Article 30 since the same protection is not given in relation to the national products.'

89 See Schwintowski, H.P., 'Freier Warenverkehr im Europäischen Binnenmarkt, Eine Fundamentalkritik an der Rechtsprechung des EuGH zu Art. 28 EGV', 64, Rabels Zeitschrift für Ausländisches und Internationales Privatrecht, 38, 54, 2000.

90 But see Arved Deringer, A., 'Zum Spannungsverhältnis Zwischen den Freiheiten des Gemeinsamen Marktes und den Nationalen Interessen der Mitgliedstaaten

in Europäische Gerichtsbarkeit und Nationale Verfassungsgerichtsbarkeit', in W.G. Grewe, H. Rupp and H. Schneider (eds), *Festschrift zum 70. Geburtstag von Hans Kutscher*, 95, 105–6, 1981.

91 But see Sacerdoti, G., 'Standards of Treatment, Harmonization and Mutual Recognition: A Comparison Between Regional Areas and the Global Trading System', in P. Demaret, J.F. Bellis and G. García Jiménez (eds), *Regionalism and Multilateralism after the Uruguay Round*, 613, 622, Brussels: European Inter-university Press, 1997 ['The mutual recognition of national standards ... is not found in GATT'].

92 McGovern, E., 'Standards and Technical Regulations as Barriers to Trade' in A. Qureshi, H. Steiner and G. Parry (eds), *The Legal and Moral Aspects of International Trade*, 207, 213–15, New York: Routledge, 1998.
SPS: Agreement on the Application of Sanitary and Phytosanitary Measures, Apr. 15, 1994, Marrakesh Agreement Establishing the World Trade Organization, Annex 1A, Legal Instruments – Results of the Uruguay Round vol. 27 (1994).
TBT: Agreement on Technical Barriers to Trade, Apr. 15, 1994, Marrakesh Agreement Establishing the World Trade Organization, Annex 1A, Legal Instruments – Results of the Uruguay Round vol. 27 (1994), http://www.wto.org/english/docs_e/legal_e/17-tbt.pdf.

93 See e.g. the excellent Mattera A., 'L'Article 30 du Traité CEE, la Jurisprudence ≪Cassis de Dijon≫ et le Principe de Reconnaissance Mutuelle. Instruments au Service d'une Communauté plus Respectueuse des Diversités Nationales', RMUE, 1992, n. 4, pp. 13–71.

94 But see Schwintowski, H.P., 'Freier Warenverkehr im Europäischen Binnenmarkt, Eine Fundamentalkritik an der Rechtsprechung des EuGH zu Art. 28 EGV', 64 Rabels Zeitschrift für Ausländisches und Internationales Privatrecht, 38, 54, 2000 [mentioning 'erosion-like' changes in companies within the Community].

95 Commission of the European Communities, Completing the Internal Market: White Paper from the Commission to the European Council, COM(85) 310 final, Luxembourg: Office for official Publications of the European Communities, 1985.

96 Single European Act, OJ 1987 L 169/1.

97 Matthies, H. and R. von Borries, 'Commentary on Article 36 EC', in Grabitz E. and M. Hilf (eds), *Kommentar zur Europäischen Union*, Supp. 10, Par. 26, Munich: Beck, October 1996.

98 Council Directive 83/89 of 28 March 1983 Laying Down a Procedure for the Provision of Information in the Field of Technical Standards and Regulations, OJ 1983 L 109/8; subsequently amended by: Council Directive of 22 March 1988 amending Directive 83/189/EEC Laying Down a Procedure for the Provision of Information in the Field of Technical Standards and Regulations, OJ 1988 L 81/75; Directive 94/10/EC of the European Parliament and the Council of 23 March 1994 Materially Amending for the Second Time Directive 83/189/EEC Laying Down a Procedure for the Provision of Information in the Field of Technical Standards and Regulations, OJ 1994 L 100/30. With regard to the medicinal sector, see Council Directive of 22 December 1986 on the Approximation of National Measures Relating to the Placing on the Market of High-Technology Medicinal Products, Particularly Those Derived from Biotechnology, OJ 1987 L 15/38.

See also the various agreements in this area: Agreement of the Representatives of the Governments of the Member States Meeting in Council of 5 March 1973 on Information for the Commission and for the Member States with a View to Possible Harmonization Throughout the Communities of Urgent Measures Concerning the Protection of the Environment, OJ 1973 C 9/1; amended by Agreement of the Representatives of the Governments of the Member States of the European Communities, Meeting in Council of 15 July 1974 Supplementing the Agreement of 5 March 1973 on Information for the Commission and for the Member States with a View to Possible Harmonization Throughout the Communities of Urgent Measures Concerning the Protection of the Environment, OJ 1974 C 86/2. Agreement of the Representatives of the Governments of the Member States Meeting in Council of 28 May 1969 Concerning Standstill and Information for the Commission, OJ 1969 C 76/9; amended by Agreement of 5 March 1973 Amending the Agreement of the Representatives of the Governments of the Member States Meeting in Council of 28 May 1969 Concerning Standstill and Information for the Commission, OJ 1973 C 9/3.

99 Council Directive of 19 February 1973 on the Harmonization of the Laws of Member States Relating to Electrical Equipment Designed for Use Within Certain Voltage Limits, OJ 1973 L 77/29.

100 According to the Council Resolution of 7 May 1985 on a New Approach to Technical Harmonization and Standards, OJ 1985 C 136/1, the bodies 'being generally considered to be the "European standards bodies which are particularly competent" ' are CEN (Comité Européen de Normalization) and CENELEC (Comité Européen de Coordination des Normes Electriques) (see Council Resolution of 7 May 1985, at 6).

101 Anselmann, N., 'Die Rolle der Europäischen Normung bei der Schaffung des Europäischen Binnenmarktes', 32, Recht der Internationalen Wirtschaft, 936, 939, 1986; Langeheine, B., 'Commentary on Article 100 EC', in E. Grabitz and M. Hilf (eds), *Kommentar zur Europäischen Union*, Supp. 7, Par. 57, Munich: Beck, September 1994.

102 Commission of the European Communities, Guide to the Implementation of Community Harmonization Directives Based on the New Approach and the Global Approach, 44, Luxembourg: Office for Official Publications of the European Communities, Lanham, Md: UNIPUB, 1994; Mohr, P.M., Technische Normen und Freier Warenverkehr in der EWG, 13–14, 1990.

103 See also the Communication from the Commission Concerning the Consequences of the Judgment Given by the Court of Justice on 20 February 1979 in Case 120/78 ('Cassis de Dijon'), OJ 1980 C 256/2:

'The Court's interpretation has induced the Commission to set out a number of guidelines – The principles deduced by the Court imply that a Member State may not in principle prohibit the sale in its territory of a product lawfully produced and marketed in another Member State even if the product is produced according to technical or quality requirements which differ from those imposed on its domestic products. Where a product "suitably and satisfactorily" fulfils the legitimate objective of a Member State's own rules (public safety, protection of the consumer or the environment, etc.), the importing country cannot justify prohibiting its sale in its territory by claiming that the way it fulfils the objective is different from that imposed on domestic products. In such a case, an absolute prohibition of sale could not be considered "necessary" to satisfy a "mandatory requirement" because it would not be an "essential guarantee" in the sense defined in the Court's judgment. The Commission will therefore have to tackle a whole body of commercial rules which lay down that products manufactured and marketed in one Member State must fulfil technical or qualitative conditions in order to be admitted to the market of another and specifically in all cases where the trade barriers occasioned by such rules are inadmissible according to the very strict criteria set out by the Court. The Commission is referring in particular to rules covering the composition, designation, presentation and packaging of products as well as rules requiring compliance with certain technical standards. – The Commission's work of harmonization will henceforth have to be directed mainly at national laws having an impact on the functioning of the common market where barriers to trade to be removed arise from national provisions which are admissible under the criteria set by the Court. The Commission will be concentrating on sectors deserving priority because of their economic relevance to the creation of a single internal market. To forestall later difficulties, the Commission will be informing Member States of potential objections, under the terms of Community law, to provisions they may be considering introducing which come to the attention of the Commission. It will be producing suggestions soon on the procedures to be followed in such cases.'

104 There have been no shortage of critics: Mattera, A., 'De l'Arrêt ≪Dassonville≫ à l'Arrêt ≪Keck≫ l'Obscure Clarté d'une Jurisprudence Riche en Principes Novateurs et en Contradictions', RMUE, n. 1, 1994, pp. 117–60; Picod, F., 'La Nouvelle Approche de la Cour de Justice en Matière d'Entraves aux Éxchanges', RTDE, n. 2, 1998, pp. 169–89.

105 Joint Cases C-60/84 and C-61/84, *Cinéthèque SA* v. *Fédération Nationale des Cinémas Français* [1985] ECR 2605.

106 Case C-155/80, Summary Proceedings against Sergius Oebel [1981] ECR 1993, Recitals 11–16:

'11 ... The national Court asks whether the effects of domestic legislation on working hours in bakeries ... in regard to the export and import of fresh baker's wares are to be regarded as measures having an effect equivalent to quantitative restrictions on mports or exports within the meaning of Articles 30 and 34 of the Treaty.

12 It cannot be disputed that the prohibition in the bread and confectionery industry on working before 4 a.m. in itself constitutes a legitimate element of economic and social policy, consistent with the objectives of public interest pursued by the Treaty. Indeed, this prohibition is designed to improve working conditions in a manifestly sensitive industry, in which the production process exhibits particular characteristics resulting from both the nature of the products and the habits of consumers ...

14 The accused maintains that the prohibition on the production of ordinary and fine baker's wares before 4 a.m. constitutes an export barrier

prohibited by Article 34 of the Treaty. This is alleged to be the case particularly with regard to products which have to be delivered fresh in time for breakfast and which must therefore be produced during the night before the day on which they are offered for sale.

15 However, as the Court has already declared ... Article 34 concerns national measures which have as their specific object or effect the restriction of patterns of exports and thereby the establishment of a difference in treatment between the domestic trade of a Member State and its export trade, in such a way as to provide a particular advantage for national production of for the domestic market of the State in question.

16 This is clearly not the case with rules such as those in issue which are part of economic and social policy and apply by virtue of objective criteria to all the undertakings in a particular industry which are established within the national territory, without leading to any difference in treatment whatsoever on the ground of the nationality of trades and without distinguishing between the domestic trade of the State in question and the export trade.'

107 Case C-145/88, *Torfaen Borough Council* v. *B & Q plc* [1989] ECR 3851; Case C-332/89, Criminal Proceedings against Marchandise et al. [1991] ECR I-1027; Case C-169/91, *Council of the City of Stoke-on-Trent and Norwich City Council* v. *B & Q plc* [1992] ECR I-6635].

108 See the opinion of Advocate General van Gerven in Case C-145/88, *Torfaen Borough Council* v. *B & Q plc* [1989] ECR 3851, Recitals 17–26.

109 Case C-145/88, *Torfaen Borough Council* v. *B & Q plc* [1989] ECR 3851.

110 Joined Cases C-267/91 and C-268/91, Criminal Proceedings against Bernard Keck and Daniel Mithouard, [1993] ECR-I, 6097, Recital 16. The Court thus concludes in Recital 17: 'Provided that those conditions are fulfilled, the application of such rules to the sale of products from another Member State meeting the requirements laid down by that State is not by nature such as to prevent their access to the market or to impede access any more than it impedes the access of domestic products. Such rules therefore fall outside the scope of Article 30 of the Treaty.'

111 See the second opinion by General Advocate van Gerven in Joined Cases C 267/91 and C-268/91, Criminal Proceedings against Bernard Keck and Daniel Mithouard, [1993] ECR-I, 6097, Recitals 8 and 10:

'8. In considering this issue I will assume that the Court adheres to the broad Dassonville formula. I would point out that in the Opinion I delivered in the first Sunday-trading case, I proposed that the Court should adopt a more reserved approach towards national rules which, like the rules at issue in this case or in the aforementioned Sunday-trading case, are not intended to regulate intra-Community trade. My proposal was that Article 30 should be declared applicable to rules of this type only if they have the effect of screening or partitioning the market, that is to say if they jeopardize the interpenetration of national markets.

The Sixth Chamber of the Court did not follow my proposal. In its judgment the Court implicitly adhered to the Dassonville formula and held that the balancing of interests which must be performed under that broad formula with reference to the principle of proportionality in Article 30 is a matter for the national court. In its second Sunday-trading judgment, and even more clearly in its third Sunday-trading judgment mentioned above, the Court, sitting as the Full Court, reversed its earlier decision on the last point but not on the first. As may be seen from the passage cited (in Paragraph 6 above) from the third judgment, the Court tests the national rules concerned against the requirement of proportionality, which means that it recognizes that in principle Article 30 is applicable.

I will thus assume from now on that the broad Dassonville formula still remains the cornerstone of the Court' s case-law concerning the sphere of application of Article 30 of the EEC Treaty. In order to avoid any confusion, I think that the Court owes a duty to the national courts to make this quite clear.

10. My first Opinion in this case was delivered on 18 November 1992 and therefore antedates the Court's latest Sunday-trading judgment. Did the Court in that judgment give its case-law on the free movement of goods a more restrictive twist? I do not think so. If the Court had wished to restrict the fundamental scope of the prohibition laid down in Article 30 of the EEC Treaty, it would have undoubtedly begun by expressly referring to the Dassonville formula, gone on to restrict it and then arrived at the conclusion, for example, that the rules concerned, prohibiting shops from trading on Sundays (which the court making the reference had found to affect the sale of imported products), did not constitute a measure having equivalent effect. The Court, however, confirmed, as it had done in the previous Sunday-trading cases (*Torfaen, Conforama* and *Marchandise*), that such rules could have an adverse effect on the volume of sales of certain shops even if they affected sales of national products as much as sales of imported products and trade in products from other Member States was not therefore made more difficult than trade in national products. The Court then went on to examine again the justification for the aim of the rules in question and ended its reasoning by looking at the proportionality of the rules'.

In his first opinion, General Advocate van Gerven subsumed the disputed regulation under the Dassonville-Formular and thus being caught by the scope of Art. 30 EC, see Joined Cases C-267/91 and C-268/91, Criminal Proceedings against Bernard Keck and Daniel Mithouard, [1993] ECR-I, 6097.

112 Joined Cases C-267/91 and C-268/91, Criminal Proceedings against Bernard Keck and Daniel Mithouard, [1993] ECR-I, 6097, Recital 14.

113 Becker, U., 'Von "Dassonville" über "Cassis" zu "Keck" ', 29, Europarecht, 162, 164, 1994; Matthies, H., 'Artikel 30 EG-Vertrag nach Keck', in O. Due, M. Lutter and J. Schwarze (eds), *Festschrift für Ulrich Everling*, 803, 805, Baden-Baden: Nomos, 1995; Müllbert, P.O., 'Privatrecht, die EG-Grundfreiheiten und der Binnenmarkt', 159, Zeitschrift für das Gesamte Handels- und Wirtschaftsrecht, 2, 16–9, 1995; Reich N., 'Anmerkung zu dem Urteil "Keck und Mithouard" ', 14, Zeitschrift für Wirtschaftsrecht, 1815, 1818, 1993.

114 Regarding the criticism of the 'Dassonville'-formular see – in addition to Advocate General van Gerven – the opinion of Advocate General Tesauro in Case C-292/92, *Ruth Hünermund and others* v. *Landesapothekerkammer Baden-Württemberg* [1993] ECR-I 6787, Recitals 9–11.

115 Joliet, R., 'Der Freie Warenverkehr: Das Urteil Keck und Mithouard und die Neuorientierung der Rechtsprechung', 43, Gewerblicher Rechtsschutz und Urheberrecht Internationaler Teil, 979, 984, 1994.

116 Case C-260/89, *Elliniki Radiophonia Tileorassi AE* v. *Dimotki Etairia Pliroforissis and Sotirius Kouvelas* [1991] ECR I-2925, Recitals 41–43:

'41 With regard to Article 10 of the European Convention on Human Rights ... it must first be pointed out that, as the Court has consistently held, fundamental rights form an integral part of the general principles of law, the observance of which it ensures. For that purpose the Court draws inspiration from the constitutional traditions common to the Member States and from the guidelines supplied by international treaties for the protection of human rights on which the Member States have collaborated or of which they are signatories ... The European Convention on Human Rights has special significance in that respect ... It follows that ... the Community cannot accept measures which are incompatible with observance of the human rights thus recognized and guaranteed.

42 As the Court has held ... it has no power to examine the compatibility with the European Convention on Human Rights of national rules which do not fall within the scope of Community law. On the other hand, where such rules do fall within the scope of Community law, and reference is made to the Court for a preliminary ruling, it must provide all the criteria of interpretation needed by the national court to determine whether those rules are compatible with the fundamental rights the observance of which the Court ensures and which derive in particular from the European Convention on Human Rights.

43 In particular, where a Member State relies on the combined provisions of Articles 56 and 66 in order to justify rules which are likely to obstruct the exercise of the freedom to provide services, such justification, provided for by Community law, must be interpreted in the light of the general principles of law and in particular of fundamental rights. Thus the national rules in question can fall under the exceptions provided for by the combined provisions of Articles 56 and 66 only if they are compatible with the fundamental rights the observance of which is ensured by the Court.'

117 Möschel, W., 'Kehrtwende in der Rechtsprechung des EuGH zur Warenverkehrsfreiheit', 47, Neue Juristische Wochenschrift, 429, 431 [stating that Keck could be seen as following the shadow of the subsidiarity principle]; Ress, G., 'Abschied von Cassis de Dijon und Dassonville?', 4, EuropÄische Zeitschrift für Wirtschaftsrecht, 745, 1993 [stating that Keck could be interpreted as a sign of 'judicial self-restraint']. See however Becker, U., 'Von "Dassonville" über "Cassis" zu "Keck" ', 29, Europarecht, 162, 164, 1994 [stating that there is no evidence to interpret Keck as resembling the concept of subsidiarity].

118 Joined Cases C-267/91 and C-268/91, Criminal Proceedings against Bernard Keck and Daniel Mithouard [1993] ECR-I, 6097, Recital 13.

119 But see (with regard to TBT) Sacerdoti, G. 'Standards of Treatment, Harmonization and Mutual Recognition: A Comparison Between Regional Areas and the Global Trading System', in P. Demaret., J.F. Bellis and G. García

Jiménez (eds), *Regionalism and Multilateralism after the Uruguay Round*, 613, 623, Brussels: European Interuniversity Press, 1997.

120 Appellate Body Report on 'European Community – Measures Affecting Meat and Meat Products (Hormones)', 16 January 1998, WTO Doc. WT/DS26/AB/R, WT/DS48/AB/R, Par. 165: '... It is clear to us that harmonization of SPS measures of Members on the basis of international standards is projected in the Agreement, as a goal, yet to be realized in the future. To read Article 3.1 as requiring Members to harmonize their SPS measures by conforming those measures with international standards, *guidelines and recommendations*, in the here and now, *is, in effect, to vest such international standards, guidelines and recommendations (which are by the terms of the Codex* recommendatory *in form and nature) with* obligatory force and effect. The Panel's interpretation of Article 3.1 would, in other words, transform those standards, guidelines and recommendations into binding norms. But, as already noted, the SPS Agreement itself sets out no indication of any intent on the part of the Members to do so ...' [emphasis in original].

121 Case C-5/94, *The Queen* v. *Ministry of Agriculture, Fisheries and Food, ex parte: Hedley Lomas (Ireland) Ltd.* [1996] ECR I-2553. Simplified, in this case the ECJ ruled that a Member State can not invoke Article 36 of the EC Treaty to justify a limitation of exports of goods to another Member State (here refusing to issue licenses for the export to another Member State of live animals for slaughter on the ground that their treatment in slaughterhouses located in that Member State was contrary to a Council Directive on stunning of animals before slaughter) on the sole ground that, according to the first State, the second State is not complying with the requirements of a Community harmonizing Directive which pursues the objective which Article 36 is intended to protect.

122 Panel Report on 'United States – Restrictions on Imports of Tuna', GATT B.I.S.D. 39S/155 (not adopted); Panel Report on 'United States – Restrictions on Imports of Tuna', reprinted in 33 I.L.M. 839 (1994) (not adopted). Both cases dealt – simplified – with import restrictions on Mexican tuna harvested by employing techniques which resulted in a high incidental killing rate of Dolphins. It has to be noted, however, that neither report was adopted by the then Contracting Parties – which was necessary to give 'teeth' to the recommendations made by the respective panels.

123 Panel Report on 'United States – Import Prohibition of Certain Shrimp and Shrimp Products', WT/DS58/R (15 May 1998), modified by Appellate Body Report on 'United States – Import Prohibition of Certain Shrimp and Shrimp Products', WT/DS58/AB/R (12 Oct. 1998). Whereas the panel (see Panel Report, Par. 7.45) found that it was not possible for a WTO-Member to impose restrictions on imports due to the production method of the banned product – harvesting shrimps without a turtle excluder device – the Appellate Body stated that '... [the Panel's test] ... finds no basis ... in the text ...' and that import restrictions imposed on a product due to certain processing methods of that product could be allowed in principle (see Appellate Body Report, Par. 121).

124 Tietje, C., Normative Grundstrukturen der Behandlung Nichttarifärer Handelshemmnisse in der WTO/GATT-Rechtsordnung, 210, Berlin: European

Interuniversity Press, 1998. But see Howse, R. and D. Regan, 'The Product/Process Distinction – An Illusory Basis for Disciplining Unilateralism in Trade Policy', European Journal of International Law, 2000.

125 Roth, W.H., 'Wettbewerb der Mitgliedstaaten oder der Hersteller?', 159, Zeitschrift für das Gesamte Handels- und Wirtschaftsrecht, 78, 89, 1995.

126 Articles 2 (2) and 2 (7) TBT provide the following:

'Article 2
Preparation, Adoption and Application of Technical Regulations by Central Government Bodies
With respect to their central Government bodies: ...

2.2 Members shall ensure that technical regulations are not prepared, adopted or applied with a view to or with the effect of creating unnecessary obstacles to international trade. For this purpose, technical regulations shall not be more trade-restrictive than necessary to fulfill a legitimate objective, taking account of the risks non-fulfillment would create. Such legitimate objectives are, inter alia: national security requirements; the prevention of deceptive practices; protection of human health or safety, animal or plant life or health, or the environment. In assessing such risks, relevant elements of consideration are, inter alia: available scientific and technical information, related processing technology or intended end-uses of products. ...

2.7 Members shall give positive consideration to accepting as equivalent technical regulations of other Members, even if these regulations differ from their own, provided they are satisfied that these regulations adequately fulfill the objectives of their own regulations.'

127 Art. 4 (1) SPS provides the following:

'Article 4 Equivalence

1. Members shall accept the sanitary or phyto-sanitary measures of other Members as equivalent, even if these measures differ from their own or from those used by other Members trading in the same product, if the exporting Member objectively demonstrates to the importing Member that its measures achieve the importing Member's appropriate level of sanitary or phyto-sanitary protection. For this purpose, reasonable access shall be given, upon request, to the importing Member for inspection, testing and other relevant procedures.'

In addition Art. 2 (1) and (4) provide the following:
'Article 2 Basic Rights and Obligations

1. Members have the right to take sanitary and phyto-sanitary measures necessary for the protection of human, animal or plant life or health, provided that such measures are not inconsistent with the provisions of this Agreement. ...

4. Sanitary or phyto-sanitary measures which conform to the relevant provisions of this Agreement shall be presumed to be in accordance with the obligations of the Members under the provisions of GATT 1994 which relate to the use of sanitary or phyto-sanitary measures, in particular the provisions of Article XX(b).'

3
Mutual Recognition in Goods and Services: An Economic Perspective

Jacques Pelkmans

Introduction

Mutual recognition is a remarkable innovation facilitating economic intercourse across borders. In the EU's internal goods market it has been helpful in tackling or avoiding the remaining obstacles; namely, regulatory barriers between Member States. Mutual recognition (MR) is widely appreciated for the original and simple fashion in which it can solve what seemed long an intractable and infinite steeplechases of overcoming obstacles for thousands of products. It also underlies ingenious ways to facilitate the free movement of services. This general appreciation has spread beyond the Union to other continents and the WTO. The notion of MR has travelled beyond disciplines, too, from European law and the domain of regulatory specialists to economists worldwide.

However, there is a curious paradox. It has turned out to be difficult to get MR accepted with all its consequences, despite the almost universal acclaim of its great merits. The widespread recognition on its own has neither led to a sweeping liberalization of the internal market, whether in goods or services, nor to much of a deeper analytical economic understanding. Not surprisingly, this has frustrated its initial supporters in policy circuits. During the mid-1990s the disenchantment with MR was so strong that UNICE (the European confederation of industry) recommended a return to harmonization as a superior option. And in services it has turned out that MR is not so easy to apply. As to analysis, economic work on MR is scant. Economic literature on trade or the internal market often mentions MR but usually merely in passing or with just a few telling cases (like the German beer case).

This disenchantment and neglect is most regrettable. Mutual recognition opens up many and great opportunities, and it deserves better recognition in economics and more widespread application in Union practices. The purpose of this chapter is to provide the economic and strategic arguments for such recognition and application, especially for goods and services markets. In the process I also hope to clarify why MR, simple as it would appear to be at first sight, nevertheless entails considerable complications. These complications can lead to high transaction costs, and lowering those is a painstaking and involving process. The Union is developing this process (as I shall set out) and thereby gradually rendering MR more attractive. Indeed, I argue for a *'mutual recognition culture'*, especially at the level of national authorities, which would stimulate permanent exposure to healthy competition throughout the single market, without in the least sacrificing justified concerns of health, safety and consumer protection.

The structure of the chapter is as follows. First I define MR and its place in the internal goods market. The legal and regulatory detail is minimized so that the essence becomes more clear for the economic reader. Crucially, MR cannot be understood in isolation; it can be indispensable for free movement (liberalization) and substitutes for or complements harmonization. The strategic economic advantages of MR in the new regulatory strategy of the Union are then set out. In allowing a much less costly regulatory system to emerge, these strategic advantages probably far outweigh the direct economic benefits of applying the principle. A micro-economic analysis of the direct (welfare) benefits is provided, showing its pro-competitive nature unless strategic games are played on quality. The drawbacks of MR are then considered. It is little known or understood that the proper application of MR implies large and deep-rooted transactions costs, and these costs are spelled out in some detail and illustrated. MR in services is then discussed. MR or the related 'home-country control' principle has clearly yielded strategic as well as direct benefits in some service sectors like transport and financial services; yet in other sectors the gains are spurious or MR is largely irrelevant.

The discussion then turns to regulatory competition and its (de)merits. The case for regulatory competition is conditional and indeed more problematic than MR, its prerequisite. Casual empiricism suggests that it is not widely practiced in Europe despite many fears, which brings us to the ambivalent attitude of European business to MR which is explored. The final section concludes.

Mutual recognition in the internal goods market

After decades of experience with 'deep' market integration in Europe, the concept and place of mutual recognition can be clearly defined. There are basically three ways of realizing free movement (here, of goods) in the internal market: liberalization, approximation and mutual recognition. All three have limitations and no single method can suffice for all cases. In that sense they are complements. Liberalization amounts to the imposition of free movement by prohibitions for Member States to intervene in cross-border trade in direct or even indirect ways. These prohibitions derive either directly from the Treaty and the European Court of Justice (ECJ) jurisprudence, or from EC regulations or directives building on such provisions. Approximation is the adaptation of national laws in such a way and to such a degree that cross-border trade is no longer hindered in a direct or indirect way. This approximation avoids, therefore, centralized rules but aims to bring national laws into 'harmony' (hence, the French wording 'harmonization' in Arts 94 and 95, EC, where the English text speaks of 'approximation'). Approximation can be justified as a complement to liberalization where market failures have to be overcome by regulation. In extreme cases of very high risk where uncertainty or discretion could have unacceptable consequences, such market failures might be addressed by centralized rules, but otherwise, and hence in the overwhelming majority of regulatory issues, approximation will suffice. The goal must then be commonly defined (because the purpose of directives is to remove or overcome market failure throughout the EU) and the instruments (that is, the detailed technical provisions) only insofar as they might hinder, directly or indirectly, intra-EC trade.

Mutual recognition starts from the idea that member states have equivalent regulatory objectives in safety, health, environment and consumer protection (SHEC) which, in actual practice in Europe, is very often correct. But if and when objectives are equivalent, and thus the market failure is addressed, approximation should no longer be necessary and free movement could prevail. The notion of mutual recognition refers to the implication for national customs or inspectors or regulatory agencies or policy-makers that a good entering this member state from another EU country must be allowed unhindered access, even if the detailed specifications in the relevant domestic regulation differ from those in the country of origin, as long as the regulatory objectives are equivalent: from a narrow regulatory point of view it would thus seem as if the importing country 'recognizes' the regulatory regime of the exporting country. Because the principle has general application for the internal market, this 'recognition' is 'mutual'.

Before explaining MR a little more precisely in the EU context, it is crucial to appreciate a few properties. First, mutual recognition must always be understood as an alternative or complement to liberalization and/or approximation. Therefore, when EU authorities say that MR is a leading principle of the internal market, this should not be interpreted – as some ill-informed economists have done – as meaning that it is the sole or overriding principle. Economists ought to analyse the economics of MR in the proper regulatory context. Second, the reliance on MR in the EU is greatly facilitated by the forceful treaty principle of free movement, a principle that does not exist and cannot be expected in international trade law or in economic regionalism elsewhere (whether NAFTA, the ASEAN free trade area, Mercosur, and so on). Free movement goes much beyond free trade in that the former implies a *right* to enter national markets. National discretion to intervene only exists when there is an explicit derogation in the treaty. Thus, when the derogation does not apply or when it is narrowly interpreted by the ECJ (which has typically happened in the EU) free movement prevails automatically. And when derogations do apply, the objectives and key aspects can be approximated by common decision-making. The originality of 'mutual recognition' was that, before rushing into thousands of approximation exercises, one should first ask the question whether the objectives of national regulation, falling under the derogation, are not equivalent to begin with. If so MR applies, because the purpose (that is, overcoming the internal market failure) is then fulfilled and free movement should prevail, irrespective of the details that might differ between those national rules. Third, a supranational ECJ is neither present in the WTO regime nor in other regional trade regimes. It is the combination of these last two aspects (that is, the principle of free movement rather than free trade, and a 'supreme' court) which makes it doubtful whether MR, with all its profound consequences, can be exported to world trade or other trade blocs.[1]

The remainder of this section endeavours to set out more precisely the mutual recognition regime of the Union in its regulatory context. The aim is to have the reader understand that MR can only flourish in a well-defined and hierarchical legal regime. As will be shown later, even this is only a necessary, not a sufficient condition for a smooth application in the internal market, genuinely lowering transaction costs of intra-EU economic intercourse.

The principle of mutual recognition has been developed by the ECJ in its case-law. In its famous *Cassis de Dijon* case the ECJ held that, in principle, a Member State must allow a product lawfully produced and marketed in another Member State into its own market, unless a prohibition of this product is justified by mandatory requirements, such as health and safety protection (see later).[2] This means that Member States cannot apply certain specific details of national regulation to intra-EC imports of goods, if the *objective or effect* of the relevant law in other member states is *equivalent* to that of the importing country. The idea behind mutual recognition is that all member states care for their citizens and cannot be assumed to produce, for instance, unsafe or unhealthy products, merely because technical specifications differ. Hence the principle of mutual recognition plays a pivotal role in the internal market since it ensures free movement of goods (and services) *without* making it necessary to approximate/harmonize national legislation. Since free movement of goods is essential to the internal market, it is not surprising that the burden of proof of 'non-equivalence' of objectives is on the member state which is unwilling to allow the import of the products concerned. Where the regulatory objective or effect are *not* equivalent, free movement can be impeded. In such cases, however, the Treaty offers a remedy to the free movement by allowing for the approximation of precisely those objectives or effects under Article 95 EC (ex Article 100a EC), under qualified majority voting.

In order to fully grasp the role and significance of mutual recognition one needs to understand how liberalization, mutual recognition and approximation work together to ensure free movement. This interrelationship is summarized in Table 3.1. Article 28 EC gives expression to the general principle of free movement of goods by prohibiting member states from imposing quantitative restrictions on imports or measures having an equivalent effect. The treaty language is a misnomer, probably drafted by trade diplomats. The phrase should be, 'regulatory barriers', as the Court acknowledged in *Dassonville* (1974). In *Dassonville*, the ECJ removed all uncertainties about the interpretation of the concept of 'measures having equivalent effect' by declaring that trading rules enacted by Member States which are capable of hindering, directly or indirectly, actually or potentially, intra-Community trade are also to be considered as measures having an effect equivalent to quantitative restrictions.[3] This economic interpretation paved the way for a very broad interpretation of measures of equivalent effect.[4]

In its famous *Cassis de Dijon* ruling, the ECJ further refined the principle of equivalence and ruled that products lawfully produced and marketed in one member state must be admitted by another Member State, save where refusal is justified by virtue of mandatory requirements.[5]

Table 3.1 Interaction between liberalization, mutual recognition and approximation

	Article	*Nature*	*Main features*
1	28 EC (ex 30 EC)	LIBERALIZATION	Prohibition of quantitative restrictions on imports or measures having an equivalent effect (regulatory barriers)
		Extended: (ground work for mutual recognition)	• *Dassonville* Ruling of 1974: widening of prohibition to all regulatory barriers: '[a]ll trading rules enacted by Member States which are capable of hindering, directly or indirectly, actually or potentially, intra-Community trade are to be considered as measures having an effect equivalent to quantitative restrictions' • Enhances liberalization
2	28 EC (ex 30 EC)	MUTUAL RECOGNITION	• *Cassis de Dijon* Ruling of 1979: further refinement of the principle of equivalence: Member States must allow a product lawfully produced and marketed in another Member State into their own market, unless a prohibition of this product is justified by mandatory requirements (see point 3) • if regulatory objectives or effects such as Safety, Health, Environment and Consumer Protection (SHEC) are equivalent Member States must mutually recognize each other's legislation • obligation to include a mutual recognition clause in national legislation (*Foie Gras* Ruling and Dir. 98/34) • if not equivalent, then approximate (see point 4, below) • enhances liberalization even more
3	30 EC (ex 36 EC) and	DEROGATIONS to liberalization and	• all grounds mentioned in Article 30 EC, which are restrictively interpreted, and

Continued

Table 3.1 *Continued*

Article	*Nature*	*Main features*
28 EC (ex 30 EC)	mutual recognition	• other 'mandatory requirements' developed in the ECJ's case-law, notably the *Cassis de Dijon* Ruling ('rule of reason') • all derogations are subject to a proportionality test
4 95 EC (ex 100a EC)	APPROXIMATION	• where national (SHEC) objectives are *not* equivalent, approximation unifies those objectives
	'New Approach' (broad and/or horizontal)	• wide sectors covered (e.g. machines) • or horizontal issues covered (e.g. directives on food additives or general product safety)
5 95 EC (ex 100a EC) only if not applicable: 94 EC (ex 100 EC)	APPROXIMATION 'Old Approach' (specific and/ or vertical)	• all other (product) approximation: for instance: ○ involving high risk (chemicals, cars) ○ precision in rules required (measuring instruments) ○ specifying certain product compositions, such as jam and marmalade and cocoa and chocolate

Sources: Pelkmans, J., E. and L. Mauro, 'Reforming Product Regulation in the EU: A Painstaking, Iterative, Two-Level Game', in G. Galli and J. Pelkmans (eds), *Regulatory Reform and Competitiveness in Europe*, vol. I, Cheltenham/Northampton (USA), Edward Elgar, 2000.

In its 1985 White Paper on the Completion of the Internal Market, the Commission adopted the principle of mutual recognition as its main strategy to achieve the internal market, with far-reaching consequences.[6] In addition, it proclaimed its intention to concentrate its approximation activities mainly in areas where trade barriers were justified according to the criteria determined by the Court.

The principle of mutual recognition thus implies that member states, when drawing up commercial or technical rules liable to affect the free movement of goods, may *not* take an exclusively national viewpoint and take account only of requirements confined to domestic products. In this way, the mutual recognition case-law boils down to *regulatory reform* because exposure to competition from elsewhere in the Union is enhanced, without compromising the purpose of regulation; namely, overcoming the safety, health, environment and consumer protection (SHEC-type) market failures. According to the ECJ's case-law, Member States are moreover required to include in their national legislation a so-called *mutual recognition clause*, in order to allow the acceptance on their territory products which are in conformity with the legislation of another Member State.[7] This requirement stems from the implementation of the notification procedure laid down in the Information Directive (Directive 98/34/EC) (see later).

In emphasizing the objective(s), rather than the detailed specifications, in a national product law or decree, the national regulation as well as the regulation of Member States where the imported product comes from are *forced to concentrate on overcoming the market failure*. This will tend to make regulatory failure unattractive. A widespread instance of regulatory failure in Europe was overregulation in the sense that national product laws would extend to aspects that had nothing to do with the market failure. At the same time, however, it assumes that the grounds in Article 30 EC (ex Article 36 EC, referring mainly to health and safety) represent market failures. If one includes the so-called 'rule of reason' interpretation of the ECJ of Article 28 EC (ex Article 30 EC) which justifies national regulation involving environment and consumer protection, and observes that almost all the relevant product regulation, related to Article 30 EC (ex Article 36 EC) is about health and safety protection, this assumption is broadly correct. These combine to form SHEC (safety, health, environment and consumer protection) which covers practically all relevant market failures for goods.

Where mutual recognition fails because of non-equivalence, the EU can decide to take up regulation approximating national legislative provisions in order to ensure the free movement of goods. In an attempt to overcome the drawbacks of the 'old approach' to the abolition of technical barriers to trade followed by the Council since 1969,[8] the Commission launched in 1985 its 'New Approach to Harmonization and Technical Standards'. The new approach restricts approximation to stipulating *essential* health and safety requirements, whilst the specification of these requirements in technical standards is left to the European standardization bodies (CEN, CENELEC and ETSI). The distinction between the essential SHEC requirements (the regulatory objectives) and technical specifications constitutes the main characteristic of the new approach. This new approach is often denoted as 'minimum harmonization': what this refers to is not that regulation is somehow (too ?) minimalist, but that all that is to be approximated are the objectives and their essential links with voluntary, preferably common, standards, but no more than that.

Once these objectives are approximated, the rest is subject to MR. Common – though voluntary – standards are then desirable instruments to drastically lower information costs and uncertainty for business and technical designers in clarifying what critical specifications are presumed to be in compliance with these (often quite general) SHEC objectives. However, innovation is not throttled because new solutions may be tested and certified as well, as long as they comply with these objectives. The new approach, with much lower costs and far fewer blockages in the Council, has thus been greatly facilitated by the emergence of mutual recognition.

The new approach is far superior to the old, rigid harmonization approach the Community applied before 1985. But would regulatory competition, as a logical corollary of MR and precisely because it might overcome market failures at least cost, not be still better than approximation? Approximation suggests that there is no prior equivalence between objectives of national regulation, otherwise mutual recognition should apply. A lack of equivalence could be due to the fact that some Member States have barrier-prone regulation and others have not, or that objectives of all existing national regulation of a product do differ 'too much'. Under the 'new approach', approximation can be viewed as a written agreement in Council on equivalence. In actual practice, it turns out to be far more complex, because the new approach defines the objectives over wide product groups. As soon as the objectives have to be operationalized in mandates for European standardization, great differentiation and some precision is often required, hence directives (have to) go further than just equivalence of objectives. Indeed, the ECJ speaks about objectives *or effects*. Some economists have attempted to show that regulatory competition between Member States, driven by free movement under mutual recognition, can be (economically) superior to approximation. Given the equivalence of objectives, 'the market' (rather than civil servants and ministers) would reveal consumer and user preferences, and in this way the desired specifications could be 'discovered', which can then be codified in directives to facilitate trade. Although this might possibly be correct in comparison with the 'old' approach, it is unlikely to be superior to the 'new approach' (Sun and Pelkmans, 1995[9]). In any event, where the new approach fails because no qualified majority on objectives (or effects) can be found, regulatory competition fails as well, because free movement would be blocked. The issue of regulatory competition will be addressed below.

As Table 3.1 shows, liberalization, MR and approximation cannot be understood in isolation but only within the notion of a regulatory strategy. MR and (new approach) approximation can be substitutes or complements, and they may well serve different needs.

The strategic advantages of mutual recognition

The advantages of MR are of two types, strategic for the overall realization of the internal market and the manifold benefits this implies, and direct (net) welfare benefits of the application in specific cases. It would be a serious mistake to narrow down the economic analysis of MR to the comparative static of applying MR to a particular traded good as the strategic gains almost certainly greatly outweigh the direct benefits.

There are four strategic economic advantages of mutual recognition in goods markets. First, the internal goods market can be (and indeed has been) established far more easily and more quickly than would have been possible with old and new approaches of approximation combined with technical and unsatisfactory judicial review. Second, the propensity to overregulate for vested interests or bureaucratic reasons is severely constrained both as to EC directives and at the national level. Third, even if regulatory competition does not seem to be pursued actively in the EU, mutual recognition creates the prerequisites for it; this potential for regulatory competition exercises an additional disciplinary effect on national regulators. Fourth, the interaction between MR and approximation under the new approach (under qualified majority voting) forces member states to rethink their national regulatory solutions and focus on what is essential (the objectives) and what can usefully be subject to common (but voluntary) standards; in so doing, time and again, regulators have to think in terms of mutual recognition (for all that is not 'essential'). This prompts a process of learning among Member States about 'best-practice' regulation and reinforces the incentives to raise the quality of regulation at both levels in the European public interest.

These strategic advantages stem from the systemic implications of the notion of mutual recognition, not from the pure judicial application by the ECJ itself. It is important to see that a mere judicial application of MR (*à la Cassis de Dijon*) would have been no more than a welcome handmaiden to the promotion of free movement in some selected product sectors. Its main application would have been limited to food products, with a few scattered instances in other markets as well. Only once one begins to understand its influence on the design of the new regulatory strategy of the Union (after the White Paper of 1985 and the Single European Act) and its crucial role in that strategy, is it possible to discern and appreciate the strategic economic meaning of the principle.

Table 3.2 The Union's new regulatory strategy

Political	*Judicial*	*Regulatory*
Qualified majority voting (with a few exceptions)	Judicial mutual recognition (given equivalent objectives or if Art 30 does not apply)	→ free movement → no internal frontiers → subsidiarity → minimum approximation / harmonization → regulatory mutual recognition
	Proportionality (member states)	Proportionality (EC level)

Source: Pelkmans, J., *European Integration, Methods and Economic Analysis*, Harlow, Pearson Education/Financial Times/Prentice-Hall, 2001.

The strategy consists of a triptych of a political, a judicial and a regulatory panel (see Table 3.2). The regulatory panel, in turn, is made up of a quintet. With due account of the political and judicial panels, this *regulatory quintet* is central to the establishment and proper functioning of the single market, the economic hard core of the Union.

The Single Act removed the veto obstacle. For most internal market matters qualified majority voting (QMV) was *de jure* and *de facto* introduced. This altered the conduct of member states representatives in Coreper and Council. No longer could every detail and every deviation with other Member States be imposed on the Community: compromises were either needed to obtain some concessions from others or they were indispensable to form a blocking minority. QMV thereby reduced the costs of 'how' the EU regulated, while significantly lowering the probability of deadlock, so that the internal market could be built much faster.

The judicial panel has its roots in the 1970s, albeit only for goods markets, in the *Dassonville* and *Cassis de Dijon* cases. This *judicial form of mutual recognition* is remarkable because, in effect, it undermines the regulatory autonomy of a Member State with respect to intra-EU imports.

Judicial mutual recognition proved capable of declaring inapplicable to intra-EU imports a very large number of regulatory specifications in food laws, and some in machine safety regulations, construction products, and others. In and by itself, it made superfluous a lot of tedious approximation that was deadlocked on the technical specifications, *not* on the regulatory objectives sought. Just as qualified majority voting did after the Single Act, judicial mutual recognition altered the behaviour of member states. First, it came to be understood that the 'need to act in common' (a required step of the subsidiarity test) at EU level often did not apply where health (and other) objectives were the same. This had the practical effect of *reducing the EU regulatory burden* (that is, less approximation) while exposing national overregulation (with technical specifications) by free movement. In one stroke, therefore, *the probability of costly regulatory failure diminished greatly* at both levels of government. Or, to put it in a less abstract way, the potential total number of products waiting for EU regulation before free movement would become a reality for business and consumers was drastically curtailed. Moreover, existing, often detailed national regulation as well as possible future refinements became unenforceable *vis-à-vis* intra-EU imports.

Second, it led to a rethink of how approximation could best be tackled whenever there was doubt about the equivalence of regulatory objectives. Approximation was minimized to the 'essential requirements' of health, safety, environmental or consumer protection. Beyond these regulatory objectives, Member States were free to regulate more strictly, but mutual recognition (and thus free movement) would apply. This *regulatory mutual recognition* solved the problem of (business) uncertainty about 'equivalence' by defining common minimum requirements in rather general terms, while imposing free movement and mutual recognition 'beyond' those requirements. This had the great advantage that agreement in the Council would be far easier to achieve as, in Europe, regulatory objectives hardly diverge in the large majority of cases. It meant that the establishment of the internal market became politically feasible.

The Court also introduced another principle, that of 'proportionality'. Because judicial mutual recognition may confuse consumers, as they are confronted with products from different regulatory regimes, it did accept labelling requirements as a 'least restrictive' measure to protect the consumer. Previous very costly measures such as complete import bans (for example, beer into Germany; pasta not fully made from durum wheat into Italy, and so on) had to be removed. Thus asymmetric information can be solved at very little cost and without impeding free movement.

The regulatory panel of Table 3.2 emerged from this evolution. With the Single Act's removal of internal frontiers and the Maastricht treaty's adoption of subsidiarity, the quintet was complete. It is hard to overrate the economic significance of the regulatory quintet. The combination of free movement, no internal frontiers and mutual recognition as well as proportionality at the Member States' level have led to a far greater and more intense competitive exposure of national goods markets than before the Single Act. Should common regulatory action be necessary, it is nevertheless still bound by the combination of subsidiarity (as in the treaty, Art. 5-EC), minimum approximation and EU-level proportionality.

There is one caveat. Establishing the internal market while overcoming market failures and minimizing regulatory failures should improve economic welfare, as a rule. But this conclusion cannot be fully generalized. Consider the case of EU countries having very large differences in preferences: in some health, safety or environmental objectives they diverge sharply. An inconsiderate application of free movement would preempt the satisfaction of the strictest local preferences (in say, environmental regulation). Art. 30, EC should prevent this from happening. But approximation may similarly suppress such preferences if QMV overrules the relevant Member State(s). This might mean that common regulation to overcome market failure would *lower* welfare in some member states. Assuming that the overruled preferences expressed in Council are widely held by the voters in these countries and do not merely reflect overt protectionism, this would be a serious drawback.

There are two possible responses to this problem. First, in Art. 95, sub. 4 an escape clause is formulated, under strict conditions, allowing a member state to maintain stricter legislation *without* mutual recognition. This clause has hardly been invoked thus far showing that it is not a pressing problem in actual practice. Second, a Member State may maintain or enact stricter legislation, but of course subject to mutual recognition. In economic terms, the effect will be that *the regulatory costs will fall on the suppliers in the member state itself*. If such preferences are truly widespread in the country, the satisfaction of these preferences may well offset the regulatory costs.

The economic welfare analysis of mutual recognition

The direct benefits of MR can be clarified with the help of rigorous welfare analysis, be it under somewhat restrictive assumptions. Realizing that regulatory barriers are very different from tariff barriers or quotas, there are essentially two (different) ways of approaching the direct economic effect of MR. First, one can regard national standards and regulations as *cost-increasing entry barriers* and MR will then alter the competitive exposure of domestic firms, hitherto operating in fairly sheltered national markets. Second, one can regard national SHEC rules or voluntary standards and (tough) conformity assessment as *quality signalling*. In such a setting, the cost differential may simply reflect quality competition and a need to invest in reputation-building. These two contrasting perspectives can both be relevant, dependent on the nature of the goods market. With the steady Europeanization of standards, whether linked to directives or not (hence, MR), the problem could be expected to fade away in another one or two decades (except perhaps in building products where also the USA continues to have perennial barriers in its internal market).

First, our analysis will focus on a simple three countries/one-good model, with constant costs for the rest of the world (ROW) and increasing costs for the two EU countries, *L* and *H*. Consider Figure 3.1[10] showing the market in *H*. The good is homogenous between *ROW*, *L* and *H* (no quality differences), but regulations between *L* and *H* differ, causing adjustment costs.

The high-cost country *H* is not fully protected by the Union's common external tariff (CET) and *CD* of imports from *ROW* enter. The low-cost country *L* could easily export to *H* over its excess-supply curve (as drawn in the *H* market) $S_{H + exc. / L}$.[11] Its potential exports to *H* would be *FE*; if so, *ROW* would be squeezed out of the market as in simple customs union theory. However, with non-harmonized and non-recognized national technical regulations, *L* incurs an adjustment cost, in Figure 3.1 assumed to be the vertical difference between $S_{H + exc. / L}$ and

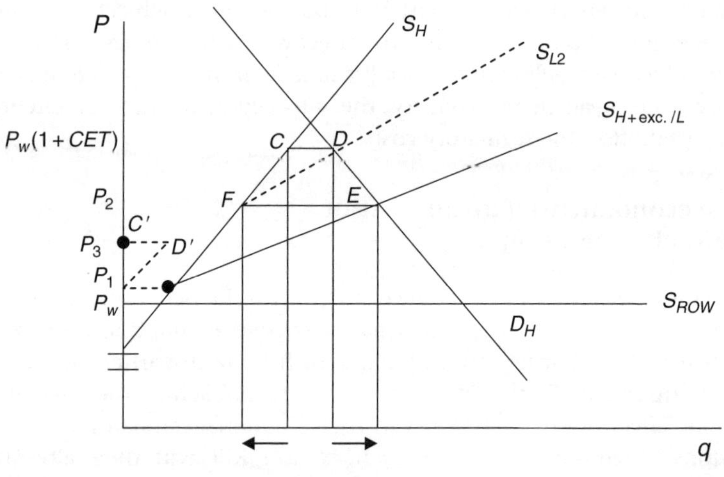

Figure 3.1 Mutual recognition and homogenous goods

Source: Adapted from Abraham, F., 'Building Blocks of Europe's Single Market', *Tijdschrift voor Economie en Management*, vol. 36, no. 4, 1991, pp. 6–15.

S_{L2}, hence, a given percentage of the cost price. It is (arbitrarily) drawn such that it goes through *D* and leaves enough exports into *H* so as to squeeze out *ROW* at the price $P_w(1 + CET)$. Would the adjustment be a little higher, *L* firms would refrain from exporting to *H*. Thus, in the internal market for homogeneous goods, still characterized by regulatory barriers, we find that:

(a) trade diversion may still occur, but, dependent on the (cost-increasing) barriers, it may also be reduced or absent; it also depends on whether the world price does or does not include similar adjustment costs as *L* experiences when entering *H*;
(b) both *L* and *H* keep very high domestic market shares when regulatory barriers are not tackled; indeed, dependent on the cost of adjustment to the regulation in *H*, the internal market may well remain segmented;
(c) the consequence of partial or complete segmentation is price disparities in the EU, despite tariff-free trade in the EU and the homogeneity of the good; if S_{L2} were relevant, or if it were situated even higher, the price prevailing in *H* would be $P_w(1 + CET)$; in *L* the domestic market clearing price would be P_1 and adding excess supply *CD* (= *C'D'*) would increase it to P_3; hence a considerable price disparity would arise.

Note that 'old-approach' type of harmonization (as distinct from mutual recognition or, as in Figure 3.1, from cost-increasing barriers only for exports to *H*, yet not domestically) would, due to vetoes and technical specificities, probably lead to 'maximum' requirements for standards and/or testing, in other words, close to or identical with those of *H*. The effect of this is not visible in the graph as nothing would alter in *H* but in *L* it would cause a price-hike. It would wipe out the competitive advantages of *L*, clearly something companies will fiercely resist. This simple analysis shows one major drawback of the 'old approach': it provides power to *protect* a high-cost industry, protected by regulatory barriers,[12] *rather than a 'liberalization'* of the internal market. The seductive plea for a 'level-playing field' may be very costly and throttle (potential) intra-EU trade.

The introduction of 'mutual recognition' (assuming that 'equivalence' is not a problem) drastically alters the picture. In Figure 3.1, *L* no longer incurs an adjustment cost and will export *FE* to *H*. The market share of domestic *H* producers is more or less halved (an absolute decline of sales, for a larger total quantity) which will prompt rationalization and restructuring. Consumers in H gain with the price fall, but consumers in L lose as the EU will now enjoy one price (P_2). Note that, if the restructuring of H-based firms does not lead S_H to shift down considerably (an improvement of technical efficiency), these firms cannot exploit mutual recognition by exporting to L. Trade diversion would now be certain in Figure 3.1.[13]

In this simple analysis, therefore, mutual recognition boils down to a *pro-competitive* regulatory regime.

Second, our analysis will stylize a case where SHEC regulations can be considered as quality signalling. Let us assume that domestic regulations refer to national standards which reflect quality; different national standards reflect quality differentials. The distinction between regulations and standards is crucial – without mutual recognition, the regulations constitute barriers, but with mutual recognition (hence, equivalence as to the 'essential requirements') only the voluntary quality standards remain, and hence the price/quality combinations are determined by consumers and users. So, quality refers to 'non-SHEC requirements' like solidity, guarantees, materials, ingredients (including 'recipes' in the case of food products), technical sophistication, durability, design or after-sales service. Now consider Figure 3.2 which links (cost) prices to levels of quality

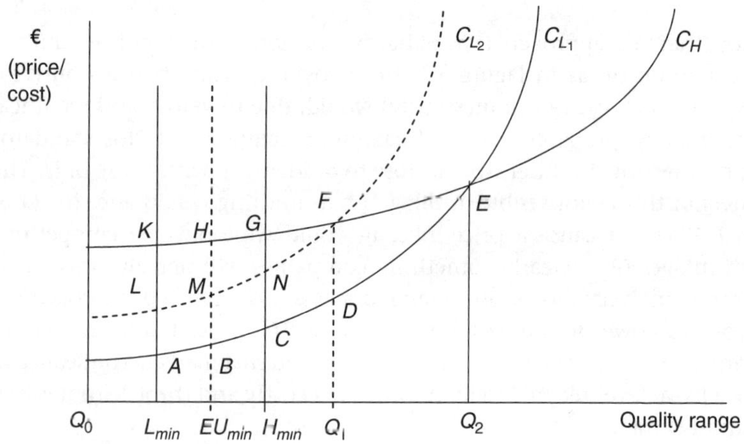

Figure 3.2 Mutual recognition and quality signalling

Source: Adapted from Falvey, R., 'Trade, Quality Reputations and Commercial Policy', *International Economic Review*, vol. 30, no. 3, 1989, pp. 607–22, and Abraham, F., 'Building Blocks of Europe's Single Market', *Tijdschrift voor Economie en Management*, vol. 36, no. 4, 1991. Note that there is no volume in this graph.

in L and H (*ROW* is ignored). Both countries have (different) minimum qualities L_{min} and H_{min}. The price/quality curves are convex, expressing the idea that ever higher quality becomes increasingly expensive. However, dependent on soft and hard infrastructure as well as experience, given domestic preferences (themselves a function of per capita income levels), H is a typical high-cost producer in the low-qualities range (between L_{min} and Q_2) and L in the high-qualities range (beyond Q_2 or E).[14]

With intra-EU trade opened up, under regulatory barriers, L can sell in H only beyond H_{min} up to Q_2 (that is, over *CE*), and H can sell in L only beyond Q_2 (or E). This squares with the notion that differentiated goods will generally sell in both markets.

Now mutual recognition is introduced. For simplicity we take this to mean that all qualities at or beyond L_{min} can be sold in the internal market. For L producers, the extra business opportunity is to sell now in H in the $L_{min} - H_{min}$ (*AC*) range. Seizing this opportunity depends, however, on the effectiveness of the quality signal. Consumers in H may mistrust the lower price of the L product for lower quality compared to H products in the same range. This lack of confidence is caused by the disappearance of the *H*-testing mark or certificate, so that consumers have an information problem. Beyond H_{min} this is less of a problem because H quality traditions are adhered to; still, convincing consumers of this very fact might require extra effort (for example, voluntary certification). In other words, L will need to invest in reputation-building or it would systematically ensure that its products are tested and certified to compliance with H standards.[15]

These efforts shift the C_{L1} curve to C_{L2}. L producers will now sell in H any quality between L_{min} up to Q_1 (over *LF*) but lose competitiveness *vis-à-vis H* firms in the range *FE*. Another interesting effect has to do with the fear of a 'race to the bottom'. In Figure 3.2 the opposite occurs – it leads to what David Vogel (1995)[16] has called, 'trading up', a convergence to higher quality levels.

If, in contrast to the earlier assumption, we assume that SHEC objectives play a role to set a minimum quality (say, of safety; or an emission ceiling), then one obtains a combination of minimum harmonization, and mutual recognition beyond it, based on quality. This could represent a stylized 'new approach'. In Figure 3.2, EU_{min} represents the regulatory minimum, in the light of SHEC objectives, but this (often) says relatively little about the overall quality properties of machines, toys, and so on. As shown, this could lead to the exit of producers in the very low-quality range between L_{min} and EU_{min}. Whether this is a welfare loss depends on whether L_{min} did or did not fully overcome the market failure.[17]

Box 3.1 Mutual recognition and imperfect competition

Advanced economic analysis has ignored mutual recognition, with a few exceptions. In Lutz (1996)[18] harmonization and mutual recognition are compared in a model of vertical product differentiation, which builds on work by Shaked and Sutton (1982)[19] and Ronnen (1991),[20] for the two-countries case. Duopolistic firms face quality-dependent fixed costs and compete in quality and price in two segmented markets. When firms have identical cost functions, the introduction of mutual recognition yields the maximal sum of regional welfares, compared to harmonization or 'no regulation'. A harmonized regulation, maximizing the sum of national welfares, will lead to a reduction of welfare in *H*. But when costs of the *L* firms increase (and indeed increasingly with higher quality, as in Figure 3.2), these results are partially reversed. Indeed, with a high enough cost differential, harmonization with only one firm in the market is superior in welfare.

The exit of *L* firms is in the overall (welfare) interest of the country. Lutz is capable of showing, be it in a highly stylized fashion, that entry deterrence by strategically choosing quality is possible (see also Herguera and Lutz, 1998[21]).

A somewhat different two-stage game, with Cournot duopoly and two countries, is presented by Suwa-Eisenmann and Verdier (2002).[22] It is an extension of the well-known Brander and Spencer model (1985)[23] and introduces a political support function (i.e. the government only looks at producers' interest). Mutual recognition is interesting once the 'institutional capacity' of *L* and *H* differs in supporting all what such recognition takes (in quality and conformance infrastructure) at low costs. This would tend to move implicit regulatory protection towards an asymmetric increase in the cost of *L* producers exporting to *H* (in other words, it favours *H* as if it were a tariff).

Analytical work in more sophisticated models is still scant and the results are not comparable because of disparate approaches. Box 3.1 provides a flavour of this kind of economic research. The conclusion is that mutual recognition in homogeneous goods markets tends to be strongly pro-competitive, whereas in differentiated goods markets there are likely to be forceful incentives for 'trading up', the opposite of a race-to-the-bottom. However, in models of imperfect competition (and given that mutual recognition requires equivalent objectives of domestic regulation, including reliable conformity assessment) there is scope for strategic quality games. In such games the competitiveness of low-cost lower-quality suppliers might sometimes be affected.

The costs of mutual recognition

After two decades of judicial MR and one and a half of a regulatory application of the principle in goods markets, the picture emerging is one of great ambiguity.

On the one hand, there can be no denying the great merits of introducing this innovative principle. Many instances of silly and *de facto* protectionist import bans have been removed. An entirely new approach to food law has been developed at EU level which is solely focused on SHEC objectives or effects, without – as a rule – specifying the individual products concerned. When the *quality* of goods – beyond 'essential' issues of SHEC – is concerned, the consumer disposes, based on mere labelling requirements (so as to remove asymmetries of information). Beyond food and beverages, it is possible to identify a range of goods markets where MR applies. Based on the Atkins Report for the Single Market Review,[24] it is estimated that nearly 50 per cent of intra-EU goods trade is subject to MR and the rest is covered by the old and new approaches. Of the 50 per cent covered by MR some 20 per cent refers to unregulated goods (say, teaspoons), and another 30 per cent to nationally regulated goods (say, beer, pasta, carpets, and so on).

Yet, one has to answer the questions whether this figure means that (1) without MR these markets would not enjoy free movement?; (2) with MR they do enjoy unhindered market access? Both questions should be answered with a qualified 'no'. The completely unregulated markets would probably enjoy free movement without any problems. But the nationally regulated ones would cause higher costs of intra-EU trade or force local establishments or block trade. So, the identifiable gains should be looked for only in those markets. However, when question 2 is considered, it turns out that there are numerous practical problems in enjoying market access, even when MR should formally apply. These problems can cause a great deal of anxiety and uncertainty, and have indeed engendered a sense of disenchantment with the principle. We shall discuss the generic 'costs' of mutual recognition and what to do about them in this section; together with a brief review of the belated strategy at EU level to reduce these costs. Later in the chapter the more specific costs which tend to fall on business are set out, with some examples from goods markets. There is also evidence that MR in those service markets where the principle could matter is little exploited by business.

Mutual recognition turns out to have fairly high information, transaction and compliance costs. Apart from some specific costs to business (see later in chapter p. 114), there are six reasons for these costs to be high:

- First, MR is not 'visible'. For a particular tradable good in markets, MR is a distant abstraction. What makes it even more difficult is that the national rules in a country are usually well-known and can be easily verified, yet they are overridden by this abstraction. It is obvious that in many cases such a configuration cannot be expected to lead to the required degree of legal certainty in day-to-day business throughout a big internal market trading many tens of thousands of goods. Perhaps one could best regard MR as a 'regulatory' principle with several layers: whereas the general principle will necessarily remain abstract, if only for its applicability in a wide variety of cases, the sufficient conditions for low-cost applicability amount to several layers of much more practical guidelines which should be easily verifiable. This is confirmed by the other five reasons for the generic costs of MR.

- Second, there is no rule-book for MR, indeed, if anything MR applies the negative of a rule-book. Clearly, for inspectors, certifiers and indeed traders themselves this can be a drawback when one realizes how fast modern markets and exchange works. The EU authorities and possibly national ones as well could undoubtedly be proactive at this 'lower' layer of MR. As we shall see this has finally been realized by the Union during the last few years.
- Third, one important reason for the gap between the principle and its application in day-to-day business is the lack of clarity about the equivalence of *effects*. The ECJ has always spoken about equivalence of 'objectives or effects'. Although objectives can cause difficulties occasionally, even when the leap to approximation is not taken, the interpretation of effects risks (re-)introducing a good deal of the regulatory specifications that should be of little or no significance under MR. Hence, the importance of the new approach where voluntary standards deal with the effects in a useful but not restrictive manner. But where MR applies in the presence of some national regulation, the 'effects' clause creates a grey area which raises the costs of MR. Again, these costs can be reduced by proactive policies.
- Fourth, the costs of monitoring are very high. It is out of the question to monitor each and every individual case of MR. The high costs of monitoring may even prompt strategic behaviour on the part of some authorities in some specific cases, not least when viewed in combination with the next drawback.
- Fifth, judicial review in the EU is slow because of the overload of the ECJ and the huge increase in the requested 'preliminary rulings' (not seldom on MR cases). Of course, this drawback is not specific to MR but the application and indeed the conduct of national regulatory authorities and testing/certification institutes is likely to be directly affected by it.
- Sixth, the application of MR has turned out to be much more complex than originally envisaged. The more complicated its

interpretation and the more 'grey areas' and special cases, the more it approaches an EU-based regulatory system, whereas the idea is precisely to avoid EU rules and allow diversity to be combined with free movement. Once again, the complexity calls for a proactive policy of information and lowering of transaction costs.

In discussing what the Union has done in order to lower the costs of MR, one should distinguish the activities and debates about *existing* regulatory barriers and the EU infrastructure about *newly emerging* regulatory barriers due to new legislation in Member States.

As to the existing regulatory barriers, the doubts about the effectiveness of MR in goods markets began after the EC 1992 programme was completed. Following regular complaints from European business and an *ad hoc* conference in Copenhagen between the Commission and European business on a Danish list of no less than 400 instances where MR had allegedly failed, two initiatives were taken to address the issues. The Molitor Report (1995) on simplification of European regulation[25] recommended that the actual benefits of MR were often outweighed by the costs of uncertainty, hence approximation would often be better. The 1995 UNICE report[26] took a similar stance. The Atkins Report on Technical Barriers (1998) in the Single Market Review (see note 24) documents both deep scepticism amongst economic agents in markets about MR, and analyses in seven case studies how rarely MR works out the way (naive?) economists might be led to believe (see also p. 114 this chapter). A 1999 Commission report[27] finally acknowledged that MR requires a far wider, deeper and proactive infrastructure in the single goods market to make it work. One can also infer from this report that there is no, what I call, '*MR culture*' yet in the Union.

Such a culture would comprise at least three 'soft' but critical ingredients which are nowadays still lacking:

(1) economic agents well-informed about the 'rights' MR implies for their business, trade or consumptive activities;
(2) confidence between Member States, and more specifically their various regulatory, inspection and/or certification agencies, about specifications and actual enforcement; and
(3) incentives for whatever national bodies having a direct or indirect impact on free movement (under MR) to think and act 'European' rather than national – the point here is that the incentive structure is tilted the other way around.

This *information – confidence – Union-mindset* combination could do much to render MR far more effective. However, this would require deep and permanent investments and possibly some restructuring.

The Barcelona European Council (15/16 March 2002) asked the Commission to report (once again!) on technical barriers to trade, which signals a persistent concern about MR when it comes to its day-to-day enforcement in the single market. The Commission opened the SOLVIT initiative in 2002 for infringement cases where the reason seems to be 'misapplication' of EC law in goods and services – often, a matter of MR. In May 2002, such cases numbered no less than 681![28] This is likely to be only the well-known tip of an iceberg of unreported frustrations of free movement.

More specifically, the second Commission report on MR[29] comprises for the first time a much more proactive approach with activities such as regular conferences and round tables, the publication of guides and guidelines and detailed case studies as the basis for common interpretation. At the same time, this report testifies the complications of MR in all areas. Nevertheless, the Commission is more adamant than ever to ensure better and more widespread compliance with MR, for the better functioning of the internal market.

The EU has done much better in permanently *preventing new regulatory barriers* from arising year after year. The infrastructure consists of a little known yet crucial committee, backed up by exceptionally strong information powers as well as strict obligations of member states to accept EU priorities in their national legislative processes. The 98/34 Committee (formerly known as the 83/189 Committee) deals with all national draft laws having a bearing, actual or potential, on regulatory barriers in goods markets. The Committee does this *before* these drafts reach national parliaments and under automatic or discretionary 'standstills' (of the national legislation process) of anything between three and 18 months! Member States and the Commission give 'detailed opinions' if regulatory barriers are suspected or expected and, in any event, 'equivalence' and/or MR clauses have to be incorporated in every such law. In doing so, new regulatory barriers are nipped in the bud and MR is not only allowed to work, it is encouraged by explicit references to equivalence. In effect, therefore, the 98/34 committee protects MR for all new laws of member states. Only in very rare cases that no equivalence exists will the Commission propose an approximation directive. With hindsight it is clear that this committee has rescued the functioning of the internal goods market. Without this infrastructure a singular focus on the existing barriers, even with MR, would have been hopelessly ineffective given the extremely high rate at which Member States add new sources of barriers where MR could lead to uncertainties. The work of this committee also shows that a proactive approach, based on firm powers, is the only way to render MR effective and (via equivalence clauses in national law) transparent.

The functioning of this low-key but critical committee has revealed to what extent Member States have turned into 'regulatory machines' (see also Pelkmans, Vos and Mauro, 'Reforming Product Regulation in the EU: A Painstaking, Iterative, Two-Level Game', in Galli and Pelkmans (eds), *Regulatory Reform and Competitiveness in Europe*, vol. I, Cheltenham/ Northampton (USA), Edward Elgar, 2000 for a detailed analysis). In recent years, the 15 Member States have produced, year after year, some 650–700 laws and decrees (or non-trivial amendments of them) which have to pass the Committee. If that number isn't reason to pause and wonder whether market functioning is genuinely improved by such a regulatory 'turnover', one ought to realize that (a) this only refers to goods markets,[30] and (b) Member States are not allowed to draft laws in 'approximated' markets, other than implementation of the directives.[31] So these 700-odd laws or decrees only deal with MR-type markets, covering a mere 30 per cent of intra-EU goods trade! After 18 years of the operation of this Committee the beginnings of an 'MR culture' can be discerned. However, the national instincts and incentives to come up with a lot of new regulation, year after year, remain forceful. It is also unclear whether the incipient MR culture in the Committee spills over to tackling existing barriers where MR should apply. Fortunately, to the extent that the Committee is a success, the area of existing barriers should no longer grow and a proactive MR policy by the EU might become effective in lowering the generic costs of MR in those goods.

Mutual recognition in services markets

It took some time before mutual recognition came to be applied to services in the internal market. In 1979 – the year of the *Cassis de Dijon* ruling – the liberalization of cross-border services had hardly begun and was therefore far behind the progress in goods markets. By the time the EC 1992 programme was designed, services had become more prominent and the question was rather how to tackle the many services markets that were regulated, and indeed differently regulated in different types of services markets.

The basics in the Treaty looked like those in goods, in that there is a clear obligation to remove restrictions on the free movement of services

(Art. 49, EC; then Art. 59) and that non-discrimination is the rule. As for goods, there are derogations from non-discrimination (Art. 46, then Art. 56) and these tend to be narrowly interpreted by the ECJ. The analogy with goods also extends to the judicial approach to restrictions of a non-discriminatory kind in the 1991 *Saeger* case,[32] just like the famous *Dassonville* ruling of 1974 in goods. Hence, these restrictions should be judged from an economic perspective: restrictions 'liable to prohibit or otherwise impede' cross-border services of the 'temporary' type are not allowed. This economic approach covers measures affecting the ability to provide, those increasing the costs of the relevant service (a very wide-ranging prohibition, as in *Dassonville*), those discouraging its provision and those preventing consumers from receiving the service.

It is then a small step to introduce the *Cassis de Dijon* analogy, that is, the notion of judicial mutual recognition.[33] A member state cannot normally prohibit the provision, in its own territory, of a service lawfully provided in another member state, even if the conditions in which it is provided are different in the country where the service provider is established. As with goods, this mutual recognition even applies in case of derogations as long as the legitimate objectives pursued in different member states are equivalent.

Nevertheless, it would seem that the practical economic significance of judicial MR in services is fairly limited. The wide derogations of Art. 46, EC and a host of other objectives (often under the 'general good' doctrine, a kind of rule-of-reason approach developed by the ECJ) can be legally compatible with the Treaty, even though free movement of services is thereby severely curtailed. The ECJ will verify this compatibility using three tests: a restrictive justification test (overriding reasons of public interests); a non-duplication test (for statutory conditions, if equivalent, already satisfied in the home country); and the proportionality test (barriers should be indispensable and least-restrictive). The ECJ approach has helped to remove all kinds of arbitrary protectionism or overregulation. In and by itself, however, judicial MR and the compatibility tests of derogations have not resulted in truly free movement of services in most markets.

To understand why this is so, three crucial properties of services provision in the internal market should be considered. First, many services markets are regulated. Although judicial MR might sometimes suffice to obtain free movement, the information, confidence and transaction costs of MR are likely to be much higher in the case of services than for goods. Services are not storable and are also intangible, which renders it difficult to assess quality. Services are typically not 'search goods' (where the buyer can verify quality before consumption, as in goods markets), but either 'experience goods' (evaluation of quality only possible after consumption) or 'credence goods' (quality cannot even be assessed after consumption). Such markets tend to suffer from asymmetries of information and this can lead to a range of inefficiencies (including moral hazard and adverse selection). Suitable regulation ought to ensure a proper functioning of such markets. The gradual establishment of the internal market for services in the EU has shown that the reduction of these costs of MR may require a regulatory approach to MR, that is, Directives specifying the objectives and (main) effects, beyond which MR applies.

Second, most of the larger (non-governmental) services markets fall under special regimes in the Treaty which assume priority before free movement of services (Art. 49, EC) applies. This renders services incomparable to goods trade in economic terms. Financial services, transport services (all six modes) and all services in network industries (including telecoms, broadcasting, postal and the distribution services of gas and electricity) have special Articles or Chapters in the EC treaty. All of these tend to be heavily regulated (both for services and for establishment) and a judicial form of MR cannot easily be expected to be workable. The internal market will require either far-reaching approximation of rules and supervision, or regulatory MR, or some combination of the two.

Third, the economics of services provision, such as the simultaneity of production and consumption of services (in many cases), the frequently inevitable proximity of supplier to the customer (both in B2B and B2C) and the importance of reputation and confidence, strongly suggests that the determinants of the volume and nature of cross-border services are not comparable to those of goods trade. To put it simply, the formal removal of regulatory barriers may well prompt a much greater response in goods trade than in services trade, even if everything else were equal. But everything else is not equal in at least two respects: many services sub-markets are characterized by some degree of market power (for reasons such as product differentiation, reputation, consumer loyalty, existing networks and so on), and this is probably a greater obstacle to market penetration than in goods markets in a number of instances, and the incentives to substitute service provision through local establishment for cross-border provision is far stronger than in goods trade precisely because of proximity and confidence reasons.

Like in goods, mutual recognition applies only to a limited number of cases. However, in services there is no such thing as the 'old' approach of total and detailed harmonization. It is true that, for a long time, the

Transport Council was split on how much (intrusive) harmonization would be required before free movement of transport services would apply, but no decisions of the 'old'-approach kind were actually taken. Once the Council had been convicted (!) by the ECJ in 1985 (on request of the European Parliament, *nota bene*) for its failure to establish a common transport policy, as the Treaty clearly prescribed, the EC pursued a 'new approach' with minimum approximation and mutual recognition (see later). Compared to the categorization of goods trade falling under either judicial MR (unregulated or equivalence) or the old approach (no scope for any MR due to uniformity) or the new approach (approximation only of 'objectives' and key issues of 'effects' if any; mutual recognition beyond it), a somewhat different categorization is best used in services as Figure 3.3 sets out.

Whereas most goods are tradable there exists a large category of services which is not, including pure governmental services, local private services (a haircut, for example), all non-distance education (a major sector) and a very large part of health services. The tradable services have to be split into non-regulated services where MR is not necessary (such as tourism, the service sector with the biggest turnover in Europe, and business services such as consulting and voluntary conformance services), and regulated ones. Regulated services, in turn, can be divided into network industries and non-networked services. The former services depend critically on physical or logistical networks with enormous sunk costs and are typically subject to public (or universal) service obligations. The liberalization and proper pursuit of competitive cross-border services in network industries is complex and requires sophisticated combinations of approximation, supervision (by 'regulators') and competition policy (see European Commission, 1999,[34] 2000;[35] Pelkmans, 2001b[36]). Within strict limits, selective and/or residual instances of MR (for example licensing) remain possible.

It is in the realm of non-networked regulated services that mutual recognition has regulatory and economic significance and two distinct approaches are employed. In financial services and (non-networked) transport services a regulatory form of MR, based on approximation of 'essential requirements', coupled to 'home-country control' has been opted for. Home-country control adds another innovative twist to the originality of mutual recognition. In financial services the EU has chosen to differentiate between the institutions supplying services (that is, banks, insurance companies and merchant banks and the like) and the services themselves. Knowing that approximation of the essential requirements of the services themselves might be very difficult and slow

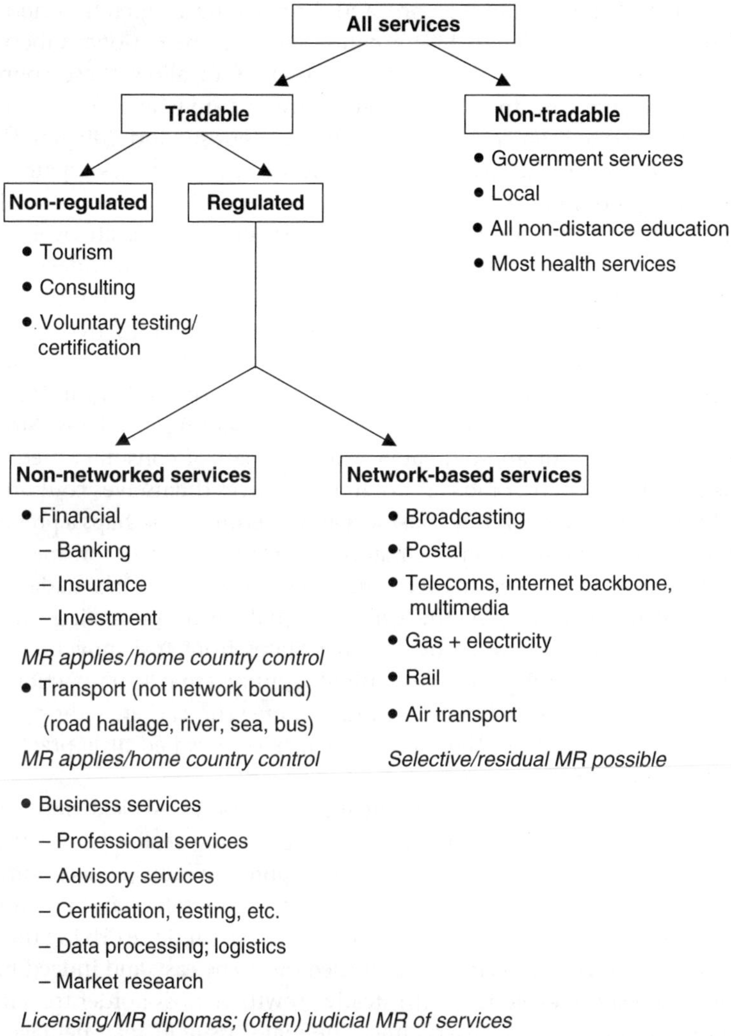

Figure 3.3 Services, trade and mutual recognition

(indeed, a 'new approach' might not be feasible, certainly in the mid-1980s before the wave of financial innovation and large-scale application of IT to financial services), the financial soundness of institutions was tackled as follows. Approximation of the key rules for financial soundness and the obligations of national supervisors to verify this on a permanent basis was achieved (think of minimum capital, solvency, large (risk) exposure, and so on) and far-reaching cooperation about automatic access to detailed information between the national supervisors established, which provided a solid basis to allow these sound financial institutions to do cross-border business anywhere in the internal market (at a distance or via simple branches or support offices in the host country). No authorization in the host country is necessary unless one changes to full subsidiaries. Thus, the bank or insurance licence in one Member State becomes a 'passport' to do business all over the Union. The mutual recognition refers to the authorization/supervision regimes amongst the Member States so that confidence in country B in a financial institution offering services there but originating from country A, can be based on the 'home-country control' (under common rules, to be sure) in country A. Close cooperation and information exchange among regulators irons out any remaining problems. Since the services are not approximated (except a part of consumer credits) one might ask whether judicial MR in the services themselves could not yield substantial cross-border business and, eventually, perhaps a process of regulatory competition facilitating a 'new approach' or market-driven convergence. The answer here is that the ECJ itself has made this very difficult by developing the 'general good doctrine' protecting a host of regulatory interventions by Member States from free movement.[37] Although this doctrine is now increasingly confined to B2C transactions – as asymmetries of information are much more serious there – the application of judicial MR to the services themselves has had little practical impact thus far.[38]

In road haulage as the dominant mode of non-networked transport services, the so-called common transport policy now realized consists of mutual recognition of licensing based on approximation (hence, home-country control as well) and approximation of the safety and environmental requirements of the vehicles (that is, goods) and the driving times of the drivers. Free movement has turned out to be easy and indeed has been aggressively exploited, with steady growth of cross-border trucking ever since the EC 1992 programme. The major issue in road haulage is the appropriate allocation of user costs of infrastructure in countries refusing to have tollroads, which has nothing to do with MR.

In business services regulation is uneven and generalizations are dangerous.[39] The present chapter is not the place to analyse the problems, but for the sake of comparison one might say that the application of judicial MR is the rule, yet has turned out to be exceedingly difficult in actual practice. Where licensing plays a role in these markets, the mutual recognition tends to be of a different nature; namely, based on

MR of diplomas. There is an old and a new approach in diploma recognition but it is doubtful how well each of them really facilitates cross-border provision, especially but not only in professional services.[40]

In conclusion, mutual recognition has been applied to services with ingenuity, based on analogous case law (as in goods) and the notion of 'home-country control'. The sector where this has worked best is least known for MR; namely, road haulage. The reason is presumably that regulation of services and firms in road haulage is relatively light, whereas truck regulation falls under goods rules. In financial services MR of 'home-country control' has undoubtedly been a clever regulatory innovation, but it has served as little more than a necessary, not a sufficient condition to boost cross-border services provision. That 'deeper' regulatory commitments were required was recognized by all the EU players and lawmakers when the Financial Services Action Plan was adopted in 2000, for completion in 2005. As far as MR of the financial services themselves are concerned, the 'general good' doctrine has been a far too wide and almost open-ended inhibition of cross-border service provision. The limitation of the doctrine to B2C transactions is an improvement, but the doctrine itself should be reconsidered. A third reason why MR in financial services is of limited economic significance has to do with the relatively great need for proximity to customers for reasons of trust, consumer loyalty and service quality. The link between FDI and service provision is therefore very strong.

This is also the case in business services. Nevertheless, in business services there are numerous opportunities for irregular cross-border services trade without foreign direct investment (FDI) but the practical problems are still considerable. The link with diploma recognition for all professional services and some other ones as well, an array of local regulations, problems with FDI and a litany of obstacles about contracts for 'posted' workers (essential for occasional contracting), not to speak about the reluctance of small and medium-sized enterprises (SMEs) to complain are amongst the more important issues.

Altogether, in services even more than in goods, MR requires proactive policies. It should be realized that there is no committee like 98/34 in goods and, until recently, the European Commission did not pay systematic attention to cross-border services problems. The member states, the regions and local authorities hardly display anything like a 'MR culture'. The underutilization of MR and the lack of competitive challenge across borders is not particularly helpful for Europe's dynamism in services. Proactive policies, embedded in an EU-driven infrastructure to follow this systematically, are badly needed.

Assessing regulatory competition

Regulatory competition between Member States would seem to be a natural consequence of mutual recognition, under free-movement obligations. MR will expose national regulation to the forces of arbitrage: consumers may choose between domestic regulation and that of any other member state by importing the relevant *goods or services*. To the extent that even production factors find it profitable to respond to regulatory differences, mutual recognition and free movement may induce cross-border *factor* flows. All this should improve welfare on account of greater variety and additional output in the EU. But, since mutual recognition is a static notion, no more than a one-time adjustment would take place.

Regulatory competition is dynamic and takes this process further. It is defined as changes in national regulation in response to the actual or expected impact of cross-border mobility of goods or services on national economic activity, itself prompted by MR (Sun and Pelkmans, 1995[41]). Behind this alteration of national rules one may find complex business–government interactions. Jurisdictions with costly regulations may find businesses pressing for reductions in their regulatory burden when faced with import competition from jurisdictions with 'light' regimes. Alternatively, local businesses and governments may agree on strategic de-regulation with the aim of boosting certain activities in the internal market. Since this may also be practiced, or responded to, by other member states, iterative processes of regulatory competition may develop. Where Member States would *maintain* ambitious regulation, the costs will fall on that Member State's economy; this can be interpreted as meaning that the local benefits of satisfying these preferences are more than worth the local costs. Quality or other non-price determinants induced by this regulation would make products from other jurisdictions poor substitutes, and hence would protect local business from suffering too much from import competition. When factor mobility is at issue, location benefits (after taking account of sunk costs of establishment) would apparently outweigh the benefits of relocation at the margin. The notion of regulatory competition implies that the maintenance of regulatory differences despite exposure to arbitrage would be economically justified in view of disparate preferences.

As a rule, however, one would expect a process of regulatory competition to induce 'market-driven' regulatory convergence in the EC. The condition for optimality is that this should *not* be allowed where negative externalities produce the relevant market failure as this would lead to fragmentation of the internal market or too low regulation (exposing the environment, for example, or failing to deal with discriminatory measures), but it would be suitable if information asymmetries or other 'internalities' are the problem. At the end of a process of regulatory competition, the market-driven convergence could be codified in essential requirements in EC approximation. This economic 'model' of regulatory competition can be shown to be of some but not great practical relevance in the EU (with respect, for example, to equivalence). There is also little empirical evidence that intra-EC regulatory competition does take place (see for example Neven, 1996).[42]

Initial fears in the Community that regulatory competition would create a 'regulatory gap' (Bourgoignie, 1987, pp. 171–2)[43] or a race to the bottom have not been borne out. This is indeed what proper understanding of mutual recognition – the prerequisite of regulatory competition – would lead one to expect. After all, mutual recognition only applies if the objectives or effects of regulations in different member states are equivalent. A race to the bottom, removing regulation justified by market failure would clearly violate the equivalence test. Perhaps it may well work the other way, at times, as Vogel (1995 and 1997)[44] and Genschel and Plumper (1997)[45] attempt to show; namely, pushing regulation 'upwards', especially in environment and food law. This 'trading up' prompts the question whether it indicates a regulatory failure, *ex post*, or a failure to tackle a market failure, *ex ante*. If the political economy is not disciplined by regulatory quality requirements, there is a risk that regulatory failure may occur; that is, overregulation beyond what is needed to overcome the market failure.

A cost/benefit analysis of regulatory competition in the internal market is best made in comparison with that of EU regulation (here, approximation). However, it is crucial in such a comparison to compare regulatory competition *not* with the 'old approach' (and easily declare victory), but with the new approach. Table 3.3 summarizes the main costs and benefits of EU regulation and of regulatory competition.

The three benefits of regulatory competition are often mentioned and presumably require little elaboration. The third one, inspired by a Hayekian view of competition, is difficult to evaluate. I would submit that its empirical significance is so unclear that it leads to extremely difficult policy dilemmas. Its appeal is perhaps more relative than absolute, that is, in cases where the costs of regulatory rigidity (for example product harmonization before 1985 in the EU) are evidently very high, or where radical reform is going to prompt upheavals and far-reaching adjustment anyway (for example, EU telecoms before 1998), risky experiments and liberal processes of 'discovery' tend to become more acceptable.

Table 3.3 EU regulation and regulatory competition: costs and benefits

Costs	*Benefits*
Regulatory competition	
1 Open-ended and distortive	1 Greater choice of regulation 2 'Disciplining effect' on national regulatory systems
2 Sub-optimal regulation (too little, or, too much)	3 Strategy for discovery, experimentation and innovation
3 National regulatory drift	
*EU regulation**	
1 Regulation disproportionate to market failure	1 Removal of distortions, with (more) certainty for business 2 Flexibility (with EC-92), through various modes, intensities and differential scope
2 Rigidity, once in place (esp. before EC-92)	

* here, approximation.
Source: Based on Sun, J.M. and Pelkmans, J., 'Regulatory Competition in the Internal Market', *Journal of Common Market Studies,* vol. 33, no. 1, March 1995.

The costs of regulatory competition may well be considerable. Sun and Pelkmans show by means of a detailed decomposition of the process in the EU as well as illustrative case-studies (one for goods, one for services) that regulatory competition may well be open-ended and distortive. Also, the well-known argument that too little regulation may result, should not be dismissed, in contrast to the conclusions of Siebert and Koop (1990)[46] and Oates and Schwab (1988).[47] The point is that regulatory competition is not the same as fiscal competition where a 'race to the bottom' might never occur under 'fiscal equivalence'. Insufficient regulation will allow the reemergence of the market failure which regulation was originally designed to overcome. Similarly, too much regulation may occur as Peltzman (1976) has shown.[48] Finally, alteration of laws as a means of discovery has a price, quite apart from possible distortions; namely, national regulatory drift. An extreme example is the drift in US state liability laws in the 1980s and early-1990s where hundreds of changes created great uncertainty, so much so that some markets failed or collapsed.

Shifting to the costs and benefits of EU regulation, it should first be noted that the picture here has changed quite radically since the mid-1980s. The *relative* attraction of regulatory competition has decreased since the new regulatory strategy of the EU has come to be accepted. The strategy has no doubt reduced the two types of costs in Table 3.3: the highly detailed and otherwise excessive regulation, often disproportionate to the market failure (but pre-1985, under unanimity, inevitable for the free movement in such products), and the rigidity, once EC Directives were in place.[49] With minimum approximation, only of objectives ('essential requirements'), reference to voluntary standards[50] and options to comply even with the help of other standards, the dated anecdotes about the jam or chocolate Directives or the hill-farming-tractor Directive no longer form the benchmark to compare regulatory competition.

On the benefit side, the first effect (removal of distortions) has probably not changed in nature, yet drastically in scope. Beginning with the long delayed, proper implementation of the 1973 Low-Voltage Directive in the early-1980s, EC-1992 has widened enormously the range of products benefiting from free movement with often fairly 'light' and flexible Directives. This change was a function of the wide product scope of crucial EC-1992 Directives (for example toys, machines, electromagnetic compatibility) and some horizontal ones (such as product liability), as well as the sheer number of industrial and agricultural product Directives (some 160). Also, the flexibility of EU regulation has greatly improved, after the bitter and costly lessons from the past had been learned. In fact, a conscious differentiation has taken place amongst a wider range of partial or complete alternatives, such as a greater reliance on framework Directives, sunset legislation, Council recommendations with a call for (constrained) self-regulation, and so on. In Regulations (unlike a Directive, an EC Regulation has direct effect throughout the Union and is, in that sense, 'centralist'), regional or national differentiation has also been introduced to a greater extent.

The most interesting aspect is perhaps that regulatory competition and EU regulation act as *complements* in all cases where SHEC objectives justify regulation. So, the upper and lower panels of Table 3.3 are no longer independent in a large number of cases of products and services. To understand this, remember that, beyond the 'essential requirements' in EC Directives, regulatory competition is allowed, if not implicitly encouraged. Unless a blocking minority insists on detailed specifications of 'essential requirements' (which has become rare, except in the environmental field), *the threat of regulatory competition exercises a disciplinary effect* on national regulators. Qualified majority voting and the no-frontiers accomplishment make this threat credible. This permanent discipline was identified as a great strategic advantage earlier in this chapter.

Business' ambivalence about mutual recognition

It is well-known that business has a Janus-face when it comes to regulation and protectionism. Particular barriers protecting narrowly defined product markets may be strongly preferred by specific interests whilst, at the same time, joining the overall lobbying against 'overregulation' and barriers in the internal market. In this sense one can almost never speak of one consistent business view. Even when this caveat is taken into account, however, it would seem entirely appropriate to call attention to the deep ambivalence business in Europe has developed about mutual recognition. With analogies of peeling an artichoke or sailing to the horizon on a big ocean, business expresses the sentiment that mutual recognition appears to be a promise which materializes in actual practice only very slowly. It is often suggested that MR has to be 'conquered', almost case by case, and is therefore not so radically different from approximation. Such utterances tend to be heavily biased towards the remaining problems since, where MR functions or approximation is satisfactory, nothing is heard. Given the practical difficulties of measuring progress in applying the principle in so many sub-markets in goods and services, the voices of frustration are not put into perspective by a clear overall picture. Nevertheless, the problems business still encounters on a daily basis are simply too serious to be ignored or belittled. It is also narrow-minded, indeed costly, to have a mythical confidence in the judicial and enforcement system of the EU as the sole source of removal of the many barriers as the Internal Market scoreboards and a range of legal sources testify to this.[51] Much more cost-effective would seem to be the regular 'package meetings' the Commission holds with each one of the member states where numerous instances of non-application of MR can be resolved.

This section aims to illustrate the market realities of MR for business. After a few short examples from the Atkins Report, three cases in goods markets will be presented with a little more detail, followed by illustrations from the markets for business services. These illustrations help to illustrate the sharp contrast between the praise for an innovative principle and the scorn from business in Europe when entering markets.

A few case studies from the Atkins (1998) Report[52] may give some impression of what the uphill struggle means if one would insist on the right of free movement and market access:

Electric cables No formal barriers, but a private mutual recognition agreement between selected certification bodies having a 'monopoly' in each of the 16 Member countries (so, not the Global Approach for conformity assessment accompanying the 'new approach' of approximation, and presumably anti-competitive, the main motive being quality, but this could 'raise rivals' costs' unduly).

Cement Little cross-border trade because of regulatory and non-regulatory barriers (hence, complex infringement cases, one by one) and a cartel severely limiting cross-border trade discovered in 1998; solutions to be found under the Construction Product Directive which moves very slowly because of building codes (etc.); it implies that MR is partly substituted by approximation and common standards.

Pesticides Strong technical barriers; high costs of compliance; MR does not work and neither does approximation (in 1996/97). MR here is legal fantasy. The only reason that goods are not approximated is disagreement among Member States precisely about 'essential requirements'.

Carpets Regulatory (fire-testing) and non-regulatory barriers; high compliance costs; MR does not work but embryonic private MR agreement now exists.

Zooming in on three other examples only confirms the complexity of MR application and helps one to appreciate the scepticism in business circles. All three are markets with considerable turnover and anything but marginal or exceptional.

The first case is 'fortified food or drinks'.[53] Typically these products claim to provide extra energy (for example for sports) or vitamins or otherwise be good for health. The central problem here is 'non-equivalence' of objectives or effects (mainly the latter) between Member States. So, MR cannot work fully. Approximation had failed at least up to 1998. The elegant triptich of the EU's regulatory system (free movement through prohibitions to Member States, mutual recognition; approximation) breaks down and a seemingly chaotic battery of restrictions fragments the internal market. Non-equivalence is hard to tackle via the ECJ because the scientific evidence of 'effects' is unclear and in such cases the ECJ gives the benefit of the doubt to the country imposing restrictions. The inconsistencies are many. Take margarine: whereas France applies a ban to fortification, it is compulsory in the Netherlands! In many product categories there are labelling problems since the claims about health or other effects are often hard to substantiate; member states differ in drawing the line between permissible and misleading claims. Parallel imports are usually not tightly controlled – giving the impression that MR does work – but this can prompt liability claims. Yet another inconsistency is that some member states employ positive lists and others negative lists.

Bicycles is a second case.[54] Until recently the internal market for bicycles did not function properly. Unlike cars there is no technical approximation (neither the 'old' approach as in cars nor a 'new' approach) for bicycles. But MR was not allowed to work well either. The greatest problem is that national standards (which are, by definition, voluntary) in France and the UK have been referred to in domestic laws as compulsory. In Germany, with greater subtlety, exactly the same effect resulted because product-liability insurance requires retailers to provide a 'voluntary' certificate of compliance with the DIN standard. The Danish concerns about theft go so far as to impose an obligation for an indelible mark/stamp for purposes of tracability. Since this creates problems for the import of painted bikes (it is costly to paint separately at the sales location) it serves as a regulatory barrier and would be convicted by the ECJ. After several decades of growth, partly as a result of innovation (mountain bikes, and so on), demand is stagnating and the threat of import competition from East Asia has increased. In the second half of the 1990s the EU imposed anti-dumping duties, and some trade diversion was captured by EU producers behind these duties and a (high) tariff of 15 per cent. It would seem that the mounting evidence of weak competitiveness of the Union's bicycle industry and an awareness that some barriers might not be enforceable once tested before the ECJ have finally prompted action, driven by the largest intra-EU exporter, Italy. A consistent application of MR would lower costs for the industry and thereby enhance competitiveness. The approach taken is interesting. While avoiding approximation, mutual recognition will be based on the withdrawal of national standards but only once a European (CEN) standard is agreed (which is expected). This standard is given legal force by publishing it under a general directive for safety which serves as a fall-back for instances where there is no product-specific directive.[55]

The third example is about the Danish beer fortress. In the internal market for beer, MR might be believed to have prevailed ever since the famous 1987 case against Germany (and, little known, Greece as well). Not only is MR merely a necessary, yet far from sufficient condition to penetrate national beer markets (because of anti-competitive structures due to ownership or tied-finance-and-exclusive-distribution of beer houses contracts as well as numerous anti-competitive conduct cases and problematic mergers), dubious restrictions have long remained in place which make a mockery of mutual recognition. The celebrated case is what can be denoted as the Danish beer fortress. Ever since Denmark became an EC member state (1973), several laws have been introduced creating cost-raising barriers for beer exporters from other Union countries. The Commission's vigilance prevented these measures from taking effect or ensured their withdrawal. The measures were also seen as suspect because in those days Denmark had a tight duopoly of Tuborg and Carlsberg with a joint market-share at home of over 90 per cent. The ingenious attempt to create a new regulatory barrier in 1981 proved harder to fight because it was tied up with an environmental cause: beer (and some other beverages) could only be sold (hence, also imported) in reusable bottles, thereby blocking all canned-beer imports and, significantly, raising costs for importers of bottled beers. It would go too far for the present illustration to enter into the details of this case. The crux of the matter was whether environmental objectives could serve as a derogation of free movement (based on MR). But three circumstances spoke strongly against this: the clear protectionist intent (shown by this law being another attempt in a series), the fact that it was not least-restrictive (violating proportionality) and, worst of all, shielding a tight domestic duopoly (soon to alter into a monopoly due to a merger). Also, the distortive effect was demonstrated when the duopoly continued to produce huge exports of canned beer for the internal market, while its competitors could not sell canned beer in their Danish home market. The ECJ, in a stunning ruling, allowed the derogation in 1988 despite strong evidence in the Cecchini Report (published five months before the ruling!) of the import-blocking effect of the law.[56] The protectionist intent was moreover proven by the lifting of the law during a long strike at both Tuborg and Carlsberg in 1985/6 when imports dramatically increased, only to reduce to close to zero once the strike was over and the law restored. Was the environmental objective no longer valid during the strike? It was only in 2002 that Denmark finally agreed to accept imported beer not packaged in reusable bottles. This case shows clearly that MR requires extreme vigilance by the EU authorities and does not preclude clever instances of regulatory capture.

Mutual recognition in services equally requires deep supervisory investment and vigilance. In the Commission's view, services 'are much more prone to Internal Market barriers than goods and are harder hit'.[57] A compact but incomplete explanation is insightful:

> Because of the complex and intangible nature of services and the importance of the know-how and the qualifications of the service

> provider, the provision of services is often subject to much more complex rules covering the entire service activity than is the case for goods. Furthermore, while some services can be provided at a distance, many still require the permanent or temporary presence of the service provider in the Member State where the service is delivered. Whereas with goods only the goods themselves are exported, in the case of service provision it is often the provider himself, his staff, his equipment and material that cross national borders. As a result some or all of the stages of the business process may take place in the Member State where the service is provided and be subject to requirements differing from those in the Member Sate of origin. This also means that barriers at a single stage of the business process cannot be looked at in isolation; their cumulative impact throughout the service activity must be considered. (*Ibid.*)

Note that this worrying conclusion refers mainly to business services, the category at the bottom of Figure 3.3 where the application of MR should be expected to work.

This chapter is not the appropriate place to delve deeply into the maze of restrictions and the scope, actual or potential, for effective application of MR to business services. An arbitrary selection of examples might hammer home the point that much remains to be done to exploit MR,[58] while at the same time it also means that the permanent welfare gains to be had from exposure to greater competitive pressure from cross-border origins should be quite significant.

Although monopolies are (now) rare in business services, all kinds of sweeping restrictions remain with analogous effects such as *numerus-clausus* rules for geographical areas, territorial restrictions or even a single-establishment obligation (medical laboratories in a member state) which implies the giving up of an establishment in the Member State of origin! Authorizations and registration requirements tend to be annoying, unnecessarily costly or next to prohibitive. Duplication (hence, going against the ECJ jurisprudence, as discussed earlier, p. 102), multiplicity (bakeries in one country tend to become a 'collector' of licenses because licenses do not refer to the nature of the business but to many individual products), long duration, too much discretion of the part of local authorities and recommendations from bodies made up of local competitors (!) are amongst these barriers and would appear to express the very opposite of a 'mutual recognition culture' that the internal market for services requires. Because of the need to employ local establishments, the very considerable fiscal problems of cross-border business, precisely for SMEs without professional fiscal departments, should not be underestimated.[59] Similarly, because cross-border services by nature often involve temporary work across borders, the actual profitability of a contract is more often than not dependent on the extremely restrictive treatment of 'posted workers' where disproportionate requirements and duplication seem to be viewed as legitimate. If, in addition, companies make use of workers from employment agencies, additional difficulties may arise.

Insofar as professional services are concerned, not only do the cumbersome MR of diplomas amount to a severe obstacle, but frequently a range of additional, often subtle barriers flowing from codes of conduct (self-regulation of an anti-competitive nature) as well.

The consequences of these practices fall disproportionately on SMEs and on users who (rightly) take free movement serious. Practices are resistant to change because companies, especially SMEs, shy away from litigation against local authorities. This leads to what the Commission calls 'arrangement practices' (not seldom with local competitors) or evasion ('black market strategies'). It goes without saying that a lot of cross-border business simply gets discouraged by the number and arbitrariness of the barriers.

All the illustrations, even if selective, feed the ambivalence of business about mutual recognition. Much as they would like to compete across borders and deepen the economic meaning of the Single Market, firms find themselves unwillingly appointed as the guardian of the Treaty (here, free movement under MR), chasing violations at their own costs. For business, the legal access to national markets represents only one among several possible costs of gaining market share, besides different tastes, other marketing strategies and perhaps different pre- and after-sales service. Given the costs and uncertainties of MR in some goods and many services markets, the risks of testing MR are simply not assumed and what ought to be a single market remains too often fragmented.

Concluding remarks

Mutual recognition has taken root in EU law, policies, enforcement and, at least for goods, infrastructure. The introduction of mutual recognition has induced a focus on essential requirements, thereby reducing the intrusiveness of approximation or avoiding any EC directive altogether in thousands of cases. Indeed, as we have shown, the great strategic advantages of MR can be found in the systemic upheaval it prompted in the regulatory system of the EU. These strategic advantages are worth spelling out once again: a much more rapid realization of the internal market, severe constraints to overregulation by Member States, additional disciplines on national regulators by the further option of regulatory competition, and a search for 'best-practice' regulation among member states, whether for national purposes or for Directives. In addition, the direct 'welfare' benefits are likely to be considerable as MR is pro-competitive, without sacrificing essential regulatory objectives such as health, safety, environment and consumer protection. Only when quality is extremely demanding might a risk exist that the needed investment in reputation is so costly that entry barriers are even strengthened in the internal market. The conclusion is that mutual recognition is highly beneficial and that many of the gains are permanent.

However, the application of MR in the internal market for goods and services is not an unambiguous success story. Applying the principle turns out to have fairly high information, transaction and compliance costs. We identify six cost elements including, among other things, the abstract nature of MR when inspectors or indeed business itself are confronted with well-specified national law which might be overridden by this 'invisible' notion; the absence of a 'rule book' for MR for market participants; the lack of clarity about the 'effects' (much more than 'objectives'); the very high costs of monitoring; the low speed of EC judicial review (which invites strategic or opportunistic behaviour); and the increasing complications in MR interpretation, especially in services. Focusing on existing barriers, lowering these costs has not been aggressively pursued by the EU until very recently. When it comes to the prevention of new regulatory barriers, the picture in goods is completely different: already for 18 years, and with increasing effectiveness, a low-key committee stops Member States from further fragmenting the internal market. This highly valuable piece of infrastructure does not exist for services.

Mutual recognition covers about half of intra-EC industrial trade, but it only matters for the 30 per cent of intra-EC trade for which national regulations exist. A selection of examples, some with considerable detail, illustrate the practical problems for business when relying on the MR principle. Business in Europe is disenchanted with MR as it works in actual practice. Firms find themselves unwillingly appointed as the guardian, or at least front-soldiers, of the Treaty, chasing violations at their own costs. Although hard overall figures are not available, the situation in services is probably graver. As Figure 3.3 clarifies, there are many tradable services where MR is pointless or of very limited significance. In financial and business services it applies but leaves much to be desired for reasons of information, compliance and the crucial meaning of a link with FDI in services. In road transport MR works well and is exploited dynamically. The analysis has also explored the role regulatory competition could play, as a dynamic complement to MR. Compared with the 'new approach', expectations should not be set high because regulatory competition may well be distortive and because in actual practice it cannot fully substitute for approximation (due to the lack of 'equivalence').

The manifold benefits of MR for Europe are too great to allow the present ambiguities to continue. The EU needs much more proactive approaches as proposed in recent Commission documents and should create permanent monitoring infrastructures for MR in services. Above all, what is required can be called the development of a 'mutual recognition culture'. Such a culture would have to improve and deepen the triptich of *information–confidence–Union mindset* for national policy-makers and compliance officers. It is in this spirit that the new Commission and other initiatives should be assessed so that the Union can better enjoy the fruits of its own regulatory ingenuity.

Notes

1 Pelkmans, J., 'Comments', in A. Sykes (ed.), *Product Standards for Internationally Integrated Goods Markets*, Washington, DC, Brookings Institution, pp. 154–68, 1995.

2 Case 120/78, *Rewe-Zentrale AG* v. *Bundesmonopolverwaltung für Branntwein* [1979] ECR 649, although this principle was only explicitly developed in Case 113/80, *Commission* v. *Ireland* [1981] ECR 1625.

3 Case 8/74, *Procureur du Roi* v. *Dassonville* [1974] ECR 837.

4 See, more recently, for instance, Cases C-238/89, *Pall-Dahlhausen* [1990] ECR I-4827; C-362/88, *GB-INNO-BM* v. *Confédération du Commerce Luxembourgeois* [1990] ECR I-667, C-126/91, *Schutzverband gegen Unwesen in der Wirtschaft* v. *Yves Rocher* [1993] ECR I-2361. See however the ECJ's more restrictive approach in Court Cases C-267 and 268/91, *Keck and Mithouard* [1993] ECR I-6126.

5 Case 120/78, *Rewe-Zentrale AG* v. *Bundesmonopolverwaltung für Branntwein* [1979] ECR 649.

6 Commission of the European Communities, *Completing the Internal Market*, White Paper from the Commission to the European Council, COM(85) 310 final, 1985.

7 See Case C-184/96 *Commission* v. *France (Foie Gras)* [1998] ECR I-6197.

8 Adopted on 28 May 1969, OJ C 76/1. For the drawbacks see Pelkmans, J., 'The New Approach to Technical Harmonization and Standardization', *Journal of Common Market Studies*, vol. 25, March 1987.

9 Sun, J.M. and J. Pelkmans, 'Regulatory Competition in the Internal Market', *Journal of Common Market Studies*, vol. 33, no. 1, March 1995.

10 Figure 3.1 extends the notion of 'cost increasing trade barriers' (emphasized by Pelkmans, J. and L. A. Winters, *Europe's Domestic Market*, London,

Routledge, 1988, pp. 18–20, as distinct from tariffs which are revenue generating, and this property is crucial in customs union theory) to mutual recognition.

11 Beyond the market clearance price P_{L1}, its excess supply is horizontally added to *H*'s domestic supply schedule.

12 Not rarely, the barrier may have relaxed the cost minimization discipline of external competition (so the stakes to keep it, become more entrenched over time), or, indeed the barrier is fully endogenous, in the sense that regulators have been captured to 'tailor' the barrier so as to protect sufficiently.

13 Clearly this was one fear behind the 'fortress Europe' campaign of the USA in the late 1980s. In actual practice, one has to be careful to draw this conclusion. The ECJ has been quite liberal here: thus if *ROW* would obtain acceptance of its product in any Member State of the EU, mutual recognition would apply in full throughout the internal market.

14 Note that, compared to Figure 3.1, no (further) adjustment costs are assumed.

15 Note that, here, there is no CE marking since this only applies to an EC Directive. CE marking is completely independent from the (EU) country of testing and certification.

16 Vogel, D., *Trading Up: Consumer and Environmental Regulation in a Global Economy*, Cambridge, Mass., Harvard University Press, 1995.

17 The problem with market failures such as safety and health objectives is that they are not independent from local preferences and income levels, hence the risk/price preferences matter to some degree.

18 Lutz, S., 'Trade Effects of Minimum Quality Standards With and Without Deterred Entry', *CEPR Discussion Paper*, no. 1384, April, London, 1996.

19 Shaked, A. and J. Sutton, 'Relaxing Price Competition through Product Differentiation', *Review of Economic Studies*, vol. 49, 1982, pp. 3–13.

20 Ronnen, U., 'Minimum Quality Standards, Fixed Costs and Competition', *Rand Journal of Economics*, vol. 22, no. 4, 1991, pp. 490–504.

21 Herguera, I. and S. Lutz, 'Oligopoly and Quality Leapfrogging', *The World Economy*, vol. 21, no. 1, January 1998.

22 Suwa-Eisenmann, A. and T. Verdier, 'Reciprocity and the Political Economy of Harmonization and Mutual Recognition of Regulatory Measures', *CEPR Discussion Paper*, no. 3147, London, January 2002.

23 Brander, J. and B. Spencer, 'Export Subsidies and Market Share Rivalry', *Journal of International Economics*, vol. 18, 1985, pp. 83–100.

24 Atkins, W.S. 'Technical Barriers to Trade', *Study for the Single Market Review*, Subseries III.1, Office for Official Publication of the EC (OOPEC), Luxembourg and London: Kogan Page, 1998.

25 Molitor, B. *et al.* (1995) 'Report of the Group of Independent Experts on Legislation and Administrative Simplification', Brussels, COM (95) 288 of 21 May 1995.

26 UNICE (1995) *Releasing Europe's Potential through Targeted Reform*, Brussels, November.

27 COM (1999) 299 of 16 June 1999, *Mutual Recognition in the Context of the Follow-Up to the Action Plan for the Single Market.*

28 *Internal Market Scoreboard*, no. 10, May 2002, p. 10.

29 COM (2002) 419 of 23 July 2002, *Second Biannual Report on the Application of the Principle of Mutual Recognition in the Single Market.*

30 And a small category of 'information services'.
31 Anyway, these are not notified to this Committee.
32 Case C-76/90.
33 The following paragraphs are based on an interpretative communication by the European Commission on the free movement of services, *Official Journal EC*, C 334 of 9 December 1993.
34 Commission of the European Communities, 'Liberalization of Network Industries', *European Economy*, Reports and Studies, no. 4 (Special Issue), 1999.
35 Commission of the European Communities, *Services of General Interest in Europe*, COM (2000) 580 of 20 September 2000.
36 Pelkmans, J., 'Making EU Network Markets Competitive', *Oxford Review of Economic Policy*, vol. 17, no. 3, Autumn, 2001.
37 For a revealing analysis, see two Communications by the Commission in Official Journal EC C 209 of 10 July 1997 and *idem* C 43 of 16 February 2000.
38 The reader is referred to the contribution by Hertig, G., 'Regulatory Competition for Financial Services', in D. Esty and D. Geradin (eds), *Regulatory Competition and Economic Integration*, Oxford, Oxford University Press, 2001.
39 For a detailed analysis of barriers to cross-border trade, see COM (2002) 441 of 30 July 2002 on the state of the internal market for services.
40 See the chapter by Kalypso Nicolaïdes in this volume.
41 See note 9.
42 Neven, D., 'Regulatory Reform and the Internal Market', in OECD, *Regulatory Reform and Regulatory Market Openness*, Paris, 1996.
43 Bourgoignie, T., 'Consumer Law and the EC: Issues and Prospects', in Bourgoignie, Th. and D. Trubek, *Integration Through Law. Consumer Law, Common Markets and Federalism in Europe and the US*, vol. 3, Berlin/New York, W. de Gruyter, 1987.
44 Vogel, D., *Trading Up: Consumer and Environmental Regulation in a Global Economy*, Cambridge, Mass., Harvard University Press, 1995, and Vogel, D., *Barriers or Benefits? Regulation in Transatlantic Trade*, Washington, DC, Brookings Institution Press, 1997.
45 Genschel, P. and Plumper, 'Regulatory Competition and International Co-operation', *Journal of European Public Policy*, no. 4, December 1997, pp. 626–42.
46 Siebert, H. and M. Koop, 'Institutional Competition *v.* Centralization: *quo vadis* Europe?', *Oxford Review of Economic Policy*, vol. 9, no. 1, Spring, 1990, pp. 15–30.
47 Oates, W. and R. Schwab, 'Economic Competition Among Jurisdictions: Efficiency-Enhancing or Distortion-Inducing?', *Journal of Public Economics*, vol. 35, 1988, pp. 333–54.
48 For example, US state regulation of registered nurses. However, these state rules were affecting inter-state free movement, which is not in keeping with the MR principle in the EU. Perhaps a comparable example consists of the packaging law in EU countries. See Peltzman, S., 'Towards a More General Theory of Regulation', *Journal of Law and Economics*, vol. 19, 1976, pp. 211–40.
49 This rigidity was a result of the excessive detail in the Directives, and the heavy procedural obstacles to non-trivial changes. For elaborations, see

Pelkmans, J., 'Regulation and the Single Market, an Economic Perspective', in H. Siebert (ed.), *The Completion of the Single Market*, Tübingen, Mohr, 1990.

50 And a widespread shift from design to performance standards.

51 For a survey and trends of infringements, other compliance problems and financial sanctions by the ECJ, see J. Pelkmans, D. Gros and J. Nunez Ferrer, 'Long-Run Economic Aspects of the EU's Eastern Enlargement', *Working Document*, no. 109, The Hague, WRR, chapter 3, 2000. (see www.wrr.ul)

52 Atkins, W.S. 'Technical Barriers to Trade', *Study for the Single Market Review*, Subseries III.1, Office for Official Publications of the EC (OOPEC), Luxembourg and London: Kogan Page, 1998.

53 *Ibid.*

54 *Internal Market Scoreboard*, no. 10, May 2002, pp. 21–3.

55 The General Safety Directive 92/59 (Official Journal EC L 228 of 11 August 1992, as amended (see proposal in COM (2001) 63 of 2 February 2001).

56 See MAC Groupe, 'The Cost of Non-Europe in the Foodstuffs Industry, Case of Recycling Law of Beverages in Denmark', *Research on the Cost of Non-Europe, Basic Findings*, vol. 12, Part A, 1988, pp. 368–94.

57 Quoted from COM (2002) 441 of 30 July 2002, p. 6.

58 All examples are taken from the paper quoted in note 34.

59 See, for a detailed analysis, SEC (2001) 1681 of 23 October 2001, a special *Annex on Company Taxation in the Internal Market*, of COM (2001) 582 on the strategy Paper 'Towards an Internal Market Without Obstacles' of the same date.

4

Globalization with Human Faces: Managed Mutual Recognition and the Free Movement of Professionals*

Kalypso Nicolaïdis

Introduction

While short-term capital flows and foreign direct investment have never moved across borders so freely, neither has the international movement of people been so 'managed'. This is one of the apparent paradoxes at the heart of today's pattern of globalization. In an era of much-proclaimed liberalism, rules at the national level governing conditions for the granting of visas, work or residence permits, and ultimately permanent residence and naturalization, constitute perhaps the strongest remaining expression of state power. These rules are hardly subject to any international oversight, or even coordination, save in the restricted realm of asylum, where the national norms relating to the movement of people become subject to international human-rights norms. The paradox, of course, is only apparent. The weight of forces driving the liberalization of capital movement dwarfs those driving the free movement of people. More fundamentally, policies addressing migration, bound up as they are with the 'who is "us" ', the definition

* A substantial part of the research for this paper was conducted for the Organisation for Economic Co-operation and Development (OECD) and is contained in the Report: Nicolaïdis K., 'Promising Approaches and Principal Obstacles to Mutual Recognition', in *International Trade in Professional Services: Advancing Liberalization through Regulatory Reform*, OECD Publications, 1997. See also 'Managed Mutual Recognition: The New Approach to the Liberalization of Professional Services', Working Paper no. 97-14, Politics Research Group, Kennedy School of Government, Harvard University, Spring 1997.

of political as well as economic boundaries, and, ultimately, the flexibility or lack thereof of group identities, escape the sole constraint of economic rationality.

There is, nevertheless, a real paradox. That is that in one of the few areas where developed countries actually have domestic incentives to address the demands of the developing world, they have been so hard pressed to do so. In one guise, the international movement of people has become embedded in the global trade regime: as part of 'trade in services'. Individuals with professional training, from doctors or teachers to software engineers, form part of a growing third-world constituency seeking to provide their services abroad, more cheaply and often more diligently than their counterparts in host countries. These host countries on their part often face demographic circumstances and skill supply gaps which would make such labour supply precious. Indeed, periodically, quotas are issued in one country or another for one category of professionals or another. Yet, while globalization itself increases the need for international provision of professional services, there is no mechanism in place for the global management of professionals in a more systematic and holistic fashion. Instead, in most sectors and most countries, professionals face numerous obstacles including residency or investment requirements. Foremost among such obstacles are domestic requirements for practicing their professions.

Obviously, tackling such obstacles to the free movement of people-as-professionals is no easy mission. The difficulties that, to this day, plague efforts to do so within the European Union, the world's most sophisticated negotiating machine, testify to the greatest obstacle of all: the lack of trust between countries in their respective training and certification systems.

This chapter focuses on mutual recognition of qualification, licensing and certification requirements as the central mechanism that can be used to address the impact of national regulations on the capacity of professionals to exercise their activities across borders. Under this approach, countries or regulatory bodies recognize (conditionally of course) their counterparts' stamps as equivalent to their own and therefore the legality of their respective professionals. The chapter tackles the issue of mutual recognition at two levels. At the first, the micro level, I ask under what conditions can individual mutual-recognition deals be negotiated, what are the most promising approaches as well as the principal obstacles revealed by experiences with mutual-recognition agreements in the field of professional services. Examples are drawn from the professions of architecture, law, accounting and engineering, although lessons are generalizable across professions.

At the second level, the macro level, I analyse the broader institutional and political context with an eye to the normative implications of liberalization in this field. Mutual recognition, I believe, can and should be seen as the human face of globalization. Most importantly in this regard, I argue that we need to recognize and address the detrimental brain-drain effects in the originating countries of permanent migration – as well as to a lesser extent the kind of social polarization increasingly witnessed in the receiving countries. Thus it may be argued that designing an international regime easing the *temporary* movement of people would contribute in addressing concerns on both sides. Temporary movement, or better still back and forth movement, should maximize remittances and skill transfer while minimizing social disruption. In this light, the General Agreement on Trade in Services (GATS) should be considered as a privileged venue for experimenting with 'globalization with a human face' by better operationalizing, and promoting the distinction between temporary service-provider movement and permanent migration. Some go so far as to argue that immigration policies that focus on permanent migration should be replaced by 'mode 4'-type movements (mode 4 is defined in GATS as the provision of services by an individual moving to the exporting country). Some would argue conversely that the two regimes must be strengthened together. Whatever the spillover effects on permanent migration, however, temporary movement of service providers does represent the human face of globalization.

Three interrelated arguments will be presented about mutual recognition in the field of professional services – arguments embedded in a broader set of analysis on mutual recognition across sectors (see other contributions in this volume as well as later works by Nicolaïdis):

- *Managed mutual recognition as a process.* The European experience with mutual recognition demonstrates the value of adopting a form of 'managed mutual recognition' which does not require extensive prior harmonization of qualifications across borders. Instead, mutual recognition agreements (MRAs) can involve variations in scope, automaticity and reversibility of access to compensate for existing differences in the ways in which professions are regulated. Moreover, they should be thought of as the basis for dynamic processes of learning-by-doing and progressive liberalization.
- *'Open recognition' through proactive multilateralization.* The WTO should adopt a cautious approach to the enforcement of unilateral obligations – including unilateral recognition – by judicial fiat.

Instead, under the Doha round, it needs to create incentive for the negotiation of 'open' MRAs as well as devise mechanisms to guard against disruptive discriminatory effects and accelerate the multilateralization of MRAs, including through the drafting, updating and administration of MRA guidelines with the support of the OECD.

- *Transatlantic regulatory cooperation and regulatory development.* MRAs cannot be struck in a vacuum. Because they are vulnerable to conflicts of interpretation and changes in domestic circumstances, they must be designed to minimize risks of disruptive conflicts. They therefore require corollary regulatory cooperation in the form of ongoing and systematic exchange of information, mutual monitoring and cooperative enforcement. In this context, the USA and the EU should renew their efforts at cooperation on mutual recognition of professional services, not only as a means of reinforcing transatlantic ties, but also as the basis for expansive and conditionally open agreements including developing countries – as suggested above.

Mutual recognition in the context of overall liberalization

Unilateral and mutual recognition

Unilateral recognition conducted on an *ad hoc* basis has long been the norm for professionals wishing to practice across borders. This involves comparing the qualifications acquired by a professional in a home state with those required in a host state where the professional requests recognition, and where the competent authorities are to assess some level of equivalence according to unilaterally determined criteria. But such a way of allowing entry for foreign professionals constitutes partial and arbitrary liberalization. Partial, because most of the time the foreign professional is not granted unconditional access; arbitrary, because the *ad hoc* character of the procedure does not ensure objective and predictable assessments.

Agreements on mutual recognition turn the above procedure from a unilateral to a reciprocal one, reducing transaction costs of granting entry for regulatory bodies and reducing the uncertainty related to rights of entry for professionals (mutual recognition is sometimes referred to by professional bodies as 'inter-recognition' or reciprocity). Mutual recognition theoretically covers the various components of professional qualifications: professional education sanctioned by diploma, professional experience, and formal licensing or certification requirements – including examination and membership of professional associations. In practice, recognition agreements can focus on one or all of these elements.

Mutual recognition is a principle that can be applied to products as well as services in general and professional services in particular. Formally, mutual recognition can be defined as a contractual norm between governments – or bodies with delegated authority – mandating the transfer of regulatory authority from the host country (or jurisdiction) where a transaction takes place, to the home country (or jurisdiction) from which a product, a person, a service or a firm originate (jurisdictions are generally sovereign states but they can also be sub-national units in federal entities). This in turn embodies the general principle that if a professional can operate, a product be sold or a service provided lawfully in one jurisdiction, they can operate, be sold or provided freely in any other participating jurisdiction, without having to comply with the regulations of those other jurisdictions. The 'recognition' involved here is of the 'equivalence', 'compatibility' or at least 'acceptability' of the counterpart's regulatory system; the 'mutual' part indicates that the reallocation of authority is reciprocal and simultaneous. A mutual recognition agreement (MRA) is one in which the respective regulatory authorities accept, in whole or in part, the regulatory authorizations obtained in the territory of the other party or parties to the agreement in granting their own authorization. It is therefore a specific instance of application of the general principle, between specific parties, applying to specific goods and services and including more or less restrictive constraints and caveats.[1]

Mutual recognition agreements in practice

There are still strikingly few MRAs in the professional sector, but there is a growing sense that their development could play a key role, both to maintain the regional and international momentum for services liberalization, and to provide impetus for regulatory reform across the world (as spearheaded for instance by the OECD).[2] Mutual recognition will likely be at the heart of trade diplomacy in the next decades and should focus prominently in the Doha round. It has proved contagious since its broad-base adoption in the context of the Single Market in Europe, especially as applied to products. Its adoption generally comes in two phases. First, it is enshrined in a broader treaty or agreement as a general principle for further liberalization. As with the Treaty of Rome 40 years ago, NAFTA, APEC the FTAA and the Australia–New Zealand Closer Economic Relations Trade Agreement (ANZCERTA) all call for future negotiations on mutual recognition. At the global level, the signatories of the Uruguay Round called for the bilateral or plurilateral negotiation of MRAs both in the Agreement on Technical Barriers to Trade (TBT Article 6) and in the General Agreement on Trade in Services (GATS Article 7).[3]

Second, following these injunctions and guidelines, actual MRAs involving specific rights and obligations are negotiated at bilateral, plurilateral or multilateral levels.[4] MRAs for professional services are still in their infancy. In the wake of the Uruguay Round, the Working Party on Professional Services operating under the aegis of GATS engaged in a major endeavour to apply mutual recognition and harmonization to the field of accounting, leading eventually to the publication of a model MRA. Recognition agreements were under the umbrella of NAFTA, including on engineering in June 1995, followed by legal consultants and architecture – with a number of other professions on the way (nurses, dieticians, veterinarians).[5] One of the most far-reaching agreements is the Trans-Tasman MRA (which builds on the ANZCERTA) implemented in 1997.

What are the factors behind this drive towards mutual recognition? First, mutual recognition has a central place among the array of methods to liberalize trade in services in general, but above all professional services. Since 1995, under the auspices of the OECD Committee on Capital Movements and Invisible Transactions (CMIT), the broad range of barriers that impede the free movement of professionals across borders either in their capacity as individuals, or as professional firms has been extensively documented and analysed.[6] Lack of recognition of foreign qualifications and experience has been repeatedly cited as a core impediment to trade in professional services. Other impediments are either more basic (citizenship) and therefore addressed earlier; or they subsist in spite of mutual recognition and need to be dealt with by domestic competition law.

Mutual recognition also carries benefits beyond rights of access. First, it may be a way for the importing country to make better use of imported skills and increase its comparative advantage in certain professional fields. Second, MRAs allow the various regulatory bodies involved in granting rights to practice on a case-by-case basis to save time and resources by working together and engaging in a more effective division of labour. It is this growing awareness that is leading professional associations and licensing boards to enter discussions on MRAs on their own initiative. Third, engaging in such recognition may also enhance mutual learning and the transmission of regulatory experience, thus raising professional standards as well as the level of access to professional services around the world. Maybe most importantly, the very prospect of having to negotiate MRAs can constitute a stimulus for internal regulatory reform and the necessary adaptation of the professions to changing economic and social environments.

There are also major obstacles that need to be overcome in order to engage in MRAs. First is the mere complexity and opacity of the education and training systems prevalent around the world and of the licensing requirements that they are meant to prepare for. Building bridges between such complex systems requires in-depth individual and institutional learning. Second is the often expressed fear on the part of government regulators and professional bodies alike that mutual recognition may lead to a lowering of professional standards, both because it would mandate entry for professionals trained below the standards of the host country, and because accreditors may be tempted to enter into regulatory competition to expand their 'client base'. In addition to purely corporatist reactions, this line of argument is the main cause for the resistance stemming from the professions themselves. These obstacles lead back to the fundamental tension which is at the heart of this whole debate, that between the trade culture which emphasizes openness and competition, and the regulatory culture which emphasizes the need for constraints on such competition and the collective responsibility for mitigating the potentially harmful effects of markets. The challenge for mutual recognition proponents is to show how these two sets of objectives can be reconciled.

The European experience: emergence of managed mutual recognition

The Europeans were the first to systematically apply mutual recognition to the professions. The historical experience accumulated in the EU is worth drawing lessons from both because it illustrates alternative approaches to mutual recognition and because it provides a roadmap for what I argue is the only workable approach to mutual recognition in most circumstances, namely managed mutual recognition.

The historical sequence of alternative paradigms

We owe the formal invention of mutual recognition in 1957 specifically to professional people. The Treaty of Rome called for the adoption of EU Directives on 'the mutual recognition of diplomas, certificates and other evidence of formal qualification', both for the purpose of freedom of establishment and free movement of services.[7] The first interpretation of this injunction dominant until the mid-1970s was that mutual recognition was predicated on the equivalence of diplomas and that equivalence meant similarity: far-reaching *harmonization* of professional training standards was to be a prerequisite to the mutual recognition of diplomas. Regional integration through convergence – rather than through competition – was the rationale for this approach. On this basis, the European Commission along with Member State representatives drafted far-reaching proposals in 1969–70 concerning about 20 professions.[8] For each profession, they set out with great precision training requirements which were to be respected in each Member State, including quantitative requirements as to the minimal number of hours of courses to be delivered by degree-granting institutions.[9] With such conditions fulfilled, mutual recognition would grant full and unconditional access in the host country to all professional activities that a given diploma granted in a home country.

A second paradigm followed in the mid-1970s, replacing such quantitative harmonization with *qualitative harmonization* as a basis for mutual recognition. In other words, equivalence of diplomas should not be predicated upon their *similarity* but upon their *comparability*. This meant that broad guidelines for the content of curricula would be spelled out along with specification of the required lengths of study. A series of mutual recognition Directives did pass on this basis in the mid-1970s concerning medical and para-medical professions, but dozens of other sectoral Directives, including for engineers, accountants, professors and lawyers, reached a stalemate. Thus, of the nearly 150 professions being practised in the EU, only a handful had been liberalized in the first two decades of the EU experience. The last Directive adopted in this vein (for architects, in 1985) set out fundamental requirements in terms of skills and abilities without specifying a corresponding content of education and training. It was a precursor to the next phase of liberalization.

By the early 1980s, a third paradigm was in the making, namely *mutual recognition without prerequisite*, thus de-linking mutual recognition from harmonization. The lesson seemed clear after almost two decades of protracted negotiations in this area: if quick progress was to be achieved, the sectoral approach which had prevailed until then would need to be abandoned and measures would need to be devised to liberalize in a broad sweep, without entering into the complexities of each particular profession. In 1984, European Heads of States called for the introduction of 'a general system for ensuring the equivalence of university diplomas in order to bring about the effective freedom of establishment within the Community'. This came to be known as the horizontal approach to professional services liberalization and was embedded in the *General System Directives* (GSDs). This approach was not to the liking of most professional bodies which, during all the previous rounds of negotiations, had fiercely defended the need to deal with their particular needs and characteristics under separate legal frameworks.[10]

The horizontal approach: a multi-tiered mechanism of recognition for all the regulated professions

The General System is a stratified system based on the length and character of study or training required to have access to a profession. It is based on two separate directives, one dealing with higher-level diplomas corresponding to three or more years of studies, the other dealing with less then three years.[11] In contrast to the prevailing mechanism for unilateral recognition, the General System addresses the issue of equivalence by asking applicants to opt directly for a specific profession rather than selecting the University diploma that they consider equivalent to their own (in most European countries where registration in professional associations is based on the possession of a diploma, unilateral recognition involved ministries of education delivering certificates of equivalence between diplomas). The GSD also moves away from the diploma-centred approach of the 1970s by allowing for training and professional experience to play a concurrent role as diplomas in assessing equivalence.[12] On this basis, the horizontal approach meant not only that all categories of professions ought to be covered, but that they ought to be covered whatever the mode of their regulation in the home country – that is without setting prior conditions regarding the criteria for accreditation in the home country.[13]

This was revolutionary stuff for regulatory bodies and the culture they reflected. To make up for its basic philosophy of broad-based equivalence, the system therefore establishes a relatively complex set of distinctions between seven types of professional qualifications that may have been obtained by the professional in his or her home country.[14] Conditional equivalence is established within each category and bridging mechanisms are set out to cover cases where requirements fall in different categories in the home and host countries. The system is based on the notion of 'regulated profession', defined as the specified set of professional activities that constitute a given profession in a given member state.[15] On this basis, a State cannot restrict access to only some activities within a profession, and conversely an applicant cannot apply only to one subset of activities (for example, *'syndic de faillite'* as part of lawyer).

Assessing the new bargain

Replacing prior harmonization by a system of compensation

The core innovation of the GSD is to have done away with prior harmonization altogether. For harmonization is by definition a case-by-case cooperative process incompatible with a horizontal approach. To make up for such a lack of negotiated convergence, the GSD allows for reduced automaticity of access under mutual recognition, introducing a 'system of compensation' based on requirements of local adaptation periods and sometimes aptitude tests in order to offset the prevailing differences among national degree-granting systems (discussed later in the chapter). Such compensations create bridges between national systems that differ both as to the content of qualifications and as to how the profession itself was regulated. In short, the basic logic of the Directive is the following: national authorities should accept equivalence of qualifications as is, identify areas where there remains 'significant' knowledge gaps or 'deficits', and seek ways to compensate for these gaps on a case-by-case basis. The idea was in effect to translate the judicial notion of *proportionality* into Community secondary law, whereby criteria for assessing such proportionality would be *codified* in legislative form by Member States rather than left up to the Court of Justice (ECJ).[16]

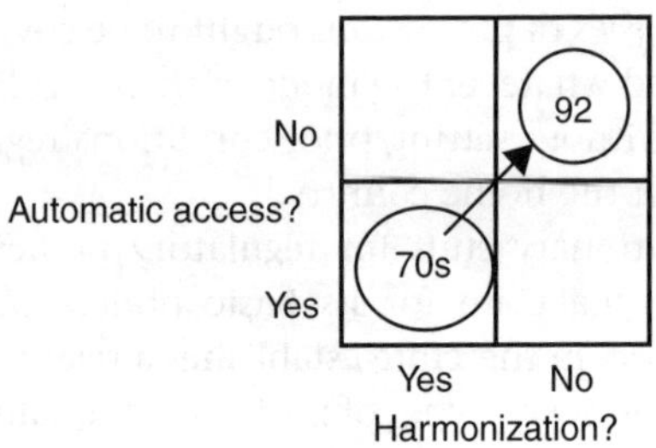

Figure 4.1 The EU horizontal approach: trading off automaticity for harmonization

The GSD turns the traditional EU approach on its head, whereby harmonization and mutual recognition are to be followed by full and unconditional market access. Instead, mutual recognition might be qualified and therefore grant only conditional market access. The system thus consists of two steps: a *premise of broad equivalence* of licensing systems, and *customized recognition* accorded to individuals.

Sustained cooperation: mutual trust in words, mutual monitoring in practice

While the GSD implies that *ex ante* transaction costs of negotiation associated with recognition are substantially lower than under the prior harmonization approach, it also implies that *ex post* transaction costs associated with liberalization have dramatically increased. The enforcement of the new system requires a high degree of sustained cooperation on the part of member states. For one, in order to decide whether and how to apply compensation measures, States need to engage in mutual monitoring or mutual oversight, draw up lists of relevant subjects and constantly update the comparison between their respective systems. This means a constant strengthening of the ties and mutual acquaintance among national regulators. As stated by the Commission, 'to aid the Member State in its task of assessing the qualifications offered and enable it to determine whether these qualifications are adequate, or whether compensatory measures are needed, cooperation is necessary between Member States'.[17] For this purpose, cooperation takes place through an information exchange and cooperation procedure both between Member States and between Member States and the Commission. With the help of the Commission, a group of coordinators appointed by each Member State is in charge of monitoring the implementation of the Directive and collecting useful information to that effect.[18]

Mutual trust between national Authorities has repeatedly been emphasized as the critical condition for success. When introducing the new system, the Commission argued that the envisaged procedures 'would have only a limited effect and ultimately be of slight practical advantage to the citizens of Europe if its application were not based on the idea of reciprocal confidence'.[19] While this is true as a minimal condition, I would argue that the GSD places at least as much emphasis on mutual monitoring through formal and informal ties as on mutual trust. Obviously the two are not mutually exclusive and may reinforce each other (mutual trust is based on mutual knowledge which needs to be constantly updated), but the introduction of compensatory requirements and the related need and right for national regulators to be able to probe into each other's system on an ongoing basis would seem to constitute a much greater factor for accepting mutual recognition than simply trusting each other's standards. As methods of training evolve, as new professions are introduced, as new requirements are added and old ones discarded, the public or private authorities competent in regulating professional markets cannot assume that equivalence at some initial point in time will be sustained. This in turns speaks to the importance of extant and new institutional mechanisms as a crucial enabling factor for the adoption of mutual recognition.

Beyond the GSD: the partial return of the sectoral logic

The two GSDs have now been in force for several years, although the fact that Member States have used different techniques to transpose them into national laws has increased the uncertainties associated with the early phase of implementation.[20] Applications for cross-national recognition did increase slightly, especially at the beginning (professionals had been awaiting the implementation of the GSD) but seem to have levelled off. Concurrently, the negotiation agenda is not closed. One piece of the legislative agenda has been to expand the GSD to craft trades and other business services. Although requirements are on average less stringent in these areas, differences between Member States are sometimes even greater than in the traditional professions. Old Directives in the health sector have also been updated in the spirit of the GSD. The EU Commission now seeks to simplify the GSD itself, in particular to address the problem of professions falling under one Directive in one country and under another in a different country, and to clarify the legitimate content of compensatory requirements.

Maybe most importantly, the GSD is far from having won unqualified approval from professional bodies. These bodies would have preferred to set criteria for equivalence on their own to be translated into sectoral Directives rather than leaving such assessment to the 'arbitrary' decisions of 'state bureaucrats'. They feel that professional associations are best able to design and update the equivalence system. For instance, in 1986, FEANI, the European Association of Engineers representing one million engineers, created a 'register commission' for engineers, hoping the initiative would serve as a basis for a sectoral Directive. This commission proposed a complex numeric formula for differentially weighing years required for three components of engineering training.[21] Under this scheme, applicants for cross-border provision of services would have been granted various types of titles of certified FEANI engineers. These efforts were at least temporarily preempted by the implementation of the GSD in 1991.

In the legal arena, the GSD has been considered at best as only a stepping stone and at worst as a drawback in the close to two-decade-long pursuit of an adequate scheme by the profession itself. It is often argued that this is the profession where host-country requirements are most justified (and where corporatist patterns are most pronounced).[22] Thus, this was the only profession to have obtained a derogation in the GSD for the host country to be able to impose an aptitude test on applicants. In the two years following the entry into force of the GSD, only a few dozen lawyers applied for recognition outside the bilateral flow between the UK and Ireland. Professional bodies have consistently argued that the GSD did not serve their needs and that they needed their own Directive. In 1997, after protracted negotiations between national Bars and between Member States, a new Directive on the right of establishment for lawyers was adopted.[23] The establishment Directive is supposed to fill the three main gaps in the GSD by (a) facilitating admission for experienced lawyers, where disagreements have focused on the exact conditions for waiving compensatory requirements; (b) granting cross-border rights to law firms in addition to lawyers, where disagreements have focused on the fate of firms not controlled by EU lawyers; and (c) allowing individual lawyers and law firms to practice throughout Europe under their home title, the most controversial issue (see discussion elsewhere in this chapter).

Preliminary diagnosis

It is fair to ask, at this most general level, whether the current European approach constitutes a first or second best when compared to the traditional approach focusing on the prior adoption of common standards. Clearly, in the short run, such an approach has a number of advantages:

1 *Expediency*: it is a more effective way to achieve progressive liberalization than seeking to bridge the structural differences between national systems.
2 *Coverage*: it was designed to cover the broadest possible spectrum of training configurations found across Member States and 2 by 2 differences found between national training systems.
3 *Standards*: it maintains guarantees on qualifications through compensatory requirements. This in effect enabled parties to go through with an agreement that might otherwise have been held hostage to the least regulated European states. By replacing *ex ante* harmonization with conditional access and the reliance on mechanisms for *ex post* cooperation, the EU achieved in three years what had not been achieved in the previous thirty years while at the same time alleviating – to some degree – Member States' fears of sub-standard competition.

But many questions remain open under the GSD. For one, even when migrants do not encounter barriers to access after review of their application, the uncertainty is still there. Isn't the system bound to deter occasional or sporadic service provision? What will happen to the mandatory updating of professional standards and the continued training required in a number of countries? Should the mandatory character of retraining also be bypassed through recognition? What will happen with the emergence of new professional sectors? To what extent can a host state be challenged for raising the stringency of its compensatory measures either when it wishes to raise the professional standards applied to its own nationals (and *a fortiori* to non-nationals) or when a home country reduces its professional standards? In part, the answer to these questions will come from the behaviour of the host States themselves and how they interpret the provisions of the GSD.

The answers to these questions also lies with the ECJ as well as national Courts who will be called upon to uphold the rights of individuals in the face of potentially arbitrary requirements imposed by host States under the compensatory system. The drafters of the new system, however, were confident that it actually created new patterns of incentives for individual states that would progressively lead to an upward convergence of standards and therefore alleviate most of the potential conflicts that could be envisaged. Because they have acquired new rights, professionals are calling for more mobility in the EU. Yet, given the customized features of compensation measures, these theoretical rights amount to very different effective rights of access depending on the characteristics of home-country standards. Professionals coming from low-standards countries and facing higher compensation than their counterparts from other countries are starting to act to upgrade the reputation of their home-country systems. Instead of a 'race to the bottom', this type of 'managed' regulatory competition is likely to create a 'climb to the top'. In short, the GSD created the conditions for an incremental loosening of host-country compensatory requirements and therefore for a progressive expansion of the effectiveness and automaticity of mutual recognition.

The four dimensions of managed mutual recognition

Drawing on the European experience as well as that of NAFTA, Australia–New Zealand and the WTO – and extrapolating from these examples – it is possible to define and describe more precisely what I mean here by managed mutual recognition and which of its features may be most appropriate in different contexts. As Table 4.1 illustrates,

Table 4.1 The main attributes of 'managed mutual recognition'

Examples	*Products*	*Professional services*	*Financial services*
Variation in: **Prior conditions:** Requirements for equivalence between national systems	a. Equivalence in health, safety and other technical standards b. Equivalence of standards of enforcement, including of testing and certification procedures c. Mutual recognition of accreditation bodies d. *Ex ante* confidence building measures	a. Equivalence of professional standards b. Equivalence of accreditation and licensing procedures c. Inter-recognition between competent bodies	a. Equivalence of prudential standards b. Equivalence of authorization and licensing procedures
Automaticity: Regulatory scope of recognition and residual entry requirements from entrant's point of view	a. Test data and inspection report v. final approval b. Additional tests and approval procedures	a. Eligibility: recognition of professional training and competence b. Compensatory requirements	a. Notification by home state b. Proof of licensing c. Additional spot checks
Scope of access: Limitations on scope of access to importing country market	Usually full scope of access except for consumer type (limitations on market access stem from other market characteristics, e.g. distribution channels, fragmented domestic jurisdiction)	a. Right to practise v. title b. Scope of permissible activity c. Rules of conduct and enforcement d. Cross-border supply v. establishment e. Temporary v. permanent right of access	a. Initial entry v. ongoing supervision b. Scope of permissible activities/ products c. Rules of conduct and enforcement d. Cross-border supply v. establishment e. n.a. f. Consumer type
***Ex post* guarantees:** Alternatives to host country control	a. Mutual monitoring b. Collaboration and accountability c. Competition law and dispute resolution mechanisms d. Case-by-case safeguards and overall reversibility		

managed recognition is analysed here with regard to professional services but can be generalized to other services sectors and products.

As an outcome, managed mutual recognition can be contrasted with 'pure' mutual recognition in the same sense as managed trade can be contrasted with total free trade. Pure mutual recognition implies granting fully unconditional and open-ended rights of access. In contrast, mutual recognition in operational terms actually involves complex sets of rules and procedures, that may serve to reduce, if not eliminate, the open-endedness of mutual recognition.

I outline below the four main dimensions along which mutual recognition can be managed or fine-tuned; namely (a) prior conditions for equivalence; (b) automaticity; (c) scope; and (d) *ex post* guarantees. On this basis, managed mutual recognition can be viewed in a static or a dynamic manner. At a given point in time, variations along each of these dimensions can be seen to indicate how far parties have travelled down the road to full recognition. Dynamically, mutual recognition can be viewed as a process, involving trade-offs between these dimensions that may change over time.

Variation in prior conditions for equivalence between national systems: is harmonization necessary?

How similar must qualification and licensing requirements be before we can consider engaging in mutual recognition? How is such equivalence determined? To address this question, MRAs must first determine the level at which equivalence is to be assessed. There are two main functions in the regulation of the professions that may be the object of mutual recognition:

1 The assessment of *qualification* through education and training of professionals, which is itself based in part on systems of accreditation to education and training bodies.
2 *Licensing, certification and/or registration* of professionals granting the right to practice.

The type of bodies responsible for these regulatory functions and the character of their intervention change from one country to the other. Diplomas delivered by Universities can serve as sole licensing mechanisms, as a mandatory input, or as an non-mandatory input for licensing. Accreditation of professional schools by professional associations and other accreditation bodies can be mandatory or only serve as an input in determining the validity of a degree as a base for licensing. Licensing bodies range from ministries to purely private associations, although the latter generally deliver certificates rather than licenses. Registration in a professional association can replace or supplement licensing undergone under the authority of an examination board. It can itself be compulsory or mandatory. In order to simplify the daunting task of assessing equivalence between such potentially different systems it is necessary to first determine to what part of the regulatory chain or process does recognition extend. Mutual recognition – like the regulations recognized – can apply to input (relied upon by the regulatory body to make its decision), determinations (agency decisions regarding the application of regulatory standards in particular instances) and legal results (ultimate decisions resting on input or determination).[24] In the professions, this means that recognition can be limited to the whole or part of the education and diploma obtained (input), the license or certification granted on this and other basis (determination), or the right to practice granted by the home country whatever the input and determination. Only under such recognition of results is there direct effect of the home-country rules on the territory of the host country, and right to practice follows not only from positive regulation but also from a failure to regulate in the home country.

Once the level of recognition is determined, a second distinction comes into play between two fundamental aspects of regulatory systems to which recognition applies:[25]

1 *Substantive requirements* ('professional standards'); that is, the criteria for determining adequate professional qualification and for accrediting training institutions, including the content of studies and licensing examinations; and,
2 *Qualification and licensing procedures*; that is, the set of procedures by which individuals are made to conform and comply with these requirements, including through examination, and the process by which the institutions that certify them are themselves accredited.

Mutual recognition in the professions technically applies to the second category: it is the process by which a professional acquires a stamp (whether of qualification or license to practice) that is recognized as equivalent. Such recognition is in turn conditional on assessing whether the underlying requirements or criteria for qualification should themselves be unilaterally or mutually recognized or harmonized (and if the latter to what extent). The GATS states explicitly that recognition may or may not be achieved through prior harmonization of the content of the relevant measures (Art. 7). Thus mutual recognition and harmonization are neither mutually exclusive nor necessarily corollaries. The 'test of equivalence' between systems that underpins recognition can be conducted concurrently or alternatively with regards to the explicit standards of education, training and licensing in and of themselves or between the procedures followed by licensing and accreditation bodies.

Equivalence of professional standards

At one extreme, parties may simply decide that their systems pass an 'equivalence test', without the need to spell out common standards and requirements for training professionals. This is the approach taken by the EU and ANZCERTA. Generally, establishing equivalence involves a prior agreement on common professional requirements between parties which may in turn involve the upgrading of their domestic requirements by at least some of the parties to the agreement. In general, the first step in most mutual recognition negotiations has been to set in motion procedures to develop such mutually acceptable standards. In accountancy – the first profession to be examined under the GATS – technical bodies outside the WTO have been busy designing international technical accounting standards (related to the characteristics of the services themselves) while the GATS has provided a framework for assessing equivalence of qualification standards *per se*. When standards concern educational requirements, experts in training and licensing for the profession first need to find ways to express common standards in the text of an agreement. The degree of specificity and detail of such criteria for equivalence may vary to include length of study, fields covered, types and content of courses required, and so on. Standardization efforts involve assessing whether the scope of the profession is comparable among parties as well as whether the training undergone for similar activities is equivalent. This specificity reflects an understanding between parties as to the degree of acceptable differences between them.

There is a growing number of initiatives among the professions themselves aimed at developing common minimal standards across borders. As one example, the Assembly of the International Union of Architects (UIA) adopted an accord on standards of professionalism for architects in July 1996 after two years of intensive discussions.[26] There are speculations that this text will serve as a model for other professions. The text defines principles of professionalism including expertise, autonomy, commitment and accountability; it defines an 'architect' and the 'practice of architecture' as well as the scope of such practice (a difficult issue). It adopts the list of fundamental requirements for registration, licensing and/or certification of an architect developed in the EU directive for architects, but adds more specific points on standards for education, accreditation, experience, examination, licensing and certification, procurement, ethics and conduct. The protocol is presented as a step towards 'inter-recognition' of national standards, but does not in itself establish procedures for assessing national conformity to these standards. It constitutes a 'basic policy framework' to be further developed into detailed guidelines that will allow flexibility for establishing principles of equivalency, 'so that requirements reflecting local conditions ... can be readily added'. The model developed here is most promising in that it sets in place a process rather than a rigid framework, and creates a dynamic of increased mutual familiarity between professional bodies. Those involved are driven by a will to 'influence the political process shaping international trade in services', presumably to ensure that diplomats do not bypass professional bodies as negotiations unfold. If there is a risk that the professions might insist on too narrow an interpretation of standards at the cost of mobility, this will be tested in the next stage of equivalence determination.

A major effort at developing criteria for equivalence of qualifications is currently being conducted under the UNESCO Convention on the Recognition of Diplomas in the Europe Region, which established a working group to contribute to a better assessment of credentials from both sides of the Atlantic.[27] In 1996, the Working Group adopted a series of general guidelines to help promote the mutual recognition of qualifications between Europe and the USA. These include greater respective participation by the parties in each other's placement and recognition processes, giving a chance to home-country specialists to review placement decisions made for applicants qualified under their system. The recommendations also expand on what types of tests should be considered as equivalent and state that:

> an individual US student's record (including the diploma for an intermediate associates degree) should be analyzed on a course-by-course basis to determine which courses completed are appropriate for meeting certain requirements of European higher education ... due consideration should be given to the quality of the program studied, the grades obtained, and the relevance of courses.

The approach recommended here requires very detailed assessments and may need to be specified if it is to serve as a basis for MRA-based commitments.

Equivalence of accreditation and licensing procedures and interrecognition between competent bodies

In addition to the standards for qualification themselves, the equivalence test can be based on recognition of equivalence between accredited bodies, accreditation and licensing bodies. At the level of accreditation, this may be done in conjunction with the setting of education standards whereby experts from the respective parties may or may not feel the need to satisfy themselves that the common criteria are actually adhered to effectively in each of the parties. The only way to verify this for accredited institutions and training programmes is often through on going interaction, field trips and on-site investigations.[28] An extreme version of this approach would be to actually require joint accreditation of educational institutions as a precondition for eligibility under MRAs.

More generally, the question that arises is whether parties ought to recognize as equivalent the bodies awarding diploma or licenses (universities or licensing bodies, boards, and so on). Public and private authority is allocated differently in different countries and professional cultures. Often in the professions, and especially in the Anglo-Saxon context, States have devolved regulatory authority to statutory bodies or associations (self-regulation), or to independent agencies as opposed to direct government oversight, or to hybrid forms of 'self regulation within a statutory framework'. MRAs need to specify authorized 'regulatory' bodies; this can be done in one of three ways:

1 Full mutual recognition involves recognizing that any body duly accredited by a home-country government is recognized as competent by the host-country government. This amounts to *transitivity* of mutual recognition from horizontal (among states) to vertical (within states) recognition: transnational recognition takes sub-national recognition as a given. Thus, if a home State chooses to delegate the regulation of a profession, the host State must recognize such a delegation even if it does not conform to its own regulatory culture. This is the core of the GSD approach.[29]

2 Recognition may be based on an enumeration procedure, both at the moment of signing of the MRA and on an ongoing basis. In this way the host country can retain some control over accreditation in the home

country, from minimal (through simple notification) to maximal (through a collective process of screening and accrediting such bodies). The procedure may be used when there are worries that alternative training routes may be abused by potential claimants, leading to a multiplication of channels of access to the benefits of recognition. In the EU, the issue arose because in the United Kingdom and Ireland, professional licensing is mainly granted by private bodies based on professional training courses rather than University degree titles. This was very much at odds with the continental culture which formed the basis for the original proposal to restrict recognition to diploma and other evidence of qualifications awarded by universities or higher education establishments, thus limiting access to the continent for British professionals while allowing professional practice by foreigners in Britain who would not fall under the authority of the associations. Ultimately, the GSD included in the definition of regulated professional activities those 'pursued by the members of an association or organization, the purpose of which is, in particular, to promote and maintain a high standard in the professional field concerned and which, to achieve that purpose is recognized in a special form by a Member State (Art. 1.d)'. In order to qualify, these associations needed to award a diploma to their members and enforce rules of professional conduct. But while all other countries fell under a generic recognition of national accreditation, the GSD listed the bodies entitled to award diploma in the UK and Ireland.[30]

3 Finally, equivalence can be attested by the accreditation and/or licensing bodies themselves who can enter into direct inter-recognition agreements. This may be done in the absence of agreements on mutual recognition/harmonization of standards between the respective countries (although it may involve agreement directly between these bodies themselves on common accreditation standards); or it may complement a general mutual recognition agreement in order to improve on it. Thus for instance, the association of European Bars (CCBE, *Conseil des Barreaux de la Communauté Européenne*) has encouraged its members to enter into an inter-Bar agreement that would provide for the possibility of all or part of a country aptitude test in favour of applicants for the professional associations that are party to the agreement (the Brussels Bar has recently concluded such agreements with the Paris and Italian Bars).

Variation in automaticity: what is recognized at the individual level?

Mutual recognition is necessarily based on an 'equivalence test' between national systems. So the degree of automaticity of access granted is first a function of the level of recognition sought as discussed above. But the question arises whether only national systems as a whole must pass such an equivalence test or whether, given some broad equivalence at the macro-level, professionals still ought to be subjected to some residual equivalence test at the individual level. Given that equivalence is so hard to establish at the macro level, most MRAs are unlikely to automatically extend the right of professionals from one country to practice in another. This is true whether or not agreement has been reached on common minimal standards. Thus MRAs need to establish procedures to deal with variations and gaps between qualification systems and must design means to bridge these differences.

MRAs vary according to the degree of automaticity of recognition which they afford and, as a result, the ease with which access will be granted to applicants. First, we need to consider *minimal interface requirements*. Fully automatic recognition means, in effect, setting a system of 'international licensing' whereby any national stamp from a country that is part of the system provides automatic access to the rest of the system, without local requirements. For example, the Trans-Tasman MRA provides for automatic recognition, whereby registration boards automatically license professionals registered under each other's jurisdiction.[31] Once registered under the TTMRA, individuals carry their occupation in the same way as anyone else registered in the destination countries (which may imply reregistration every year if this is the condition imposed in the host country). The professional need not interact with host-State authorities at all if the home State is only required to notify these authorities directly that the person in question is duly licensed and thus authorized to operate in its territory. Or verification may be limited to producing simple proofs issued by the home country. In this case, specific host-country authorities must be empowered to attest to the validity of a diploma obtained in the home state. Attempts must be made at this level to minimize bureaucratic impediments (in a number of EU countries, a high percentage of applications warranting automatic recognition was delayed on the basis of 'incomplete documentation').

In almost all cases, MRAs fall short of setting up single passports for professionals. Rather, they constitute agreed mechanisms whereby the host country '*takes into account*' the qualification obtained in the home country, and where foreign professionals are granted 'adequate opportunity for recognition'. The current EU approach has been referred to as 'semi-automatic' recognition.[32] Such lack of automaticity implies lack of predictability and remaining room for arbitrary behavior of the part of the host country. Nevertheless, MRAs provide greater transparency and above all standardized criteria for building bridges across professional licensing systems.

To simplify, automaticity depends on *two sets of factors*: the first has to do with conditions for migrants to be eligible for recognition in the first place; the second has to do with compensatory requirements that the host country can impose on migrants as a condition for granting recognition. In order to highlight the potential for negotiation, it is important to distinguish between these two dimensions analytically even if they may overlap in practice. For instance, crafters of MRAs may choose to cast a broad net through generous clauses on eligibility if they need to accommodate very different systems; this may in turn call for greater compensatory allowance; or they may choose to narrow down eligibility and leave little room for compensation if they do not have enough resources to manage the recognition mechanism.

Eligibility: recognition of professional experience and competence

Guidelines for determining eligibility of migrants have to do with determinations of equivalence of systems (see earlier discussion, p. 143) and the specific characteristics of the migrant himself. On this second count, MRAs need to specify both what host-country authorities *must take into account*, and what they are *allowed to require* from the migrant. A major step towards greater automaticity of recognition is to require the host country to determine eligibility on the basis of a broadened range of inputs, assessing equivalence qualitatively rather than quantitatively and taking into account all evidence of professional competence *beyond strict professional qualification*. This is key when a profession is not regulated or when the granting of 'diplomas' is not a condition for licensing in some of the parties to the agreement. That is when there is neither license nor qualifications to recognize. Competence can be defined as the proven ability to provide a service, through experience and the 'work credentials' acquired in the process. In the Anglo-Saxon culture where learning is supposed to occur on the job more than in the classroom, such acquired skills are much more important than formal studies. Should evidence of experience and training compensate for lack of required education credentials? The EU adopted a broadly liberal approach in this regard, basing recognition on requirements of formal qualification in other fields and professional experience in the home country (some form of qualification was necessary nevertheless). The debate was carried over to NAFTA where professional services were ultimately defined as 'services whose provision requires specialized post-secondary education, or equivalent experience and training, and for which the right to practice is granted or restricted by a Party'. In some cases, it may be relevant to also take into account experience acquired in the host country before application for recognition, either that connected to a similar but different profession, or in the same profession but under reduced scope of recognition (see earlier, p. 157). MRAs may also allow host countries to require professional experience and must specify under which circumstances. The European GSD allows host countries to require a number of years of experience in the home country when the latter does not regulate the profession and the migrant is self-trained (3 years), or has acquired some other qualifications (2 years), or has itself recognized a diploma issued by a non-EU third country (2 to 3 years), or requires training at least one year shorter than that of the host country.

In either case, how should the relevant 'competence' or 'experience' be determined? The simplest approach is in terms of number of years of experience. Other variables include (a) how far back can the experience have been obtained (10 years for the GSD); (b) the profession where competence was obtained (the GSD specifies that it must have a number of activities in common with that for which recognition is sought); (c) whether the experience must have been acquired after having obtained a diploma in the profession to be recognized; (d) the type of organizations/firms and other specified conditions of prior experience; (e) qualitative evidence of competence, such as letters from previous collaborators or employers in the home country; and (f) interviews on work premises in the home country. The second GSD had introduced the concept of 'regulated training' in the home country: that is, training with specific requirements to ensure competence at the end of the training period (this can serve to ease the professional requirements for Irish applicants). Such a notion might be generalized to cover all professions. Here again, the search for flexible equivalents is key to progressive liberalization.

Compensatory requirements

Defining deficits justifying compensation If an MRA is to adopt the 'semi-automatic' route taken by the GSD, it needs to specify under what conditions the host country is allowed to impose compensation requirements unto the migrant, in view of his or her fulfillment of eligibility criteria. These conditions amount to identifying *deficits* or *gaps* in qualifications between host and home countries, *after* eligibility requirements have been accounted for. In the EU, compensatory requirements can be imposed:

- where education undergone by the migrant is at least one year shorter than that required in the host State;
- where the matters covered by the education and training (in the respective countries) differ substantially;
- where the professions regulated in the host state comprise one or more professional activities which are not in the profession regulated in the home State, and that difference corresponds to specific education and training required in the host State.

While differences in lengths of studies are precisely specified here, assessing when differences in the content of training or the scope of the professions matter is left to the host country. Conceivably, MRAs could also allow for compensations when certain deviations from commonly agreed standards are observed, when a host state has obtained specific derogations, or when training (as opposed to education) conditions differ significantly.

Facilitated examination and aptitude test Professional qualification is traditionally assessed through written examination, including both by educational bodies and by licensing authorities. A minimal form of 'input recognition' (often taken unilaterally) consists in recognizing the equivalence of training between parties and allowing foreign professionals to take host-country licensing exams directly without having to go through a course of study.

The next step is to limit these exams to the differences between the foreign applicant's training and that required in the host county. The GSD's aptitude test, for instance, is designed on a case-by-case basis and is limited to matters that are not adequately covered by the system of education in the applicant's home country and to the host state's rules of conduct. How such differences are determined is obviously key. Can experience be taken into account? How important must such differences be before warranting examination? What are 'substantial' differences in the European or other contexts? The GSD provisions leave ample room for interpretation on the part of the host country.[33] There seems to be somewhat of a consensus that the host country should to be allowed to test for objective gaps in technical knowledge that is specific to its regulatory, natural or economic environment (for example, rules of construction for engineers or architects; anti-seismic construction rules for some jurisdictions; local law for lawyers; local diseases for doctors). It is harder to justify testing the skills of the applicants through an examination, that almost by definition cannot capture such skills (the GSD makes it possible to test for practical skills as well as theoretical knowledge). One vexing issue is whether the host country ought to be allowed to test for competency in its language (as with the use of the TOEFL in the USA) as a precondition for recognition. While this is clearly an instance where, in general, the clients ought to be able to assess the skills of the professionals themselves, there may be a case for a test when local clients do not have a choice of service-providers (teachers, doctors) or when provision of the service in a foreign language may decrease its quality unbeknown to the client.[34]

Whatever the test, the very fact of having to take exams – even if facilitated – does constitute a major limitation on mutual recognition. Professionals with 20 years of practice may have forgotten the fine points of examinations, especially if they originate from a culture that emphasized on-the-job training over academic studies. Customized compensatory tests are bound to discourage episodic provision of services. As a matter of fact, the introduction of the aptitude test was a very controversial element of the GSD negotiations opposed by most in the EU Commission. The fear is that through such a test, the requirement to adapt to host-country standards could be reintroduced through the back door, potentially emptying mutual recognition from its substance. One small step towards greater automaticity is to allow the applicant to take the test in her home country, in a familiar environment and according to local procedures. But, ultimately, a key to increasing automaticity is to seek alternatives to examination altogether.

Local professional experience and adaptation period Maybe the most promising option for reducing the automaticity of recognition in the least cumbersome way is to make it conditional on a transitional period of local practice for a specified length of time, under what could be called a '*pre-recognition status*'. The rationale for such a requirement can be seen as twofold:

1 *Training*: to provide a mechanism to help the candidate for recognition fill the deficits in his training while still granting him some kind of access.
2 *Quality control*: to enhance the quality guarantees of the service provided – and thus seek to ensure consumer protection – in this interim period. Indeed the quality of any service does not depend

uniquely on the specific competence of the service-provider but also on the organizational infrastructure and the complementary skills that characterize the local environment in which he is asked to perform.

Two basic categories of transitional requirements can be envisaged. One entails independent local practice under some reduction in scope of access, such as the use of local titles or the scope of activities (p. 157, this chapter). This approach is currently envisaged for EU lawyers. The other category consists in requiring collaboration with local professionals in a more or less subordinate capacity (from *stageur* to partner). In the EU, the approach taken for the adaptation period is that of a stage (for example, exercise of the profession under the responsibility of a locally qualified professional) not exceeding three years. In some professions, like law, apprenticeship is part of the culture; in others it may be harder to introduce. In cases where the candidate for recognition is a senior professional, local collaboration on an equal footing may be more appropriate (note that local partnership may itself be restricted in some countries in that it entails local ownership). If this second option is chosen, however, it is crucial to determine as specifically as possible what mutual obligations are entailed. Under the 1977 Directive on cross-border services for lawyers, for instance, the host state had been allowed to require visiting lawyers 'to work in conjunction with a [local] lawyer' when the cross-border service involved litigation.[35] France and Germany chose to interpret 'in conjunction with' so as to put the foreign professional and the services rendered under the effective control of local lawyers and were found to impose excessive requirements by the European Court of Justice. At the same time, the host state must be satisfied that the migrant does not use a token local collaborator to bypass the compensation provisions.

MRAs must also specify the extent to which local authorities can dictate what the applicant must actually do during the adaptation period and the process by which local authorities determine whether to grant recognition at the end of the period. Procedures for conducting the evaluation must be spelled out as well as options in case of failure.[36] Miscellaneous activities concurrent to the local practice itself can also be taken into account for the final evaluation, such as short periods of education, or attendance at courses or seminars relevant to identified deficits in qualification. These may be required or be used by the migrant to shorten the adaptation period.

In some cases, professional experience in the *home country* or in any country other than the host country can also be used as a compensatory requirement – in addition to a means to determine eligibility. In the EU for instance, it can serve to compensate specifically for at least a one-year shortfall of length of study (not the other two determinants of deficit) and cannot exceed four years or twice the shortfall in duration of education.[37] Note that professional experience and competence can be introduced as means to limit or increase automaticity, at the stage of eligibility or at the stage of compensation. Taking into account prior professional experience can make admission automatic when it previously wasn't. At the same time, requiring additional professional experience when a diploma is considered sufficient in the home country can be more restrictive than a straightforward recognition of home licensing.

Consumer protection schemes Finally, market-based compensation requirements can involve an obligation for the beneficiary of recognition to adopt various kinds of consumer-protection schemes taking into account the specific features of cross-border service provision. To start with, labelling as a minimalist form of compensation for recognition was systematically advocated by the ECJ for trade in goods and was systematized through EU regulations on 'adequate labelling' for products: is it legitimate to transfer this approach to people? Foreign service-providers can simply be required to provide potential customers with substantive information on the quality of their product in a more systematic way than required of local professionals, through various kinds of disclosures, including on past practice. Migrant professionals could be required to ensure that prospective clients be aware not only of the quality of his or her service, but also of where they obtained their qualifications and the implied differences in qualification guarantees (this is akin to the obligation for purchasers of insurance policies falling under the EU mutual recognition scheme to sign a declaration acknowledging their awareness of foreign origin). Such an obligation might constitute a least-restrictive functional equivalent to requiring the use of home-country title, although it may be vulnerable to projectionist abuses (buy local campaigns).

Beyond information-based consumer protection, discussions held at OECD level have highlighted the importance of *ex post* guarantees, based on establishing a right to redress across borders. This can be done through required professional indemnity and liability insurance schemes or client restitution funds. As a note of caution, compensation schemes based on improving consumers' capacity to assess the quality of a professional service and to insure against risk are unlikely to be very effective without increased public involvement in the making of professional policy in the first place.[38]

Issues raised by compensation provisions

Several issues arise in designing systems of compensatory requirements. First, are they cumulative or alternative requirements? It seems to make sense to allow the combination of consumer protection requirements with any of the other one. While the aptitude test, adaptation period and professional experience (as compensation) are alternatives in the EU, they could be cumulative in other contexts. Parties may consider that alternative compensatory requirements serve different functions and that they can make up for different kinds of deficits. 'Cumul' may even be more desirable from the applicant's viewpoint (who can equalize the marginal cost of alternative requirements) if it is possible to submit to the least cumbersome part of each requirement. Lawyers in the EU, for instance, would like to see some host-country experience entitle them to dispense with at least part of the aptitude test. MRAs then need to specify 'equivalency criteria' between compensatory requirements (how many years or what kind of local experience for what share of the test). For instance, as a way to placate the French who are very attached to the aptitude test, the legal profession agreed in 1995 that host-country practice of European law should not count as host-country law and thus qualify as a basis to be exonerated from the aptitude test (although European law is often directly transposed into national law).[39]

Second, if compensatory requirements are alternatives, is the choice between them up to the applicant or up to the host-country regulators? The EU solution has been to leave the choice to the professionals themselves as a base rule (except for lawyers), while countries can be allowed derogations on a sectoral basis.[40] Leaving the decisions up to the host country almost unavoidably leads to the imposition of an examination (as demonstrated by the treatment of lawyers under the GSD).[41] Conversely, candidates are unlikely to choose a test over an adaptation period. Freedom of choice is all the more valuable to the applicant for recognition if some of the alternatives are redundant with market requirements. Architects, for instance, often consider it a necessity to have a local partner familiar with the local context anyway. Nevertheless, they may still be restricted by the precise division of labour imposed by the official requirements. Moreover, as trade in services becomes increasingly possible through communication networks, requirements involving local presence may become truly restrictive.

Home-country experience or even examination may become the preferred alternative.

Third, can compensatory requirements serve to curb the potential for abuse of mutual recognition? In the first years of implementation of the GSD, national authorities have observed individuals using the system to circumvent their own national training requirements. The only case subject to an appeal in Ireland has been that of an Irish barrister who became a solicitor in England and Wales and who returned to Ireland as a solicitor on the basis of the British diploma. The applicant appealed the Irish decision to impose an aptitude test. Although the decision was repealed in light of the applicant's experience and the ECJ decision in *Vlassopoulou*, the designated authorities retained their basic objection arguing that the applicant used the Directive for a purpose to which it was not intended with the objective of circumventing national rules governing movement between the two branches of the legal profession in Ireland.[42] While such cases are rare, criteria might need to be spelled out to differentiate between circumvention and mobility.

Finally, when are the 'compensatory' conditions so rigorous as to significantly deter entry, making non-automatic recognition into an oxymoron? Given the case-by-case nature of such requirements they obviously leave room for continued restrictions on mobility through arbitrary individual decisions. Parties may vary widely in their decisions to have recourse to compensation in the first place.[43] They may also determine the content of these requirements very differently.[44] Such a margin of manoeuvre is obviously useful when MRAs include many parties. But in some cases, the differences might be so great that the freedom of manoeuvre of the host country might have to be moderated. In general, MRAs should clearly include a proportionality clause.[45] Moreover, parties may decide that the *detailed rules* governing compensatory requirements should not be left under the sole competent authority of the host state (with judicial review as in the EU), but instead be decided by joint commissions. MRAs must at least strive to mandate strictly defined ceilings for such requirements. Residual powers of host states need to be circumscribed by agreed-upon procedural guarantees for examining applications (home State certificate must be considered as sufficient evidence, the host State bears the burden of proof regarding difference, it must give a ruling within four months of each application and give reasons for its decision) and applicants must be able to seek legal redress against host-country decisions with national or supranational courts.

Variation in scope: access to what?

Mutual recognition can also be characterized in terms of its scope; for example, what is the range, mode and object of practice to which professionals benefiting from recognition actually have access. Scope can be a most controversial issue simply because modalities of access to a given market can vary from one country to the next for the locally qualified professionals themselves. Even when this is not the case, limiting scope during the initial phase of a mutual recognition process can be seen as an opportunity to create a laboratory to test the impact of liberalization. Steps towards full mutual recognition can be achieved through the progressive expansion of scope. Meanwhile, some beneficiaries of recognition might be satisfied with performing only some activities, for some period of time, as called for by reduction in scope.

Below are six ways in which the scope of access falling under mutual recognition can be circumscribed. Some of these distinctions may overlap or even be redundant but they nevertheless reflect alternative rationales that may or may not be relevant in different contexts.

Right to practise v. *title*

The first basic way to limit the scope of recognition is to grant foreign professionals the right to practise certain activities in the host territory without the right to use the corresponding local professional title.[46] The title signals to the potential client that the professional is a licensed or certified 'architect', 'lawyer' or 'accountant' with credentials equivalent to those of local practitioners and is therefore the ultimate evidence of recognition. It means in effect that the applicant has been admitted to the host-country profession. The option to withhold such a right of access to the professional label and other modes of practice has a different significance depending on the regulatory approach prevalent in the host country. In particular, countries can rely on titles as mechanisms for licensing – for example, a mandatory condition – or certification. In the first case, a country regulates a specific professional activity and the conditions under which it can be exercised, including the holding of a title. In the second case, only the use of a title is regulated, not the professional practice itself, and is usually predicated on the holding of a diploma.[47] The role of titles as signalling devices is usually more important in the latter case. In cases where some parties to an MRA have title requirements for entry into a profession and others not, the agreement may have to include a differentiated approach (for example Europe, Italy and Luxembourg are the only States that require an engineer title for all engineering activities). Title recognition may be an easier proposition in countries with two-tiered systems where a generic title is protected under the general state-enforced system while specific versions of the title may be under the purview of private bodies ('chartered architects', for example, as awarded by the Royal Institute of Architecture in the UK).

Requiring the use of the home title for certain beneficiaries of recognition is a useful device when the scope of activities or the mechanism for certification differ strongly between parties.[48] Under the GSD for instance, professionals regulated by private associations in the home country were only allowed to use the professional title or designatory letters conferred by that organization rather than the host-country title.[49] This is functionally equivalent to requiring labels of origin and turns the right to use a host-country title from a licensing (exclusive rights) to a certification method. How restrictive granting access to a right to practise is, short of access to a right to use a national title, depends on the characteristic of each professional market. It may even be the case that the use of a host-country title becomes a restrictive requirement rather than a sought after right.

Scope of permissible activity

An MRA must specify the activities that correspond to a right to practice or a given title. But the scope of activities permissible under a single professional practice or allowed under a given title may vary across national systems (for example 'barristers' and 'solicitors' in the United Kingdom *v.* generic 'lawyers' or '*avocat*' on the continent; engineers *v.* architects in different countries).[50] In theory, mutual recognition ought to imply that permissible activities are those practiced by the professional in the home country (this is how recognition has been implemented in financial services in the EU, for instance). Most commonly, however, the scope of recognition is reduced to activities allowed in the host country under the given professional label. It can even be reduced further to exclude regulated activities that are at the core of the profession in the host country, for example recognizing only foreign lawyers' right to advice on matters of foreign law.[51] The greater the asymmetries between permissible activities between parties (including when some do not regulate this aspect at all), the more likely the use of this option for limiting scope, at least during an interim period.[52]

Rules of conduct and enforcement

One of the least common domains where home-country modes of practice are likely to apply concerns rules of professional conduct, including codes of ethics, privacy issues and advertising rules. This can be attributed to a host of factors: these rules constitute lesser impediments to the mobility of professionals (easier to adapt to); equivalence may be harder to demonstrate when ethics and therefore absolutes are involved; consumers more routinely expect their own local standards to apply; and different rights for foreigners and locals may unequivocally result in unfair competition (advertising and rights to solicit clients). In addition to retaining control over the content of the rules (often reflected by an examination on the subject), the host country generally retains at least residual powers of enforcement in case of breach of compliance, both because it is likely to be better able to identify such breaches and in order to guard against moral-hazard problems (the fact that the home country may have less incentives than the host in punishing a breach that would not affect its own citizens). One configuration of mutual recognition that can be envisaged in the longer run is home country enforcement of host country standards. Note that even when host-country codes of conduct apply, cross-jurisdictional recognition of judgment passed on professional conduct ought to apply on an ongoing basis. As a result, proof of validity of home license can be time-bound, or complemented by certificates of good repute, to ensure that recognition was granted to a service-provider's current status: if a certified professional has been sanctioned in his home country for professional misconduct he should not be able to claim recognition for a right to practice which is no longer valid. Thus, MRAs may require that registration be renewed every year for certain professions.

Cross-border supply v. *establishment*

Limiting the scope of mutual recognition by limiting the choice between mode of delivery has sometimes been used as a mechanism for partial recognition, although under two different rationales. Under one rationale, recognition for the purpose of cross-border provision of services ('trade') has been deemed less problematic and requiring less preconditions, since the cross-border nature of the service itself makes it clear to the client that the professional is not a 'local'. In this vein, the first mutual recognition directive issued in the EU that required no preliminary harmonization was that related to free cross-border service provision of a temporary nature for lawyers (see discussion under compensatory requirements above). Similarly, barristers in the EU are subject to a specific directive on free provision which makes access more automatic than under the GSD framework if their activity in the host country does not involve establishment (host countries are obliged to recognize as barristers anyone authorized to practice under this title in the home country). More generally, establishment simply gives access to a bigger market and is therefore a bigger concession from a projectionist viewpoint. Yet, under a different rationale, mutual recognition may only apply to establishment, or at least involve local presence or residency requirements (short of establishment). This approach is justified as a means to ensure that local law can be enforced (in particular on rules of conduct) and that professionals are available for redress.[53]

As shown by the European experience, it may not always be easy to distinguish between cross-border offices established in support of occasional cross-border rendering of services and establishment itself.[54] MRAs that employ this scope option need to specify where service trade ends and where establishment begins.

In either case, the trade-impeding impact of restricting mutual recognition to a specified mode of delivery is a function of corollary market characteristics. The need for close and ongoing relations with clients as well as for in-depth knowledge of local markets constitute autonomous incentives for local establishment. When this is true, restricting mutual recognition to locally established professionals may not seriously impair professional mobility. On the other hand, rights of cross-border provision are especially relevant for activities that rely on information networks and economies of scale. Initial steps towards mutual recognition may differentiate between different activities within a given profession based on these technical constraints.[55] Ultimately, freedom to chose between modes of delivery is one of the clearest guiding principles that has emerged from global negotiations on services in the last few years and mutual recognition needs to be extended to all modes of delivery.[56] Both the right of local presence and the right of non-establishment are enshrined in the NAFTA (as well as in the GATS for the former while only partially for the latter). As a next step, they must be upheld in combination with mutual recognition.

Temporary v. *permanent right of access*

A closely related distinction bearing on the scope of mutual recognition is that between temporary and permanent access (temporary rights are usually associated with cross-border provision but not vice versa). In theory, recognition can be granted temporarily, in order to allow for the provision of a specific service at or until a given point in time. NAFTA specifically encourages, when possible, the development of temporary licensing regimes. Under an agreement signed in 1995, engineers licensed to practice in one country have the right to obtain a temporary licence in any other country. Temporary recognition may be an effective first step to full recognition in professions and/or contexts where professional reputation plays an important role or where individuals are identified with specific niches. Since temporary service provision usually involves collaboration with local professionals this also increases the quality guarantees associated with the right. Clauses can be included that facilitate graduation to permanent recognition.

Consumer type

Finally, the professions may borrow from an interesting approach used for the liberalization of insurance services in the EU, where mutual recognition was initially granted for the purpose of accessing specific types of customers and not others, as a function of a client's capacity to discriminate between foreign professionals. An MRA can initially allow professionals to serve clients who may be deemed sophisticated enough to be able to assess their qualification – clients with 'investigative capacity' – such as firms, hospitals, and so on. By the same token, informed consumers could be identified through self-selection by limiting recognition to dealings with 'active' consumers who initiate contact with foreign professionals not established in their state, or to dealings with existing clients originating from the home country. Barring a professional from seeking out new clients in the host country would eliminate the risk of involuntary exposure to professionals with foreign credentials.

Variation in *ex post* guarantees: alternatives to host-country control

Finally, in addition to the degree of automaticity of the recognition extended or its scope, MRAs may give different emphasis to the setting up of cooperative mechanisms between parties in order to compensate for loss of host-country control. The aim is to increase the confidence that parties have in the mutual recognition process and therefore the legitimacy and sustainability of the agreement.[57] But control mechanisms are not costless, and their development is therefore itself an object of negotiation. These mechanisms include:

Mutual monitoring

Parties need to be confident that the others abide by the letter and spirit of the agreement. Such confidence is based on the initial familiarization and continued involvement with the foreign system, including through: obligations of transparency of regulatory systems; decision-making processes; change in such systems through the continued exchange of information between licensing, registration and certification bodies; rights of regulatory oversight; and mutual monitoring that allows for the continued assessment of technical competence, capabilities and efficiency.

Collaboration

The loss of host-country control can also be compensated by the development of extant cooperative networks among parties to collectively 'manage' the implementation of mutual recognition. In this way they can help each other abide by the terms and spirit of the agreement, in particular by supporting the upgrading of standards where they are lagging (many in Mexico have expressed their aim to use MRAs as means of upgrading their professional standards). This can also include collaboration on accreditation procedures and support for inspection and evaluation that may progressively lead to a common culture on licensing standards. In this sense, MRAs should be seen as much as frameworks for mutual technical assistance and more optimal division of labour than as templates for regulatory competition. Host countries can also help home countries enforce compliance with rules of conduct by readily transferring relevant information. Transnational mechanisms for consumer protection in particular require a high degree of cooperation between host and home countries to ensure that professionals of bad repute cannot take advantage of loopholes.

Reversibility

In order to increase the incentive for parties to the agreement to enforce high-level standards of training and certification, MRAs must be designed more explicitly as contingent agreements that can be terminated should the situation change in a country that fails to produce the required professional standards. These are in effect measures against regulatory dumping. MRAs could include trial periods, periodic reviews, safeguard provisions for the temporary lifting of obligations *vis-à-vis* one or several parties, and reversibility clauses allowing parties to nullify the agreement altogether. The credibility of the system depends on (a) the possibility to observe and interpret 'the state of the world' that is the soundness of home licensing and accreditation; (b) the existence of procedures to impose safeguards under commonly agreed circumstances; and (c) the capacity of parties to reverse their initial concession in case of non-compliance, including by reverting to traditional entry procedures for licensing bodies and terminating interrecognition of accreditation. On all these counts, reversibility itself must be the object of cooperation between regulators including under conditions of crisis. It must not be an end in itself, however, and must be embedded in a reappraisal and renegotiation process. When the 1972 US–UK bilateral agreement on architectural training was terminated, no procedures had been designed to cope with the crisis and the whole cooperation process was allowed to lapse.

Competition law and dispute-resolution mechanisms

Finally, parties must invest resources in dealing with external factors that might emerge and would unduly nullify the agreement. For example, the access provided by mutual recognition may be incomplete as private anti-competitive behaviour replaces previous requirements. Private companies may continue to require local diplomas or professional registration bodies may refuse to abide by the letter of an MRA. Domestic rules restricting consumers' right to change suppliers may impede openness in spite of recognition. Cooperation in competition law must act as a supplementary lever on market openness where market forces would not take care of these problems alone. Finally, if the host country is granted the right to impose compensatory requirements, this must be subject to the proportionality principle and overseen by effective dispute resolution mechanisms. In order to make such commitment acceptable to public opinion, political, regulatory and professional accountability must be explicitly and publicly shared between home and host countries.

Trade-offs between features of mutual recognition

Every MRA needs to include provisions that pertain to the licensing, certification and accreditation system on the one hand, and to the individual professionals seeking to be recognized on the other hand. At the level of the systems, MRAs are based on prior harmonization and/or criteria for equivalence and cooperative mechanisms to make up for loss of host-country control once the agreement is in place. The individual candidate for recognition will be affected by the provisions on how automatically and on what basis the recognition is granted, and the scope of recognition set out in the MRA, that is the range and mode of practice accessible to the beneficiary of recognition. These various dimensions are obviously connected. How confident the parties are on the degree of equivalence between their systems will determine how automatically they are ready to grant recognition. How broad a scope for access is envisaged will also determine automaticity.

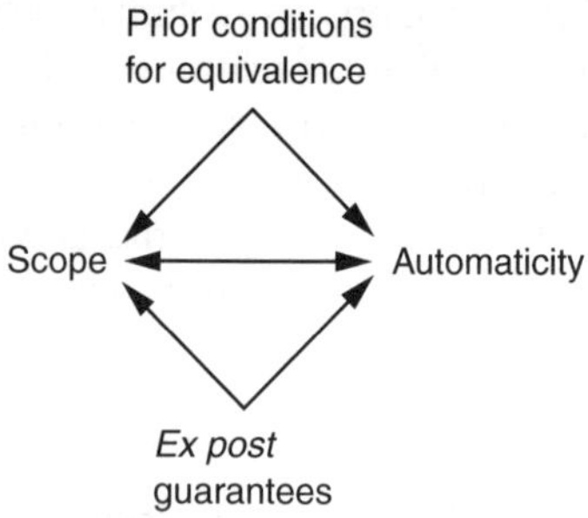

Figure 4.2 Trading-off between features of mutual recognition

The need for spelling out prior conditions of equivalence may be reduced if there are good prospects for sustaining a high level of cooperation after the agreement, and if reversibility is a plausible option of last resort.

In short, whether implicitly or explicitly, trade-offs can be exploited among the features of an MRA. The more parties are aware of these potential trade-offs, the higher the likelihood that they will reach agreement and devise solutions acceptable to all. In some cases, it may be more appropriate to relax prior conditions of equivalence and concentrate on fine-tuning automaticity (EU). In others, reducing initial scope may be considered as a way to test the grounds (NAFTA). From a dynamic viewpoint, scope and automaticity can be reduced initially to accommodate insufficient prior equivalence and expanded later on in light of *ex post* cooperation. Some of these core trade-offs are discussed briefly below (see also Figure 4.2).

Prior conditions v. ex post *guarantees*

Parties need to decide how quickly they want the agreement to come into effect and how many resources they will be able to devote to managing its implementation. This means deciding whether the regulatory cooperation that must necessarily accompany mutual recognition needs to bear fruit before the agreement is actually implemented. Although regulatory assurances are necessary before and after liberalization, if there is a sense of urgency they can focus on *ex post* guarantees. On the other hand, when resources may be insufficient to manage the guarantee mechanism *ex post facto*, it may be wiser to seek high thresholds of equivalence earlier in the process. One of the central 'twists' that allowed Europeans to respect (more or less) their 1993 deadline for the internal market has been the resort to a shift from mandatory and extensive *ex ante* cooperation and harmonization to ongoing *ex post* cooperation. This does not mean that the scheme ought to be reproduced everywhere, especially where no prior culture of regulatory cooperation exists.

Prior conditions v. *automaticity and scope of access*

If they are able to reach a high degree of prior harmonization – as with accounting under GATS – parties can aim for an ambitious and immediate full scope recognition. Alternatively, parties can also exploit the potential for customized automaticity and reduced scope, to design a step-by-step approach to mutual recognition through incremental extension of automaticity and scope conditional on increased confidence between parties after the MRA comes into force. The choice hinges on the particular professional culture, whether harmonization is feasible, the characteristics of the customers of this particular service, whether the degree of regulation varies significantly between parties, and so on.

It is also important to ask whether less than full recognition makes a significant difference in a particular context. Hence, the scope of recognition did not extend to statutory definition of functional separation and permissible activities in the EU. A French '*avocat*' is usually not able to perform in the UK the services provided alternatively by solicitors or barristers; a foreign engineer is restricted to a specific category in Germany and a psychologist authorized to prescribe medicine in Spain but not in Italy. Such restrictions would be considered much more significant limitations in the financial sector, than in the professional realm where comparative advantage has more to do with the how than with the what of service provision. That host-country rules of local conduct, including on liability, deontology or advertising have generally continued to apply also appears to have little restrictive effect.

Reconciling different valuations of scope and automaticity

There is a rich set of possible trade-offs between automaticity and scope of recognition for which the various solutions alternatively envisaged regarding the treatment of lawyers in the EU provide a textbook example. The main controversy regarding the establishment Directive has involved the right to practice under home-country title, precisely because it is associated with more automatic entry. The debate pits French and Anglo-American philosophies. According to the former, lawyers that practice in a country and advise on issues that include a component of host-country law ought to be treated as local lawyers with all the rights (host-country title) and obligations (test of local knowledge and conditions for joining the local Bar) that go along with it. The position is motivated in part by the fear of the French legal system being overtaken by the English one, to create a precedent that might extend to US lawyers. The British and American position on the other hand is to seek as extensive and unconditional rights as possible for bearers of home-country titles; for the British, operating in their capacity as 'solicitor' is not a hindrance since their comparative advantage is based on their transnational character and their specific reputation.

The crust of the debate for the last decade has been what ought to be the *quid pro quo* for introducing automatic rights of access for lawyers using their own (home-country) title. Scope limitation other than access to title can be twofold: (a) in terms of scope of practice (excluding advice on host-country law), since already, under the 1977 Directive, the scope of practice under automatic rights of access was restricted to giving advice on the law of the host or home country and on international and Community law, whereas litigation was subject to compensatory requirements; and (b) in terms of time limit, for example temporary access under home title followed by an obligation to undergo host-title requirements. The British position is obviously against time limits. But on the premise that some scope reduction might be a necessary concession, the British ask that experience acquired through local practice under home-country title be taken into account in devising the mandatory aptitude test required at the end of the time limit (through partial or total exemption). The draft directive proposed by the Commission in 1994 provided for automatic admission to the local Bar/title after three years of experience in the host country, if the experience has led to sufficient familiarity with host-country law. At the same time, it included a requirement to switch to host title or else leave the country. This 'up-or-down' approach was expectedly opposed by the British who persuaded the European professional association to counter with a proposal for an indefinite right to practice under home-country title even as requirements for the local Bar would be made harder. The so-called 'Fontaine Report' of the European parliament issued in 1996 proposed a compromise whereby a requirement to join after three years could be bypassed at the cost of being confined to advising on all law except host-country law (automaticity maintained in exchange for reduced scope). This formed the basis for the Directive.

The issues raised by mutual recognition for lawyers in Europe have an exemplary character. The negotiations pit a position favouring greater automaticity with reduced scope (UK) against lesser automaticity with full scope (France). The compromises proposed draw on the possibility for *sequencing* these options, adding restrictions with time as an incentive for local adaptation (scope of practice) and relying on local experience as the sole condition for scope expansion in terms of title. Whether it is realistic to reduce rights of access after a given period of time – that is in effect granting non-renewable temporary access for a subset of activities – is open to debate.

Options and guidelines for negotiating MRAs

Mutual recognition must be thought of as a dynamic process and the signing of an MRA as only one phase in this process. Decades can be fruitfully spent on analysing convergence between national education and training systems, but nothing can replace the virtues of learning by doing. This in turn requires that the 'doing' accommodate the various interests in place without letting any of them stall the process. As stressed by a player in the NAFTA process, 'the key is to get the professions to embark on the road to mutual recognition, an objective that is more likely to be achieved – and hence generate useful demonstration effects – if the system design remains flexible'.[58] I have sketched above a framework for designing flexible MRAs to fit alternative needs and priorities. I now turn to the broader context to consider some of the options available to enter the process of recognition.

Creating 'mutual recognition-friendly' national environments

One of the core implications of globalization is that some if not all actors concerned have to adapt to the changes required by the new competitive environment. 'Who adapts?' is therefore a key question in considering the prospect for MRAs. Systems (that is licensing, accreditation and education systems), including the organizations who shape and run them, will need to adapt in particular by becoming more compatible with their counterparts in other countries. *Mobile professionals* wishing to practice across borders bore the burden of adaptation prior to mutual recognition. In a mutual recognition environment, less adaptation to various national systems will be required (the whole point of MR), but they will have to adapt to new requirements, including for purposes of greater consumer protection. *Local professionals* obviously will have to adapt to the new competition. Finally, consumers, previously shielded from having to adapt to foreign professional practices, will now often need to invest in a greater capacity to responsibly exercise their freedom of choice between professionals presenting diverse credentials. Various versions of managed mutual recognition demand different degree of adaptation from each of these categories of actors. There may be a great level of asymmetry among countries and among actors within countries in the adaptation required. So part of the preparatory process involved in creating national environments that are mutual recognition-friendly is to enforce adaptation progressively and in the appropriate sequence.

In particular, the question of who adapts and how, raises some important sequencing issues between domestic regulatory reform and the adoption of MRAs. On one hand, MRAs will certainly be easier to negotiate for parties who have moved far enough down the road of domestic reform. The implementation of mutual recognition between states or provinces in federal systems where professions are regulated at the sub-national level can greatly facilitate international recognition. Similarly, the application of competition law to domestic circumstances where professional associations or registration boards may unduly control (through quotas for instance) entry in the profession will encourage these parties to adapt to greater competition from abroad. Minimal steps towards unilateral recognition may also prepare the ground for mutual recognition. It can start by simply increasing transparency and setting explicit standards for licensing of foreign professionals. It can include the validation of qualifications obtained abroad by nationals (this was the first step taken by the Japanese national registration and accreditation board). Unilateral recognition can be far-reaching if conducted in a broader context of domestic regulatory reform. Moreover, it can be more acceptable to certain regulatory cultures. Countries can also preempt the need for adaptation in case of mutual recognition when they develop regulatory systems from scratch by systematically incorporating foreign and international standards and including direct provisions for recognition of foreign accreditors.

On the other hand, in cases where there is significant internal resistance to regulatory reform, the prospect of recognition or the actual negotiation of an MRA may be seen as a necessary lever for change. As both the need for mobile professionals and as the competitive edge of professionals benefiting from recognition increase, a specific demand for engaging in mutual recognition may arise, in turn pushing for domestic reform. Some sub-national units, professions or specific bodies within the professions may be more ready than others to engage in the recognition process, and by doing so may then create demonstration effects for the rest of the system.

The respective role of education, accreditation and licensing organizations

Participants in mutual recognition negotiations can be governments, organizations representing the professions, or private bodies with delegated authority. Ultimately, all the actors involved in the regulation of the profession at the domestic level need to be involved in some way in the recognition process. The first step towards MRAs – that can last for years – is for all of the relevant parties to enter exploratory discussions to familiarize themselves with their respective educational systems, training, examination, certification and licensing requirements, methods of consumer protection, definition and scope of practice, and so on. On this basis, they need to assess the benefits and changes associated with mutual recognition and develop a greater awareness of the multiple options for 'managing' mutual recognition. But who ought to take the lead in the MRA negotiations themselves?

Under one vision prevalent in the European context, it is governmental bodies – for example the Commission and the committee of permanent national representatives – who are responsible for designing and enforcing MRAs with more or less cooptation of the professions in the process. Under the US lead, NAFTA proposes another vision where it is considered the task of the experts themselves (professional and licensing bodies) 'to arrive at mutually acceptable provisions given the special features of the particular profession'.[59] One of the core objectives of NAFTA in the area of professional services was to develop blueprints of rules, principles and procedural mechanisms to encourage the professions themselves to conclude MRAs (architects, lawyers and engineers). Under ANZCERTA, MRAs are largely left to professional associations to negotiate.[60] Even under this second vision, it can be argued that it is essential for governments to be able to lean on the relevant professional bodies engaged in the work of mutual recognition in instances where negotiations may have reached a stalemate.[61]

The most promising scenario may be to combine both recognition routes. Professional association and non-governmental regulatory bodies can negotiate recognition agreements among themselves which can then serve as a basis for government agreements that will provide official mechanisms for enforcing rights and obligations. Another option is to first negotiate government-to-government MRAs in order to create frameworks and floors for recognition, and then encourage MRAs between non-governmental bodies to supplement and enhance the governmental agreement. Obviously, as discussed earlier, there are many possible configurations in terms of participants and functional levels of recognition. Accredited institutions (such as schools and universities) can enter into recognition agreements that can serve as an input to recognition of accreditation as well as to the recognition of licensing or certification. Professional registration bodies can enter inter-recognition agreements which can increase automaticity of access to different degrees depending on the place of registration in the host-country system.

MRAs between accreditation bodies in particular are likely to become one of the most important building blocks in recognition systems.[62] As mentioned earlier, inter-recognition agreements between Bar associations are developing in Europe. Another interesting model is provided by the so-called Washington Accord signed in 1989 by professional engineering accreditation bodies from the USA, Canada, Australia, the UK, Ireland and New Zealand which have agreed to the mutual recognition of their respective accrediting programmes. This gives migrants recognition of their home educational qualifications for purposes of registration; it also serves as the basis for recommendations made by the member accrediting bodies to their respective licensing authorities to treat training in the other member countries as equivalent (but migrant engineers are still subject to host-country testing for licensing purposes). Accreditation bodies may also directly accredit educational institutions from abroad. This may sometimes involve the revision of their charters and certainly may require increased accreditation fees, but there seem to be few obstacles in principle. Another possible route is to accredit schools in foreign countries to train professionals to host-state standards. This half-way house is currently the dominant approach to mutual recognition in the realm of products, but is unlikely to become significant in the professions.

There are risks involved in relying on accreditation bodies to provide the first building block of recognition. First, as pointed out by Bernard Ascher, this could in itself become a basis for restriction, if foreign schools are not afforded adequate opportunity for accreditation and if accreditation standards discriminate against them. Accusation of discriminatory treatment is a staple of the accreditation world at the purely domestic level. The same types of solutions are therefore called for internationally as well as domestically: as with the domestic level, there may be appeals procedures regarding accreditation determination, accredited institutions may not have a monopoly in producing candidates for licensing, and accreditation bodies can have specific mandates to allow for accreditation at the national of institutions that do not meet their conventional standards of accreditation in order to encourage diversity provided the institution carries out the purpose of the accreditation.[63] In addition, there may be technical-assistance programmes set up internationally to help candidates to be recognized abroad, including paying accreditation fees.

A parallel question may be whether accreditation bodies that are part of mutual recognition pacts and/or start accreditation abroad are likely to enter into a competition amongst themselves to widen their market, and whether such competition is likely to lead to a lowering of accreditation standards or to the hegemony of some national standards. Mutual confidence and incentives for quality reputation, as well as collective guarantees of quality control backed up by peer enforcement, will help guard against these developments. Nevertheless, because of the risks of discriminatory accreditation and competitive accreditation, extraterritorial accreditation should be pursued with caution and mutual recognition of accreditation should be the preferred option.

Horizontal *v.* sectoral approaches to recognition

Turning to a more macro-level, which bodies are involved may in turn depend on whether the approach taken to recognition is horizontal or sectoral. The horizontal approach has been adopted in the EU and in the Australia–New Zealand context in order to ensure full sectoral coverage – even if at the cost of automaticity in the case of the EU. Sectoral recognition agreements, because they either involve some degree of coordination of education and training or can spell out criteria for recognition tailored to the sector in question, have the potential to lead to more automatic recognition for qualified professionals. In Europe, the first generation of recognition Directives in the health sector and the architect's Directive of 1985 constitute illustrations of these two variants of the sectoral approach. NAFTA has also adopted a sectoral approach to mutual recognition, although under a broad horizontal legal umbrella to cover the range of issues relevant to liberalization of professional services.[64] Under such a 'universal sectoral approach' one question is where to start. It may be easier, for instance, to start with the technical professions that are often less regulated or where regulations tend to be expressed in terms of technical norms (engineering, architecture, health). Engineering has been the first sector tackled under NAFTA.

The two approaches are not exclusive. In the EU, the second has followed the first due to the progressive realization of the cumbersome nature of the process. When this lesson has been transferred, others have skipped the first step altogether as with the case of Australia–New Zealand. But sectoral approaches can also complement horizontal approaches. Thus, the European Commission did not exclude the possibility of negotiating sectoral directives after the GSD was put in place, stating three conditions for doing so: (a) the agreement of the profession concerned; (b) wide consensus among the Member States; and (c) an advantage for using this approach rather than the GSD.

This third condition is where the Commission, with its exclusive right of initiative, possesses the greatest margin of action and can develop objective criteria. Sectoral complements could be warranted when: (a) the level of obligation set by the horizontal agreement is too vague or too low; (b) the implementation of progressive liberalization under the horizontal route may have led to convergence between national systems that may be codified in order to increase the automaticity of the rights of access; and (c), conversely, the horizontal approach has led to too many instances of entry of 'sub-standard' professionals from other members, showing the insufficiency of generic compensation mechanisms.

Multilateral guidelines for sectoral MRAs

One of the most important obstacles to the negotiation of MRAs is their apparent complexity. In a few rare cases, bilateral MRAs have been negotiated *ex nihilo*. But, generally, MRAs will likely follow from two prior steps: (a) adoption of framework agreements calling for MRAs; and (b) the crafting of detailed work programmes, roadmaps and guidelines for designing MRAs which can provide a precious basis for learning from precedents. NAFTA's professional annexes constitute a first attempt at doing so by fine-tuning and expanding the range of criteria to be considered for adoption in MRAs.

The discussions in the WTO on accountancy have provided a first forum for exploring mutual recognition at the multilateral level. In 1996, in order to support these and other incipient efforts to negotiate MRAs, followed by the European Union, the United States Trade Representative Office (USTR) submitted a proposal[65] for multilateral MRA guidelines. Multilateral guidelines for an MRA in accounting were adopted in 1997. This was to pave the way for a pledge by WTO members that the same formats and procedures be adhered to in all MRA negotiations, leading to an open and transparent negotiating system for such agreements. To ensure this result, these multilateral guidelines should be designed to be workable (not too onerous to discourage participation), broad (compatible with different regulatory systems), and open and flexible (enabling expansion).[66] At this stage of discussions, it is important to safeguard the voluntary nature of the guidelines and clearly separate out the mandatory provisions related to the treatment of third parties stemming from Art. 7 of GATS (see discussion in next section). More generally, the guidelines should encourage parties to view MRAs as a dynamic process and include provisions to that effect. These can be related to the purpose (to set in place a process for the progressive enhancement of the understanding with the ultimate goal of full mutual recognition); the combination of different mechanisms for recognition within a single MRA; indications as to how automaticity may progressively increase; maximizing the range of choice regarding compensatory requirements; drawing explicit connections between variations in scope of access (activities, title, timeframe, mode of delivery) and automaticity; and the inclusion of a reversibility clause.

Prospects for global mutual recognition

What is the prospect for worldwide mutual recognition in the professions? Mutual recognition is clearly a contagious principle,[67] and MRAs in the field of products are currently initiated in every region of the world. Recognition for the professions is likely to take more time but the same dynamics are at play. Following on the examples of the EU and Australia–New Zealand, other regional arrangements are likely to encourage their professional associations to explore the issue. There is also going to be a demonstration effect across regions as well as across professions, and part of the role of the WTO ought to be to magnify and manage the contagion effect of MRAs. In its Art. 7 on mutual recognition, GATS encourages signatories to adopt measures, by way of bilateral agreements or 'autonomously', 'to recognize the education or experience obtained, requirements met, or licenses or certification obtained in a particular country'. It has now gone one step further by supporting the development of guidelines on the form and content of MRA as discussed above.

But WTO members need to squarely address the potential contradictions between mutual recognition and the core tenets of the multilateral trading system – unconditional most-nation-nation treatment (treating all trading partners equally) and diffuse reciprocity (seeking broadly equivalent concessions but not on a *quid pro quo* basis). Bilateral or plurilateral mutual recognition deals cannot be 'multilateralized', simply because concessions based on assessing current and future equivalence of regulatory systems are not fungible. Hence, under recognition, extending MFN treatment is indeed conditional, not on some symmetrical lowering of trade barriers, but on actual compatibility of rules or equivalence of procedures of the other party. To be sure, the MFN obligation requires countries to treat service-providers of any other WTO member no less favourably than it treats service-providers of any other country in like circumstances. 'Like circumstances' means that treating an unqualified professional differently is legitimate. In short, since the extent to which foreign professionals meet domestic standards varies, recognition can be said to be compatible with the letter of the MFN obligation.

Nevertheless, in order to uphold the spirit of multilateralism and MFN, the WTO needs to ensure that the adoption of a web of MRAs around the world does not lead to greater fragmentation of international professional practice. This involves at least three types of tasks. Clarifying the line between unilateral obligations and the option to enter into MRAs; ensuring the transparency and openness of individual bilateral or regional MRAs; and providing a normative framework for resolving issues of transitivity and compatibility between these disparate agreements with the aim of eventually integrating them under a global decentralized framework.[68]

From non-discrimination to mutual recognition: Articles 6.4 and 7 of GATS

In 1995, the GATS Council established a Working Party on Professional Services whose main mission is to set out guidelines for how to ensure, *inter alia*, that licensing and certification requirements do not constitute unnecessary barriers to trade but are based on objective and transparent criteria, as mandated by Art. 6.4 of the GATS on Domestic Regulation.[69] This is paramount to asking what should be the legal obligations of the parties to GATS short of mutual recognition?

The answer to this question obviously changes the incentives for negotiating over MRAs in the first place. There are arguments on both sides. On the one hand, a broad interpretation and strict enforcement of policed national treatment (even to the point of enforcing unilateral recognition) ensures a minimal level of liberalization and may constitute an incentive for MRAs. Given their purely voluntary nature (WTO simply 'encourages'), countries (or their regulatory bodies) may simply refuse to negotiate MRAs with those that approach them for fear of competition once mutual recognition is in place. It is not even clear that WTO members are obliged to give reasons for refusing to respond to requests for MRA negotiations. In such cases, the stringency of alternative obligations must make it clear that the country cannot simply get away with it. This is the goal of the provisions under GATS Art. 6

regarding non-discriminatory regulations. They include familiar obligations to use least restrictive means, proportionality criteria, and the like, that go beyond the traditional interpretation of national treatment. But the question of whether given domestic standards and regulations conform to these obligations is likely to be extremely difficult to answer. How far is it possible in the WTO context to follow the path of the EU? There, the adoption of an ambitious approach to mutual recognition followed a progressive reinterpretation of what constitutes a 'barrier to trade' and of the extent to which Member States were directly obligated by the Treaty of Rome to provide cross-border access to people and products. In effect, mutual recognition constituted a reinterpretation and a broadening of the traditional principle of national treatment. At one extreme, some of the 'conditions' of entry into national markets applied in the form of non-discriminatory obligations to both national and foreigners can come to be considered as 'restrictions', and thus become the object of a legal obligation of recognition. In overcoming regulatory barriers to trade, where does enforcement of liberalization as a legal obligation end, and where does the need for harmonization/recognition as a political option start? The current task of 'Art. 6.4' working groups needs to be pursued in order to push the frontier of these obligations as far as possible without compromising service quality, even while some members already resort to the more ambitious MRA approach.

At the same time, a fundamental tension exists between legal and political mutual recognition. Such attempts at strengthening unilateral obligations should not overlook the fact that recognition is above all a process of mutual adaptation. Granting too much ground for imposing recognition through broad-based GATS clauses, for example judicial fiat at the multilateral level, endangers the legitimacy of the system as a whole and foregoes the benefits of regulatory cooperation that go along with recognition. The fact that even, in the EU, judicial activism has created resistance and that the WTO's dispute settlement mechanism is a main target for the political exploitation of the 'sovereignty argument' against trade liberalization ought to suggest caution. It would seem to be wiser to enforce openness to the greatest extent possible of the MRAs themselves and to resolve emerging disputes through renewed political negotiations.

Even when unilateral recognition is voluntary, the prospect of falling under MFN obligations enforceable by dispute settlement bodies may discourage parties to extend unilateral recognition in the first place. This is true for GATS where the granting of national treatment is voluntary but could theoretically result in unilateral recognition. The very fact that MFN was not made conditional on the compatibility between regulatory regimes for concessions made in national schedules has greatly decreased their utility as mechanisms for addressing regulatory barriers to trade. The obligation of unilateral recognition that may emerge from the application of Art. 6.4 and of national treatment when applicable should not be carried too far. Mutual recognition needs to remain a political contract.

Developing guidelines for MRAs: international obligations and responsibilities

How can the broad notion of non-discrimination be salvaged in the negotiation and implementation of the MRAs themselves? While the drafters of GATS have sought to ensure procedural if not actual non-discrimination in the wording of Art. 7, these attempts may be insufficient to ensure that customized rights of access granted through recognition do not become a means of discrimination between countries based on non-regulatory criteria. Three types of guarantees follow from GATS which need to be fine-tuned and reinforced on a case-by-case basis. Further efforts through the WTO need to ensure that these guarantees are enforced and eventually codified through more specific obligations under an amended multilateral treaty:

1 *Transparency.* In theory, parties to MRAs are subject to a *notification and reporting requirement* to be submitted to the WTO Secretariat 'as far in advance as possible' of recognition negotiations and when the Agreement is concluded. Concretely, the US Trade Representative Office (USTR) has suggested that parties must notify their intent to enter into discussion, the entities involved, the dates and place of the meeting. In practice, however, the degree of transparency of MRA discussions is hard to ensure when involving highly sensitive sectors, where multilateral criteria do not preexist and when there is great asymmetry between regulatory practices and cultures involved. There is also the vexing question of when do negotiations actually begin. Preliminary talks can last many years and shift progressively into negotiations. At the other end of the spectrum, when is an agreement an Agreement? Is it when it has been adopted by at least one party (even if this might be a sub-national jurisdiction), or when it is implemented? Given the still *ad hoc* nature of the process, the best that might be hoped for is greater *post hoc* transparency, in particular through requirements to establish *contact points* where details on the substance of the Agreement can be obtained by

third parties. These contact points should preferably involve the same people as those managing the agreement;

2 *Openness*. Under GATS, members who grant recognition must 'afford adequate opportunity' for other interested members 'to negotiate their accession' to existing or future bilateral or multilateral MRAs. Who decides that adequate opportunity has been granted? How extensive are these obligations? How should we distinguish between obligations to respond, an obligation to 'talk', and an obligation to negotiate? The central issue here is that negotiating over recognition is highly resource-intensive, at least when it involves thorough evaluation of equivalence and detailed mechanisms for bridging remaining differences. When discussions are conducted by private organizations they do it at their own expense and every additional partner spells an additional drain on resources. Technically, it may also be much easier to proceed incrementally rather than try to involve too many parties at once. In this light, MRAs should specify procedures for granting opportunity of access to the Agreement, while taking account of these constraints. Parties need to specify where and how requests to join should be forwarded; what information is required of the applicants; what are the alternative options for demonstrating equivalence and/or for 'graduating' into the Agreement. Openness can be progressive and granted step-by-step using the same differentiated approach as with initial parties to the Agreement. This might involve concrete steps for including third parties as observers in joint evaluation or accreditation missions, field trips and meetings and in all other discussions that can help them master the conditions for their eventual inclusion. In this regard, the OECD could contribute to more proactive non-discrimination by providing technical support on the conditions for entry into MRAs. Formally, MRAs could include a special category of 'associate parties' who are not considered to have met equivalence criteria and who thus would only be granted restricted benefits in terms of automaticity and scope but would be full participants in the MRA cooperation networks.

3 *Equitable treatment.* If third parties have been given the opportunity to apply to MRAs but do not pass the minimal equivalence test, the GATS specifies that a member must not use mutual recognition as a means of discrimination between countries (that is, the 'ins' and the 'outs') in the application of its Regulations or constitute a disguised restriction on trade in services. But obviously, it is allowed to treat professionals of different origins (covered or not by recognition) differently. Equitable treatment should therefore be conceived more proactively

to mean that MRAs should include clauses specifying the 'bridges' available to third-country applicants. In this sense procedures for progressive openness and equitable treatment should be thought of as on a continuum.

Exploring the concrete obligations entailed by the requirement of openness associated with multilateralism raises the traditional problems associated with sub-national delegation of authority which need to be addressed in a coherent manner. For the moment, commitments to least restrictive approaches and liberalization are often cast in terms of 'best endeavours', reflecting the fact that governments have often delegated jurisdiction over the professions to sub-national governments (or federations), who themselves often grant self-regulatory authority to professional bodies. How should obligations contracted by governments be transferred to region and especially private bodies with delegated public authority? In an area where liberalization entails extensive cooperation, information-gathering and analysis, asking private bodies to accede indiscriminately to the demands of any of the potentially hundreds of mutual recognition partners around the world would obviously be excessive and inoperative. At the same time, their statutory power entails obligations, including those contracted by their government internationally. Why should architects from Argentina be favoured over architects from Uruguay with the same qualifications simply because the US-based association of architects has not yet had time to attend to the latter? International organizations, including UNCTAD and the OECD need to devote resources to address this issue.

Encouraging expansion and enforcing transitivity

Finally, the practice and legal basis for MRAs ought to be progressively incorporated into the WTO framework, first by developing guidelines to enable expansion of country coverage and eventual multilateralization. According to the drafters of the current proposal, 'MRAs on a given profession should be able to fit together and be expanded into a multilateral system'. In applying this principle, WTO members need to strike a balance between flexibility and consistency. In particular, the expansion from individual recognition agreement into a multilateral system could be accelerated by enforcing more systematically the principle of transitivity. If parties *A* and *B* as well as *B* and *C* have a recognition agreement, should *A* and *C* be under consistent recognition obligations? More generally, if *A* enters a mutual recognition with *B*, and *B* is part of a federation or a regional trade agreement, should *A* be under an obligation to negotiate recognition with all the other parties connected to *B*? How far should GATS go in this regard?

It may be best to leave the greatest flexibility possible to parties engaging in mutual recognition. Under NAFTA, for instance, any configuration of mutual recognition agreement is conceivable in theory, in order to give parties as much flexibility as possible so as not to discourage recognition initiatives. An MRA between engineers from specific states or provinces in Canada and the USA does not need to be extended to the rest of the country, let alone Mexico. Moreover, NAFTA starts from the premise that even parties who are part of the same regional arrangements may have greater differences among themselves than with some outside third parties. The benefits of mutual recognition negotiated by one or two parties with a third parties (say between the United States and the EU) need not automatically extend to other NAFTA signatories.

Transitivity applies in principle in the EU although the issue as to whether training obtained outside the EU by EU nationals benefits from recognition was not an easy one to resolve. Here, the GSD adopted a very liberal approach under pressure from the UK, Ireland, Luxembourg and Greece whose nationals often pursue their professional training abroad. It states that, if an EU state has recognized a foreign diploma, such recognition will apply throughout the EU, provided the applicant has acquired three years of professional experience. The same logic has not been extended to non-EU nationals.[70]

The most important issue for the WTO is whether there should be a presumption of transitivity across bilateral or regional MRAs: if the USA negotiates an MRA with the EU and with some APEC countries, to what extent are the EU and the concerned APEC countries obliged to recognize each other's regulations? Transitivity would preclude the need for 'rules of origin' in mutual recognition zones and increase the consistency between such zones. Parties may be allowed to object to transitivity because the actual access benefits may not be balanced under the new configuration or the compounded regulatory differentials through chain recognition may surpass their threshold of 'acceptable' differences. But in this case, asymmetries in trade benefits and regulations must be significant and the burden of proof should be born by opponents of transitivity. This should not preclude the use of safeguards and allowance for generous confidence-building periods to allow regulators to set up networks for mutual monitoring. By enforcing such transitivity the WTO could help decrease the closed nature of MRAs, 'plurilateralize' bilateral agreements, and thus prepare the ground for eventual worldwide mutual recognition.

Transatlantic cooperation as a stepping stone for multilateralized mutual recognition

The adoption, implementation and enforcement of MRAs in the professional sector requires overcoming a host of obstacles. If it is based on sustaining the quality of services provided and current levels of consumer protection – even as the definitions and regulation of professions change at a growing pace – the process of recognition is likely to be highly resource-intensive. MRAs cannot be crafted overnight or follow some grand design; they need to be adapted to the requirements of the particular professions and countries involved. At the same time, they need to be consistent with one another. Ensuring such consistency while spearheading faster and more efficient negotiations of mutual recognition agreements worldwide could be the object of new transatlantic action. Regulatory cooperation between the USA and the EU regarding professional services could serve as a stepping-stone in the context of the Doha Round by demonstrating the potential for open MRAs.

More generally, transatlantic cooperation can contribute in creating a culture of mutual recognition whereby the professions themselves become increasingly aware of the benefits that can be had through recognition as well as the many ways in which recognition can be 'managed' to alleviate their concerns over a general lowering of professional standards in their respective countries. Such a culture of mutual recognition would underscore the notion that recognition is a process not an outcome, and that it needs to be continually updated, reinforced and reappraised. Ultimately, however, and in spite of all the possible caveats and refinements explored here, mutual recognition is a leap of faith.

Notes

1 See Nicolaïdis, K., 'Mutual Recognition of Regulatory Regimes: Some Lessons and Prospects', in *Regulatory Reform and International Market Openness,* OECD Publications, November 1996.
2 See 'Regulatory Reform Project: Professional Business Services', DAFFE, OECD, November 1996.
3 Art. 7 of GATS encourages signatories to adopt measures, by way of bilateral agreements or autonomously, 'to recognize the education or experience obtained, requirements met, or licenses or certification obtained in a particular country'.
4 MRAs in the field of products are now being negotiated or considered both bilaterally – e.g. between the United States and the European Union, Australia and New Zealand – plurilaterally, the G4 countries – and regionally – within APEC, ASEAN, NAFTA and the FTAA.

5 See Ascher, B., 'Trade Agreements and the Professions', Paper presented at Euroservices: Transatlantic Trade in the 21st Century, US Department of Commerce, 18 June 1996, p. 4.

6 See Nicolaïdis, K., 'International Trade in Information-Based Services: Beyond the Uruguay Round', in Drake, W. (ed.), *The New Information Economy*, New York: Twentieth Century Fund, 1995; OECD Secretariat, *Liberalization of Trade in Professional Services*, Paris, OECD publications, 1995; and OECD Secretariat, *International Trade in Professional Services: Assessing Barriers and Encouraging Reform*, Paris, OECD publications, 1996 (referred to hereafter as *OECD Documents*, 1995 and 1996). Measures are recorded in the OECD Inventory of Measures Affecting Trade in Professional Services and the survey on Regulation on Access to the Professions and their Activities.

7 Article 57.1. Although the European Court decided in a series of cases in the mid-1970s that the provisions of the Treaty were to be self-executing in the absence of the Community Directives it called for, this did not extend to mutual recognition.

8 This includes pharmacists, doctors, dentists, engineers, architects, accountants, lawyers, veterinarians, midwifes, opticians, nurses.

9 Each profession was treated along the same scheme under three separate Directives concerning respectively, (a) the abolition of legal restrictions on freedom of movement; (b) the mutual recognition of qualifications; (c) and coordination of conditions for the taking up and pursuit of the professions.

10 For more details, see Jean-Eric de Cockborne in *OECD Documents*, 1995; and Nicolaïdis, 1996.

11 Directive 89/48/CEE completed by 92/51/CEE. The first general Directive entered into force in January 1991 and the second in 1994. For a detailed description, see for instance, *Vademecum sur le Systeme de Reconnaissance Des Qualification Professionnelles Instauré par la Directive 89/48/CE et Complété par la Directive 92/51/CEE – Rapport Final – Clifford Chance*, Brussels, 1994.

12 Article 3 the GSD stipulated that, 'where, in a host Member State, the taking up or pursuit of a regulated profession is subject to possession of a diploma, the competent authority may not, on the grounds of inadequate qualifications, refuse to authorize a national of a Member State to take up or pursue that profession on the same conditions as applied to its own nationals: (a) if the applicant holds the diploma required in another Member State for … the profession in question … (b) if the applicant has pursued the profession in question full time for two years during the previous ten years in another Member State which does not regulate that profession, … and possesses evidence of one or more formal qualifications … awarded by a competent authority … which show that the holder has successfully completed a post-secondary education course of at least three years duration … and where appropriate that he has successfully completed the professional training required in addition to the course, and which have prepared the holder for the pursuit of the profession.'

13 This is in keeping with the general philosophy set out in the Court's judgment *Cassis de Dijon* (1979) where any alcoholic product was to be allowed free entry in any Member State if 'lawfully produced and marketed' in another member state.

14 The first three correspond to alternative levels of training and constitute the basic organizing categories; the next two have been added by the second

GSD to cover particular cases (attestation de competence and title FGEPS). The last two – title of training and regulated title of training – cover qualifications acquired in a home state that does not regulate a profession.

15 In virtually all the Member States regulated professions are concentrated in the same fields: education, healthcare, shipping, law and finance. But social and cultural differences explain variance beyond this core. A professional activity is considered as regulated under two conditions: (1) the regulation is issued by public authority or private authority with delegated public authority, and private professional authorities must be deemed competent to deliver a certificate under the MR system; (2) the regulation must be aimed at conditioning access to the practice of a profession – directly or indirectly – to the possession of a stated type of qualification.

16 A year prior to the passing of the GSD, the Court had indicated how proportionality ought to apply in the case of salaried activities, stating that host States were required to 'take into account' training received in the country of origin and could not refuse access if such training complied with a number of criteria of equivalence. While the case concerned free movement of workers (EEC Treaty, Art. 48), it was interpreted as applicable by analogy to the professions. Case 222/86, Heylen judgment of 15 October 1987, ECR 4116.

17 Commission of the European Communities, 'Explanatory Memorandum', Bulletin of the European Communities, Supplement 8/85, p. 7.

18 Article 9, GSD. In addition, the Commission committed itself to stepping up its support for Community-wide education databases such as the information centre on the academic recognition of diplomas and period of study established in 1976 by the Council.

19 'Explanatory Memorandum', see note 14, p. 7.

20 Some States have chosen to adopt a general horizontal measure, transposing the GSD's general principles and appointing competent authorities, with detailed rules for each profession awaiting secondary legislation; others have chosen to transpose vertically, profession by profession. See Economic Advisory Group, *The Impact and Effectiveness of the Single Market*, 30 October 1996; Commission of the European Communities, 'Communication from the Commission to the European Parliament and Council', DGIII and accompanying background information in *The 1996 Single Market Review*, 15 November 1996.

21 See Orzack, L., 'The General Systems Directive: Education and the Liberal Professions', in Hurwitz and Lequesnes (eds), *The State of the European Community*, Boulder, Lynne Rienner, 1991.

22 For an extensive analysis, see Coyne, S., *International Trade in Legal Services*, Little, Brown & Co., 1996.

23 Commission of the European Communities, *Proposal for a European Parliament and Council Directive to Facilitate Practice of the Profession of Lawyer on a Permanent Basis in a Member State Other Than That in Which the Qualification Was Obtained*, COM (94) 572 final, Brussels, 21.12.1994, 94/0299 (COD); *Amended Proposal*, Com (96) 446 fin. For a description of the negotiations, see Coyne, S., *International Trade in Legal Services*, Little, Brown & Co., 1996.

24 See Leebron, D. in OECD Proceedings, *Regulatory Reform and International Market Openness*, 1996.

25 These correspond to technical standards and conformity assessment procedures for goods.

26 'UIA Accord on International Recommended Standards of Professionalism in Architectural Practice', adopted by the UIA Assemby in Barcelona, Spain, 9 July 1996. The agreement builds on an accord between the USA and Canada, first signed in 1978 and expanded in the Annex on Architecture in the US–Canada Free Trade agreement. The FTA established the need for common standards on accreditation without spelling out these standards specifically. A process of recognition under the FTA has actually been set in motion between the National Council of Architectural Registration board and the Commission of Canadian Architectural Council.

27 The Convention was signed between UNESCO (CEPES), the Council of Europe, and the European Union, through their respective national information networks on academic recognition, such as the European National Information Centres on Academic Recognition and Mobility (ENIC). See Uvalic-Trumbic, S., 'Guidelines and Recommendations from the Working Group on Europe–U.S.A.: Mutual Recognition of Qualifications', CEPES-UNESCO, 1996.

28 In the current discussions towards a possible MRA in architecture between Mexico, the USA and Canada, teams of experts from each country have been given the task of visiting schools in Mexico. They will then meet to go over the results and assess whether the schools are actually up to standards.

29 When there is no further precision and specific provisions are mentioned the term GSD refers to the first Directive.

30 To ensure that the system would not be abused, the United Kingdom added an explanatory statement that the associations and organizations recognized in a special form were those which are incorporated under Royal Charter (Statement 9). The lists provided by Ireland and the UK includes Institutes and Chartered bodies supervising Accountants, Loss Adjusters, Management Accountants, Chartered Secretaries and Administrators, Insurance, Actuaries, Bankers, Surveyors, Planning, Physiotherapy, Chemistry, Psychology, Libraries, Foresters, Building, Engineering (structural, civil, mining, electrical, gas, mechanical, chemical, production, marine), Energy, naval Architects, Aeronautical Society, the Institute of Metals, the Institute of Measurement and Control, the British Computer Society.

31 In land surveying and pharmacy they have done so for 100 years! Architects have automatic registration since 1990. Automatic cross-registration is currently being implemented for teachers, veterinary science and dentistry and is underway for radiography. See Australian Government Publishing Services, 'A proposal for the Trans-Tasman Mutual Recognition of Standards for Goods and the Professsions: A Discussion Paper Circulated by the Council of Australian Governments and the Government of New Zealand', April 1995.

32 See de Cockborne, J.E., *OECD Documents*, 1995.

33 An element of clarification was attempted in the Statement 15 added to the Directive: 'the Council and the Commission agree that matters differ substantially ... where the activities in question cannot be pursued satisfactorily in the host Member State unless they have been mastered'.

34 This was a controversial point in the GSD negotiations. Ultimately, the right was not included in the Directive but the object of an informal understanding under Statement 3, 'the Council and the Commission agree that applicants must possess the linguistic knowledge necessary for the pursuit of their profession'. How far member states could go in enforcing language requirements was thus left unclear and subject to ECJ review. In a well-publicized case regarding a foreign teacher in Ireland, the Court did allow for language requirements on the grounds of preserving national identity.

35 Council Directive of 22 March 1977, OJ n. 78, 26.3. 1977.

36 At this stage it is important to ensure that the host country does not reintroduce an entry test through the backdoor. Under Statement 11 of the GSD, for instance, the adaptation period is the object of an assessment on the part of host-country regulators, provided that this assessment only pertains to the activities under supervision and 'in no case' takes the form of a formal written or oral test.

37 The formula is actually more complex, with X and Y as respectively lengths of studies in home/host countries (years), T as years of training, C as years of controlled practice, P as maximum years of professional experience which can be required as a compensatory measure: $Y = X + aT \Rightarrow P = 2x(a)$; $Y = X + bC \Rightarrow P = b$

38 See, notably, the contributions by Knapp, U. and J. Murray, 'Liberalization and the Consumer', in *OECD Documents*, 1996.

39 See Coyne S., *International Trade in Legal Services*, Little, Brown & Co., 1996.

40 EU member states are allowed to derogate from the right to choose: (i) for the legal profession; (ii) 'for professions whose practice requires precise knowledge of national law in respect of which the provision of advice and/or assistance concerning national law is an essential and constant aspect of the professional activity (Art. 4)'; (iii) for all professions, subject to a notification procedure with the Commission (Art. 10). France for instance asked for a derogation in tourism and professions requiring a detailed knowledge of national law (e.g. industrial property consultant). See Directive 89/48/EEC, Art. 11 Reports (1991/1992), member states reports.

41 See Art. 11 Reports (see previous note).

42 See the Ireland Report in Directive 89/48/EEC, Art. 11 Reports (1991/ 1992), Member States' reports. The French Report also cites French nationals trained as psychotherapists in Belgium.

43 This is evident in the EU Member States' reports on the implementation of the GSD which are due every two years after the implementation of the GSD on 6 January 1991. In the first two years, the rate of automatic acceptance varied greatly across pairs of countries and professions. Even between the UK and Ireland where there is probably the highest flow, the automaticity rates ranged from 96% for solicitors, to a third for secondary school teachers. The UK's rate of 75% automatic acceptance was the highest reported.

44 A good example can be found with the legal profession in Europe. In Germany the test consists in two written exams covering respectively a compulsory topic and a topic in an area selected by the candidate, and an oral on professional rules. In France the National Bar council reviews each applicant's qualification and in light thereof requires the applicant to take from one to three oral exams, sometimes complemented with a four-hour written

exam. In the UK the Aptitude test consists of two three-hour written exams on property law and litigation, and short exams on professional conduct and accounts, and principles of the common law.

45 See, for instance, Statement 15 of the GSD: 'The Council and the Commission agree that neither the adaptation period not the aptitude test should constitute a disguised means of imposing upon applicants a more stringent requirement than is necessary'.

46 More generally, regulations and therefore rights of access can apply to the activity *per se* or to certain modes of practice (in addition these include the use of titles, the reimbursement of professional acts in the field of health or the right to added compensation, such as a government subsidy due to a collective agreement). Access to these other modes of practice can be a precondition for local practice or simply an added bonus.

47 The distinction may be more or less important to different countries. In architecture, for instance, there is a great difference of culture between the Napoleonic tradition of granting a title as a precondition for professional practice, and the Anglo-Saxon culture where the title is protected by law but not practice. In the UK many bodies carry out the function of architect under other professional labels such as engineers, quantity surveyor and building surveyors or technicians.

48 The use of titles as signalling devices was introduced in the EU 1975 medical Directives, where host states were allowed to require use of home state title followed by the name and location of the establishment or examining board which awarded it; in cases where the home title 'may be confused' with a host state title, implying training which the person concerned had not undergone, the host State could require adaptation of the title through the introduction of 'suitable wording'. In addition, formal certificates of training were to be used only in the language of the member state of origin.

49 Other beneficiaries can use both the professional title of the host member state or the academic title of the home state. In the latter case the host State may require the applicant's title to be followed 'by the name and location of the establishment or examining board which awarded it'.

50 One of the traditional purposes of regulating professions has been to establish constraints on which activities could be exercised by whom. Compartmentalizing functions and services serves to limit professionals' capacity to prescribe their own services. Different professions are designated to provide specific services where there may be conflict of interest (e.g. accounting and legal services). It also allows the imposition of different degrees of regulation which may lead to higher controls in some countries. Thus law counseling (solicitors) is more regulated in common law countries. Similarly, the right to represent clients is distinguished from the task of recording acts in many countries, and the right to request construction permits reserved to architects not surveyors or engineers. See Nelson, S., *OECD Documents*, 1996.

51 See Ehlermann-Cache and Knapp, U., *OECD Documents*, 1996. The scope of 'foreign law' can itself be a matter of interpretation. According to USTR, lawyers with an office in the EU ought to be allowed to practise EU law since it is part of European law. Europeans countered that EU law often takes effect as the domestic law of Member States.

52 There are countries where titles serve as evidence of a level of training and allow for even more differentiated access, such as Germany. Certain types of organizations are free to reserve certain activities to 'doctorate engineers' rather than 'graduate engineers'. In this case, full recognition implies that such distinctions cannot apply to foreign engineers.
53 In another vein, lawyers traditionally needed to be accessible to the court and thus it was normal that they maintain an establishment within its territory. Nelson, S., *OECD Documents*, 1996.
54 In the *Gebhard* case, the ECJ denied that the 1977 Directive on cross-border provision allowed a German *Rechtsanwalt* to keep an office in Milan, to service nationals of the host country, 'on a stable and continuous basis'. Case C-55/94, European Court of Justice Judgment of 30 November 1995.
55 An interesting example is the combination of an obligation to establish for audit while cross border provision is accepted for book keeping. See Knapp, U., 'Inventory of Measures Affecting Trade in Professional Services', *OECD Documents*, 1996.
56 For a discussion of the importance of this idea in the context of the Uruguay Round, see Drake, W. and Nicolaïdis, K. 'Ideas, Interests and Institutionalization: "Trade in Services" and the Uruguay Round', in *International Organization*, vol. 46, no.1, Winter 1992, pp. 37–100.
57 This line of thinking can be presented under the general category of 'securing insecure contracts'. For a discussion, see Nicolaïdis, K., 'Mutual Recognition of Regulatory Regimes: Some Lessons and Prospects', in *Regulatory Reform and International Market Openness*, OECD Publications, November 1996, pp. 18–20. This section draws heavily on this chapter.
58 Sauvé, P., 'The Long and Winding Road: NAFTA and the Profession', *OECD Documents*, 1995.
59 See Ascher, B., 'Trade Agreements and the Professions', Paper presented at Euroservices: Transatlantic Trade in the 21st Century, US Department of Commerce, 18 June 1996, p. 7.
60 See Piggott, R., *OECD Documents*, 1996.
61 Under the NAFTA model, the NAFTA Commission, meeting at the ministerial level, is supposed to review and monitor progress. See Sauvé, P., *OECD Documents*, 1995.
62 See Ascher, B., 'Trade Agreements and the Professions', Paper presented at Euroservices: Transatlantic Trade in the 21st Century, US Department of Commerce, 18 June 1996, p. 8 and our earlier discussion, in p. 146.
63 For instance, the American Bar Association that accredits Law Schools in the USA adopted such a waiver. See ABA, *Standards for Approval of Law School and Interpretations*, Standard 802, October 1991 (ex. 18).
64 See Sauvé, P., *OECD Documents*, 1995.
65 United States Trade Representative Office, 'Multilateral Guidelines for Mutual Recognition Agreements on Professional Services', Draft Proposal introduced by USTR, 4 March 1996.
66 Ascher, B., 'Trade Agreements and the Professions', Paper presented at Euroservices: Transatlantic Trade in the 21st Century, US Department of Commerce, 18 June 1996, p. 7.
67 For an early discussion, see Nicolaïdis, K., 'Mutual Recognition: The Next Frontier of Multilateralism?', *Project Promethee Perspectives*, July 1989. See also

Nicolaïdis, K., 'Mutual Recognition of Regulatory Regimes: Some Lessons and Prospects', in *Regulatory Reform and International Market Openness*, OECD Publications, November 1996.

68 This section draws extensively from Nicolaïdis, K., 'Mutual Recognition of Regulatory Regimes: Some Lessons and Prospects', in *Regulatory Reform and International Market Openness*, OECD Publications, November 1996.

69 The same language appears in the FTA (Art. 1403: Licensing and Certification), NAFTA (Art. 1210: Licensing and Certification).

70 In the field of law, for instance, the USA requested that the EU grant US lawyers the same treatment accorded to English solicitors (e.g. right to advise) on behalf of all non-EU lawyers. US negotiators may have been ill-advised to make such a universal demand, for this was seized upon by the EU to refuse to consider the request. Under the draft establishment Directive for lawyers, non-EU lawyers who qualify as English solicitors by passing the English Qualified Lawyers Test (e.g. from Canada, the USA or Australia) or as *Avocat* by passing the French Special Exam would not be entitled to the benefits of the Directive unless they were EU nationals. See Coyne, S., *International Trade in Legal Services*, Little, Brown & Co., 1996.

5
Mutual Recognition, Unemployment and the Welfare State

Fiorella Kostoris Padoa Schioppa

Introduction

Apparently the principle of mutual recognition seems able to promote the four fundamental freedoms foreseen by the Treaty of Rome. However – unlike what happens in the commodity, service and capital markets – not only is it far from being adopted in the labour market, but the European Union endorses in this sector an opposite principle, named 'equal treatment', while labelling the mutual recognition as a form of 'social dumping'. Given that labour market problems cannot be discussed without a joint consideration of social protection policies, one has also to add that European welfare states generally utilize host rather than home-country rules, contrary to the principle of mutual recognition. However, there are no deep, logical reasons for using opposite principles in one of the four fundamental European freedoms. Quite the reverse; on logical grounds it is unlikely that, in spite of different standards and legislations, European Member States are able to be equivalent in protecting health, environment and the cultural heritage, but not workers' rights. Thus, Nicolaïdis (2000) seems correct in saying that:

> Formally, mutual recognition can be defined as ... a transfer of regulatory authority from the host State (or jurisdiction) where a transaction takes place, to the home State (or jurisdiction) from which a product, a person, a service or a firm originate. This in turn embodies the general principle that if a professional can operate, a product be sold or a service provided lawfully in one jurisdiction, they can operate, be sold or provided freely in any other participating jurisdiction, without having to comply with the regulations of these other jurisdictions.[1]

In what follows we will analyse the main reasons for the observed facts concerning the advantages of mutual recognition in three out of the four European freedoms. We will then see the disadvantages of using an opposite principle in the Union's labour markets and welfare states, and some possible extensions of the principle of mutual recognition in these fields will be proposed. Using a simple theoretical game-theory model, the positive implications on labour mobility and on the fight against the classical European unemployment will be shown, followed by some policy conclusions.

Rules and regulations on mutual recognition in the European Union markets

As is well-known, mutual recognition[2] entered the judicial and applicative *corpus* of the Union in an irreversible way after the famous European Court of Justice (ECJ) ruling, *Cassis de Dijon* (Court of Justice, 1979).[3]

In the absence of common rules, the ECJ, though recognizing that each Member State has the right to autonomously legislate the sale of products within its own territory, affirms that this national regulation cannot counter Art. 28[4] of the Treaty (ex Art. 30), which would be violated whenever the import of a good[5] lawfully produced and marketed in another Member State is impeded, unless this is justified by 'emergency measures'.[6]

Before 1979, the existing European regulations were identically utilized both for domestic and imported goods and services, and this seemed to have no discriminatory or protectionist implications within member states. In practice, on the contrary, by hampering the access to national markets of commodities produced elsewhere in Europe with different standards, they eventually proved discriminatory. The Court underlines that not only the Union body of laws prohibits any restriction to intra-Community trade, but also stresses a positive task,[7] that is, mutual recognition between member states. As a consequence, legal harmonization is not always necessary for European construction, and the substitution of national with Community norms is not a must. Delor's White Paper on the internal market[8] strongly reiterated that the harmonization of national laws through the definition of common rules at the European level should remain an exception limited to specific areas, stating in particular for the goods market that:

> in the future, legal convergence (Council Directive pursuant to Art. 100 [Art. 94 since the Treaty of Amsterdam]) will be limited to

> the setting of the main requisites in health care and safety which will be mandatory in all Member States ... Whenever harmonization of legislations is not considered essential either in terms of health care or safety or in terms of industry, the immediate and full recognition of different quality standard rules, of different provisions on food composition, etc. must be the rule.

Thus, harmonization must limit itself to minimum, sometimes only optional, standards and has to concern only fundamental aspects.

Reciprocal recognition of technical rules, procedures and certificates within the Union assumes that there exists a similarity in the level of protection of different Member States or, that there exist equivalence, compatibility or at least acceptability of the counterpart's regulatory system. This aspect is thoroughly illustrated in many European official documents. For example, the European Council in July 1984 states that 'the objectives pursued by the Member States are generally equivalent'.[9]

Thus, it is sufficient for member states to share their public interest and regulatory goals, in order to accept mobility flows and promote trade. This is, indeed, an ongoing process for three out of the four freedom areas defined by Art. 14 (ex Art. 7A, point 2) of the European Community Treaty referring to the internal market. This strong implication of the principle of mutual recognition is often reiterated by the European institutions, although with some oscillations and ambiguity. For example, the Commission's Communication of June 16 1999, states that:

> the principle of mutual recognition plays a central role in the Single Market by ensuring free movement of goods and services without making it necessary to harmonize national legislation ... The principle of mutual recognition plays a key part in opening the Single Market in all the sectors which have not been the subject of harmonization measures at Community level or which are covered by minimal or optional harmonization measures ... It is perfectly in keeping with the Single Market philosophy, whereby the home State principle prevails.[10]

Equal treatment and social dumping

Today, mutual recognition in Europe is adopted in (almost) all markets of goods (a partial exception concerns pharmaceuticals), services (based on higher education diplomas or on professional equivalence), while the capital market already enjoys quasi-perfect mobility and globalization. It is not, however, extended to the labour market and social protection, where assimilation is the general rule: specifically, an individual who decides to move from one European member state to another to reside and be active has the right to work[11] in the host state under the same conditions of a national (Art. 3, par. 1, letter c; Art. 14 (ex Art. 7A); Art. 39 (ex Art. 48); Art. 43 (ex Art. 52) of the Treaty, Community Regulation no. 1612/68 of the Council and Regulation no. 1251/70 of the European Commission). In particular, Community workers must be treated as national workers in terms of job conditions, wages, firing and hiring clauses (Regulation no. 1612/68 of the Council, Art. 7, par. 1 and 4), social security benefits and contributions, housing opportunities, minimum income support, family allowances, and loan (Regulation no. 1612/68 of the Council, Art. 7, par. 2 and 3 and Art. 9) and, finally, in terms of trade-union membership and workers' representation, with the only exclusion of their participation in the management of bodies governed by public laws.

This avoids many risks (but also many more opportunities) of social competition in Europe.[12] According to this approach, the principle of mutual recognition in European labour markets and welfare states is labelled as 'social dumping': thus, a German firm today can import *Cassis* from Dijon, but if it asks Dijon workers to emigrate to Germany and produce *Cassis* in the Rhein valley, it cannot pay them the French wage, or grant the French national holiday of 14 July or promise the French pension. Paradoxically, having to pay the German wage, it can even offer less than the French minimum income because, otherwise, it would be accused of discrimination. This almost absurd situation stems from a peculiar interpretation of the principle of 'equal treatment'. Indeed, while stating in Art. 12 (ex Art. 6) of the Treaty that 'any discrimination on grounds of nationality shall be forbidden', the factual result is to protect national workers from other European workers' potential competition, letting these foreign people believe that this is the only way to protect them from any possible exploitation in host countries: inexplicably, this competition is called 'unfair', as if guaranteeing a worker coming from a European member state the economic and social settings he/she would receive in his/her home state would lead him/her to be like a third-world immigrant without guarantees. This approach would perhaps be adequate for more heterogeneous situations in the home and host countries, but it seems hard to adapt to the Single Market, where the fundamental social rights are clearly defined and are similar everywhere.

A concrete example of how mutual recognition was denied in this field on the basis of a misunderstood concept of 'social dumping' maybe seen in a well-known episode from the 1990s in the building sector, during the reconstruction of East German regions (ex-GDR). The latter was prompting large flows of foreign firms and labour, because – on the basis of the existing rules – competition was open to all Europeans. As these job-seekers were ready to accept lower wages and less privileged employment conditions compared to West German workers, the direct advantage to these unemployed would also have implied a lower cost of new buildings and therefore additional benefits for German consumers and firms. Nevertheless, the phenomenon worried German trade-union leaders who, to protect their basis, asked and obtained from the German government a law – the *Arbeitnehmer-Entsendegesetz* (Law on Posted Workers) of 26 February 1996 – imposing[13] a minimum wage for posted workers living in Germany. The result of that initiative was a loss in efficiency and well-being, also because the degree of social protection offered to ex-GDR German workers decreased. That situation gave rise to a subsequent intervention on the part of the Commission, which produced Directive no. 96/71/EC of the European Parliament and Council: though restating the principle of the free movement of workers, the legitimacy of those provisions was confirmed under the assumption that any form of foreigners' exploitation should be avoided, as indicated in what are known as European 'social clauses'.

Without denying – and indeed restating – the legal and civil value of non-discrimination, the univocal interpretation provided by the Community legislation and by the ECJ rulings on labour and social protection policies does contribute, in my opinion, to limit free circulation of persons within the European Union. So, workers who decide to move to another member state have the right to be fully assimilated in the host State, while they have no right to maintain their original home-country identities. In other words, the right to diversity is not recognized in the receiving State, assimilation remaining the only feasible solution. Equal treatment does not hold for all those who are born in the same State, but only for those who work in the same country, which means that legislation and geographical localization always coincide.

The minimum threshold

The adoption of the principle of mutual recognition in European labour markets and welfare states would not mean denying the 'equality of treatment' objective, but would mean criticizing its current European interpretation. Something different should be proposed, whereby the identities of single citizens coming from different Member States and the peculiarities of national legislations would be respected.

To this end, it is worth recalling that the principle of mutual recognition requires two well-separated phases: a minimum threshold – namely a hard 'core' common to all legislations (for example in the *Cassis de Dijon* case), the healthcare goal; plus additional elements which may differ but are accepted under the assumption that nobody tries to impose a super-identity aimed at violating the infra-identity, on the basis of the mutual confidence of different participants (individuals, communities, states) in the construction of the same social, economic and political Community.

It is, therefore, of the utmost importance to understand how to set this minimum standard in the employment and social protection sectors,[14] knowing that in order to be shared and efficient, such a minimum cannot annul the European acquisitions in terms of welfare and fundamental social rights. Conversely it must be used to support smooth and fair labour-market functioning.

Should the European economic-social convergence process take place in the absence of agreement on such a hard 'core', with only the second phase of mutual recognition remaining, the competitive game between country systems in European labour markets and welfare states would lead to a 'minimum of minima'; although this would not represent an unacceptable lack of civil cohesion or a situation of 'social dumping', as this minimum would correspond to a standard of workers' dignity and safety guaranteed by the laws of the least protective country in Europe.

Theoretically, there are various alternatives for the identification of the minimum threshold in European labour markets and welfare states. A first alternative consists of setting minimum standards through a selective harmonization process, with a Community-level concertation between the representatives of the European institutions, national governments and social parties. A second might derive from a mediation between member states through benchmarking aimed at identifying 'good or best practices' under the hypothesis of transferability. Something of this kind is underway,[15] although inspired by different purposes, through the method known as open coordination in keeping with the Lisbon strategy.[16] A third possibility consists of referring to already-existing common rules in the European Union, with reference to the labour market and social protection: the alternatives range from the very wide so-called *acquis communautaire*[17] – including the whole body of political and legal frameworks arising in the European Union in this area – to the narrower set established in the Charter of Fundamental Rights of the European Union,[18] to a possibly intermediate one, such as the Community Charter of Workers' Fundamental Social Rights,[19] or the European Social Charter.[20] If the *acquis communautaire* seems excessive as a minimum threshold on which mutual recognition should be based – and, moreover, there are too many elements in it contrasting with this principle – the recent Charter of Fundamental Rights risks being insufficient because it is too concise and ambiguous. Consider, for example, the difficulties of interpretation raised in a multi-ethnic and multi-religious society by its Art. 3, point 1, stating that 'everyone has the right to respect for his or her physical and mental integrity'. So, would those who draw inspiration from the so-called Jewish-Christian tradition be ready to respect the choice of infibulation? And why should one consider circumcision more acceptable, which is practiced by Jews and Muslims? And should not the latter have some doubts about the mental integrity of those who base their deepest love belief on a cruel act such as crucifixion?

Proposals for the introduction of mutual recognition in European labour markets and welfare states

The principle of mutual recognition is sometimes used or proposed with reference to the free circulation of human capital in European markets. Examples are in the areas of University and higher education curricula and diplomas, in professional qualifications as well as in taxation.[21] Its adoption in these fields favours – as pointed out in other chapters of this volume – the quality and the quantity of human capital. In particular, the self-employed are encouraged to move and be active within the European Union. As we have already explained, the current situation is totally different for employees, who represent the majority in the employment pool. This is why the present analysis concentrates on the potential utilization of the principle of mutual recognition more generally on the labour market and on social protection, the two being, for intuitive reasons, strictly related one to the other.

But, first, let us recall that there already exist a few examples in Europe of factual adoption of the principle of mutual recognition both in healthcare and in pension schemes, even though this is by no means the general rule. The latter is mainly found in Council Regulations no. 1408/71 and 574/72,[22] which concern social protection of employees, the self-employed and members of their families moving within the European Union.

In particular, two criteria are usually followed in European welfare states: 'affiliation' and 'totalization'. According to the former, the worker's treatment is disciplined under the legislation of one Member State; namely, the State where the individual is working[23] (even though he/she resides in another Member State). This means that, for the whole working period in one European country, contributions are paid and rights are acquired on the basis of the legislation enforced in that country.

This goes alongside the 'totalization' of the years of contribution paid throughout the whole individual life-cycle, so as to satisfy the conditions for entitlement to benefits in kind or in cash.[24] Art. 25 of the 1971 Regulation states that persons resigning from their jobs are subject to the legislation of the Member State in whose territory they reside. Art. 10 adds that 'with regard to invalidity benefits, old-age and survivors' pensions, acquired under the legislation of one or more Member States, they shall not be subject to any reduction, modification, suspension, withdrawal or confiscation'; and the recipients will not be penalized by the fact that they might reside in the territory of a Member State other than that in which the institution responsible for payment is located. Art. 19 says that, with regard to sickness and maternity benefits, European workers 'residing in the territory of a Member State other than the competent State' or who are abroad or wish to receive medical treatment elsewhere, are entitled to obtain benefits in kind or cash in a Member State other than the competent state under specific circumstances and according to specific modalities.

Existing general rules for social protection in Europe

Thus, workers moving within the European Union are usually subject to the host State's rules of social protection in general and of healthcare and pension schemes in particular, but their past contribution history is considered. This partial recognition of the worker's origin perhaps paves the way to the possible creation of a welfare system fully based on mutual recognition, which would enable not only contributions but also all the social protection eligibility criteria and benefit formulas enforced in the country of origin to maintain their validity in the destination state. In any case, the general principle of continuity, valid for all welfare instruments, marks a fundamental step in European legislation, as it lays the basis for labour mobility within the Community, without penalizing Union workers and without compromising their social security benefits. In particular, Title III 'Special provisions relating to the various categories of benefits' states this continuity criterion in the European citizen's active life-cycle: the whole working history (spent in whichever Member State of Europe) is considered, while evaluating the eligibility and contributive conditions for sickness and maternity benefits, invalidity and old-age transfers, survivors' pensions, benefits in respect to work accidents and occupational diseases, death grants, unemployment benefits and family allowances. This principle of continuity has two consequences. Firstly, in the case of social benefits covering specific risks (death grants, sickness benefits, occupational diseases or unemployment benefits), and general risks for which special benefits are provided without a fair actuarial basis contribution, the member state in which the worker is active upon the emerging of the circumstance is responsible for the payment of the whole benefit. Secondly, for funded benefits closely linked to the contributions paid by each worker, the minimum eligibility requisites must take due account of the whole active life, though it is up to each Member State to take economic responsibility for the benefit payment in proportion to the working-life portion which the citizen spent in that specific state.

The 1971 Council Regulation also comprises specific rules (Title II, 'Determination of the legislation applicable') in favour of employees temporarily posted to another member state.[25] The posting duration is important as, if the period of posting abroad does not exceed 12 months, it creates a situation which derogates to the general rule whereby, with regard to social protection,[26] employees and the self-employed are subject to the legislation of the Member State where they carry out their activities. In fact, posted employees are insured in their home Member State and continue to pay their mandatory social security contributions to their home State; however, they are entitled to all healthcare benefits in kind in the country where they work irrespective of their transferring their residence or not, and to receive the family allowances in the country where they are insured irrespective of their families' place of residence.

It already appears that, in spite of the general regulation on social protection which usually applies the host-country criteria, there are some noticeable derogations. Few additional traces of mutual recognition exist in some European healthcare and pension rules, and we now discuss these particular sectors.

Healthcare

Within the European Union, the National Health System (NHS) is the exclusive responsibility of Member States, on the basis of the principle of subsidiarity and of other norms stated in the Amsterdam Treaty. However, the Community legislation on the Single Market and some recent rulings of the European Court of Justice (the 1998 *Kohll* and *Decker* judgments and the 2001 *Smits-Peerbooms* judgment)[27] significantly influence NHS policies.

In each Member State, the NHS consists of many sub-markets subject to the European rules on the four fundamental freedoms of persons, capital, goods and services. While the impact of Union regulation has always been felt, to some extent, in the supply of healthcare services from the viewpoint of the means of production (for example, rules concerning the partially free movement of pharmaceuticals or the ongoing process regarding mutual recognition of University diplomas and medical staff), up to the 1998 *Kohll–Decker* rulings the performance of healthcare from the viewpoint of demand, namely of patients, has not been a central part of European Union legislation.

To facilitate the free movement of workers,[28] Regulations 1408/71 and 574/72 envisage a coordination of Member States' NHS. In particular, they foresee the following:

- cross-country commuting workers and the members of their families are entitled to receive healthcare both in their home country and in their host country;
- European Union citizens requiring medical attention for emergency reasons may have access to the NHS of Member States during any temporary stays abroad; and
- an individual from one Member State is entitled to medical support on the same basis as nationals in another Member State if authorized by the competent institution in his/her own State.

In these three situations, the cost of the treatment is covered initially by the Member State providing it, and then later refunded by the home country. The host-country principle is enforced, as the citizen is treated according to the conditions and tariffs of the destination state and not according to the modalities of the sending State NHS (otherwise, there would be mutual recognition of the NHS). This setting is, however, strongly undermined by the two recent judgments of the Court mentioned above.

In the *Kohll–Decker* rulings, the ECJ awarded two Luxembourg citizens the right to obtain reimbursement for healthcare services provided in another Member State on the basis of the reimbursement tariff applicable in their home country, without prior authorization having been given by these individuals' health insurance fund. The rulings also declared that the prior authorization system constituted a barrier to the four freedoms (the ECJ considers medical treatment as a service) and that Regulation 1408/71, though remaining in force, is not an exhaustive list of all cases when European citizens may have access to the NHS of other Member States.

Thus, for the time being, there is a double reimbursement system for medical costs paid in Member States other than those of 'affiliation':

- Regulation 1408/71 states that costs must be reimbursed according to the tariffs of the country where medical treatment is provided;
- the *Kohll–Decker* ECJ rulings envisage that costs must be reimbursed according to the tariffs of the home country.

These rulings apparently imply a principle of mutual recognition because, according to the procedure created by the ECJ, patients are not integrated in the host-country NHS, but they are treated abroad following the modality and tariffs of their own NHS.

The subsequent *Smits-Peerbooms* judgment of July 2001 – concerning the cases of two Dutch citizens who received medical treatment abroad without prior agreement from their healthcare providers – presents two distinct aspects. On the one hand, it reiterates that the rules on the free movement of services also concern medical treatment and services in kind, and that prior authorization is justified so as to enable member states to have an adequate planning of medical care activities, but, on the other hand, it is more innovative: indeed, the Court clarified the conditions under which prior authorization must be granted, thus narrowing the ample discretion competent bodies have had before. According to the 2001 ECJ ruling, granting authorization is no longer an exception but the rule; as for all medical treatment considered 'normal' at an international level, it may only be refused whenever the NHS of 'affiliation' can provide the same or equally effective service without undue delay or lengthy waiting lists.

Admittedly, the recent developments on the free movement of patients within the European Union, on the one hand, give hope to the adoption of the principle of mutual recognition, but, on the other hand, they require a legal intervention aimed at consistently and unambiguously specifying the conditions under which the authorization to be treated abroad must be granted.[29]

Mandatory pension schemes

The criteria of 'affiliation' and 'totalization', when applied to mandatory pensions, imply that a worker receives the benefit from each country where he/she was insured for at least one year. Each Member State calculates the overall pension benefits a worker can obtain on the basis of its own legislation, after a number of years of contribution equalling the overall seniority reached in all Member States and pays the pension share corresponding to the years spent on its own territory. A worker is entitled to single pension shares whenever he/she has satisfied the conditions (in terms of age and seniority) foreseen by each state legislation. The computation of the theoretical pension benefit is based on wages (or contributions, if national legislations envisage so) paid in each of the member states where the worker was insured, as if the worker had completed his/her whole insurance record in that country. However, the formula to revaluate wages or contributions is the one adopted in his/her country of origin according to various ECJ rulings (among which C-251/94 and C-31-32-33/96): in this case the continuity principle becomes close to that of mutual recognition.

On the basis of the above-mentioned Regulations of 1971 and 1972, of later amendments,[30] updating or extensions[31] of those provisions and of the ECJ rulings expressed through the years, one might describe in detail the mechanisms of mandatory pension schemes and their coverage for workers moving within the European Union. In particular, the most important rules concern the retirement age, the prerequisites – in terms of minimum contribution years – for pension entitlement, the general benefit formula and any minimum floor or maximum ceiling imposed on it, and finally the possibility of accumulating pension benefits with other incomes.

With regard to the first point, the effective retirement age is the one set in the host country, where the concerned person works. However, if he/she has worked in a country where the pension age is higher (lower), the right to the pension benefit or rather the pension share acquired in that country is available only upon reaching the age requisites foreseen in that State.[32]

The adoption of the 'totalization' criterion enables the contribution years paid in other Member States to be taken into account, should the insurance period in a state be insufficient[33] for entitlement to pension benefits (as confirmed by many ECJ rulings; for example, the recent judgment C-55/00 of 15 January 2002). This does not hold true for seniority pensions; that is, pension benefits based on a minimum number of contribution years. However, the Draft Reform on the coordination of pension schemes submitted by the Commission in 1998 (COM(98) 779) states that the area of application of Community provisions also be enlarged to pre-retirement pension schemes.

With regard to any possible minimum floor of pension benefits, the host-country legislation prevails. Indeed, the sum of the pensions due by the various Member States cannot fall short of the minimum amount foreseen by the State of residence, provided at least a share of the overall pension benefit was acquired in it (Art. 49). Conversely, the legislation of the country with the most generous pension scheme among those where the working activity has been carried out prevails for the application of the upper limit. Indeed, the Union provisions impose that the overall pension benefits do not exceed the highest theoretical amount which would be reached had the pensioner worked throughout his/her whole life in one single country and, in particular, in the country with the most advantageous scheme.

Regarding the possibility of accumulating pensions and labour incomes, the reduction, suspension or withdrawal clauses foreseen by the legislation of one Member State may be invoked to retirees even in the case of benefits in kind or cash obtained in another Member State (Art. 12). A derogation to that principle is found in Art. 46, whereby the reduction, suspension and withdrawal clauses cannot be applied whenever the benefit is computed *pro rata*, a method which must always be adopted if it guarantees a larger benefit as against a formula taking account of the legislation of only one Member State (on these aspects see also, among others, the ECJ judgment C-107/00 of 7 March 2002).

Supplementary pension schemes

Apart from mandatory pensions, voluntary insurance schemes have been a topic of debate in the European Union since the early 1990s, because the issue crosses many areas, from capital markets to welfare, from the transferability of vested rights to labour mobility. Art. 9 of Council Regulation no. 1408/71 states that:

> the provisions of the legislation of any Member State which make admission to voluntary or optional continued insurance conditional upon residence in the territory of the State shall not apply to persons resident in another Member State, provided that at some time in their past working life they were subject to the legislation of the first State as employee or self-employed persons ... [and besides] ... where under the legislation of a Member State, admission to voluntary or optional continued insurance is conditional upon completion of a period of insurance, the periods of insurance or residence completed under the legislation of another Member State shall be taken into account, to the extent required as if they were completed under the legislation of the first State.

This article, using the continuity principle in a way close to the home-country mechanism, mirrors the will to eliminate any obstacle to labour mobility due to the different functioning of supplementary pension schemes in Europe, thus trying to avoid the risk that the various systems 'do not speak at all with each other'. The latest proposals of the European Commission on this subject go further – although with some ambiguity – stressing the fact that the worker should be entitled to maintain the voluntary pension scheme in the Member State which he/she has originally chosen, irrespective of his/her movements within the Union. The initial supplementary pension fund is very often located in the home State, where most workers are likely to start their careers, precisely as stated by the principle of mutual recognition.

Many rules and regulations have been issued in the European Union on supplementary pensions, and they have determined some necessary but not sufficient conditions for the introduction of the principle of mutual recognition on voluntary pensions. In this area, the introduction of this principle should be even easier[34] than in mandatory pensions, as complementary ones are a form of financial saving and should share all the advantages that capital has through the smooth-functioning Single Market.

The Commission took its first initiative on voluntary pension schemes on 21 October 1991, through a Draft Directive on freedom to manage and invest pension fund contributions. The proposal was pursuing the target of strengthening free-capital circulation, which at the time was scarce in member states. However, the times were not ripe for a positive solution and the proposal was withdrawn after three years' frantic discussions.

On 17 December 1994, the Commission published a Communication titled *A Single Market for Pension Funds*, but on petition of the French government this was annulled by the ECJ on 20 March 1997 as unsuitable to impose obligations on member states.

The first fundamental step in the Community-level organization of supplementary pension schemes came on 10 June 1997, with the publication by the European Commission of the *Green Paper on Supplementary Pensions in the Single Market.*[35] This document is a well-organized and pragmatic survey, and in it the Commission for the first time clearly encourages the development of pillar 2 in the construction of European pension systems. In particular, it sets some guidelines which should be followed at both legal and economic levels, in order to prompt the gradual liberalization of pension funds and investments carried out for social security goals, taking due account of the connected labour market variables.[36] The Commission identifies two main obstacles: the first concerns the complexity of the prerequisites for eligibility to a supplementary pension scheme, for example the (long) minimum contribution period; while the second is a fiscal problem regarding the differential tax treatment[37] on pension incomes which the same worker might receive from funded insurance schemes operating in different Member States.

The first Community Directive on voluntary pension schemes was issued on 29 June 1998 (Council Directive no. 98/49/EC), intended to safeguard the supplementary pension rights of employed and self-employed persons moving within the Community. In its fundamental Articles (Arts. 4, 5 and 6),[38] it aimed at eliminating the obstacles hampering the free movement of workers, while underlining the importance of maintaining pension rights built up through both voluntary and mandatory pension schemes.

Subsequently, on 11 May 1999, the Commission Communication *Towards a Single Market for Supplementary Pensions* (COM(99)134) surveyed many relevant aspects for pension funds, including workers' freedom to choose the managing service-provider in any preferred state of the Union, and the equality of treatment for equivalent products offered by different providers. An analysis is suggested based on performance, guarantees, exposure and activity management supplied by pension funds. A coordination of supplementary pension schemes similar to the one already adopted for pillar 1 is proposed for migrant workers within the Union, together with the elimination of all possible penalizations to transfers of accumulated capitals; a gradual fiscal treatment convergence of supplementary pension schemes and of other forms of insurance investments is suggested; and the convergence of the conditions to build up pension rights is examined. Overall, the spirit of this Communication seems much nearer to the harmonization approach[39] than to the mutual recognition principle.

In October 2000, the European Commission proposed another Directive on the activities of the Institution for Occupational Retirement Provisions (IORP), with the aim of guaranteeing a high level of protection for pensioners, creating a Single Market for financial services and complementary pensions and eliminating obstacles to the cross-border provision of professional pensions. Supervision is left to the authorities of the state where the pension fund is located, not necessarily that of the country of work.

The Draft Directive was followed on 14 April 2001 by a Commission Communication (COM(2001)214) on the elimination of tax obstacles to the cross-border provision of occupational pensions, where the need to have a fully functioning Single Market for occupational pensions is stressed. As outlined in the Communication, the tax treatment of occupational pensions in different member states is very different in terms of the deduction of contributions and benefit taxation, and might give rise to double-taxation problems in the case of workers' mobility within the Union.[40] Furthermore, there are relevant differences in the tax treatment of pension funds according to whether they are national or established in another Member State,[41] which is a violation[42] of the principle of free circulation of workers, services and capital (apart from goods). From this viewpoint, the Commission advocates[43] a convergence towards EET schemes (Exempt contributions, Exempt investment income and capital gains of pension funds, Taxed benefits), which are prevailing among Member States.[44]

On June 5 2002 the ECOFIN Council reached a political agreement on the Commission Draft Directive of October 2000. In such an agreement, according to an expert's view (Capuano, 2002),[45] 'the Directive is an instrument of minimum harmonization between different complementary pension systems and tends to reach the result that all Member States adopt a common set of rules in management and control of the pension funds'. It is clear even from this wording that there is a lot of ambiguity in the ECOFIN position because, while the 'minimum harmonization' approach is consistent with the first step of mutual recognition, the 'common set of rules' is likely to be opposite to it. In any case, it appears really relevant in a mutual recognition perspective, that all European institutions seem to agree nowadays on the necessity to 'allow workers to be free, if they so wish, to choose pension funds in countries different from the one where they work, under the conditions allowed in the Directive and in national norms'.

Summarizing, as far as European complementary pensions are concerned, four major goals appear to exist in the Union at the moment: first, to identify the measures for the 'coexistence' of heterogeneous schemes (for instance, eliminating a possible differential (and double) taxation); secondly, to make supplementary pension funds consistent with free-capital circulation; thirdly, to make them consistent with the free movement of workers; and, finally, to let them be an instrument to free the welfare state from obligations which European public finances are unable to sustain in the forms and ways adopted so far for mandatory pensions. It is extremely important, in our opinion, that the Commission intends to make the portability of supplementary pension schemes set up in the country of origin during intra-Community movements really effective and inexpensive. If and when the process of mutual recognition of supplementary pension systems were to be completed, participation in pillar 2 would not be interrupted by mobility reasons and the insured worker would know that benefits only depend on the amount and on the period of contributions. This should avoid all the problems and costs connected to the transfer of individual positions from one pension scheme to another. Admittedly, portability would remain on a voluntary basis and workers might give up whenever they wish.

The creation in Europe of supplementary pension systems where workers have the option to maintain pillar 2 in their home countries corresponds to the introduction on a European scale of the principle of mutual recognition in this area. The consistency of the Union legislation on mandatory and on supplementary pension schemes seems very important in the long and medium term. Normally, pillar 2 is connected, in its structure, in its functioning and sometimes in the determination of the levels of the involved variables, to pillar 1 and to labour market regulation. Therefore a question emerges: is the long or medium-run portability of supplementary pension funds, as it is conceived by the Commission, really feasible or shouldn't some sort of portability of rights be extended to mandatory pensions, and to healthcare and labour-market variables as well?

In our opinion, an overall and thorough reform project based on the principle of mutual recognition should necessarily tackle, sooner or later, the whole employment problem as much as the welfare state. Smaller steps are, however, welcome in the short run, either in terms of fields of application (for example we can start with healthcare and complementary pension rules) or in terms of eligibility criteria (for example mutual recognition could be initially adopted only for those employees at a professional level comparable to the self-employed professionals who already benefit from these mutual recognition provisions), or in terms of number of partners involved (a strengthened cooperation in these sectors seems easier to begin in countries like the United Kingdom or Ireland, where the welfare states' competition is more appreciated).

Classical unemployment and labour mobility

We have seen that mutual recognition is not the general rule in social protection policies, but it is not even excluded from Community standards and in some cases it is even adopted. On the contrary, according to the present European legislation, mutual recognition is absolutely banned in the labour area. Thus, we deal with this problem as an area of potential reform, as the principle of mutual recognition may prove more effective than the current host-country approach to increase Union workers' mobility and employment, and to raise efficiency and equity at the same time. Indeed, this is what happens if the following three, very plausible, assumptions hold true: (a) in every European country there is some weak component of the labour force (some region, some gender, age or skill group) which is unemployed; (b) unemployment is everywhere mainly of a classical kind, namely due to a lack of entrepreneurial profitability (an excess of labour costs, due to wage and regulatory rigidities); and (c) only job-seekers are ready to migrate, provided they find a job in the receiving country. Under these hypotheses, as we shall stress later through a very simple model, the adoption of the principle of mutual recognition in European labour markets increases the mobility of the (classical) unemployed, raises labour-market competition and reduces unemployment, while importing some flexibility into European countries with relatively higher wages and more rigid regulation.

Mutual recognition and labour market rigidities: a theoretical model

The objective of the following theoretical model is to examine the impact on labour-force mobility and consequently on employment, of adoption in the labour market of two alternative principles, namely the *host*-State and the *home*-State approaches, among Union countries all suffering some (classical) unemployment, but differing in their wage and regulatory rigidities.

Consider the case of two European countries, *A* and *B*, having heterogeneous labour market and welfare settings, and suppose that country *A* (for example Italy) is characterized by high real wages and regulatory rigidities (particularly, overprotection on hiring and firing), while country *B* (Ireland, for instance) is characterized by flexibility and lower wage costs. It is well-known, even at an intermediate textbook level such as Blanchard's,[46] that there exists a one-to-one correspondence between real wage and regulatory rigidities (Blanchard's Z factor), in terms of their implications on labour costs and consequently on classical unemployment. From this viewpoint, Italy and Ireland are chosen because they are, to some extent, polar cases of rigidities[47] in Europe, as indicated by Table 5.1.

Turning now to examine a less-specific case than the one described so far, consider the worker *M* of a generic country *K* and the worker *N* of a

Table 5.1 Labour-market regulatory rigidities and unemployment

Country	*Average and standardized unemployment rate 2000 (1)*	*Nickell indicator based on the rigiditiy of 'labour standards'*[b] *1989–94 (2)*	*EPL indicator of rigidity in the OECD version 1*[c] *Late 1980s (3)*	*Late 1990s (4)*	*Freyssinet indicator of rigidity in the OECD version 2*[d] *Late 1990s (5)*
EU-14[a]	*(VII) 7.2*	...	...	...	...
Belgium	*(VIII)* 7.0	*(IV)* 4	*(VI)* 3.1	*(VIII)* 2.1	*(VII)* 2.5
Denmark	*(XI)* 4.7	*(V)* 2	*(X)* 2.1	*(X)* 1.2	*(XI)* 1.5
Germany	*(VI)* 7.9	*(II)* 6	*(V)* 3.2	*(VI)* 2.5	*(VI)* 2.6
Greece	*(II)* 11.4	...	*(III)* 3.6	*(II)* 3.6	*(II)* 3.5
Spain	*(I)* 14.1	*(I)* 7	*(II)* 3.7	*(IV)* 3.1	*(IV)* 3.1
France	*(V)* 9.5	*(II)* 6	*(VII)* 2.7	*(V)* 3.0	*(V)* 2.8
Ireland	*(XII)* 4.2	*(IV)* 4	*(XI)* 0.9	*(XI)* 0.9	*(XII)* 1.1
Italy	*(III)* 10.5	*(I)* 7	*(I)* 4.1	*(III)* 3.3	*(III)* 3.4
The Netherlands	*(XV)* 2.9	*(III)* 5	*(VII)* 2.7	*(VIII)* 2.1	*(IX)* 2.2
Portugal	*(XIII)* 4.1	*(IV)* 4	*(I)* 4.1	*(I)* 3.7	*(I)* 3.7
United Kingdom	*(X)* 5.5	*(VI)* 0	*(XII)* 0.5	*(XII)* 0.5	*(XIII)* 0.9
Austria	*(XIV)* 3.7	*(III)* 5	*(IX)* 2.2	*(VII)* 2.2	*(VIII)* 2.3
Finland	*(IV)* 9.7	*(III)* 5	*(VIII)* 2.3	*(IX)* 2.0	*(X)* 2.1
Sweden	*(IX)* 5.9	*(I)* 7	*(IV)* 3.5	*(VII)* 2.2	*(VI)* 2.6
(for reference only)					
United States	4.0	2	0.2	0.2	0.7
Japan	4.7	1	...	2.4	2.3

Sources and Notes:

[a] Luxembourg is not taken into account because there are no data on its labour-market rigidity. For data on unemployment in the year 2000 see OECD, *Economic Outlook*, vol. 2, no. 70, December 2001. The notation ... means unavailable data. European countries' rankings are written in italics in parenthesis in every column. All regulatory rigidities in Table 5.1 refer to private employment. For corresponding indicators in the public-sector European labour markets, see ISAE, Abridged Quarterly Report, April 2002.

[b] See Nickell, S., 'Unemployment and Labor Market Rigidities: Europe *vs.* North America', *Journal of Economic Perspective*, vol. 11, no. 3, Summer 1997, based on OECD, *Jobs Study*, Paris, 1994. This is a synthetic indicator on the rigidity of the legal framework on private employment. Its maximum value is 10 and it refers to 5 dimensions, namely working time, fixed-term contracts, labour protection, minimum wage and workers' bargaining rights. Each of those items has a value.

[c] Ranging between 0 (no legislation) and 2 (strict legislation): values are cumulated.

[d] See OECD, *Perspectives de l'Emploi*, Paris, 1999. This is computed as the average of the indicators referring to regular contracts (procedure difficulties, pre-notice and indemnity applicable to individual firings, firing difficulties) and to fixed-term contracts (full-time or part-time). EPL means employment protection legislation. See Freyssinet, J., 'La Réduction du Taux de Chômage: les Enseignements des Expériences Européennes', in Conseil d'Analyse Economique (ed.), *Réduction du chômage: les réussites en Europe*, Paris, 2000.

generic country *J*. The combinations of wage and regulatory rigidities analysed in the two countries are four[48]: each country can face a situation of rigidity with overprotection and high wages or of flexibility with softer regulation and lower wage costs. Unemployment is supposed to be of a classical nature,[49] being caused by rigid labour costs, independent of the unemployment rate. By assumption, some unemployment emerges in every European country even in the most flexible. Job-seekers are ready to move, provided they find a job, that is provided there exists a positive labour demand for them, as their reservation wage is assumed to be, in every country, lower than the market wage offered to them in any other European country (hence there always exists a positive labour supply – with migration – on the part of the unemployed).

Mobility here is analysed both under the host-State principle – that is, the European *status quo* – and under the home-State principle – that is, when the principle of mutual recognition is potentially adopted. If the host-State principle holds true, the scheme illustrated in Figure 5.1 emerges in the labour demand and supply game.

The cases along the main diagonal (top left – bottom right) identify situations of non-mobility, where the choice between home- and host-State principles is by definition immaterial, because the two countries are the mere image one of the other (either both rigid or both flexible): the positive labour supply (given the status of unemployed in the worker's country of origin) is counterbalanced by the null demand, as there is an excessive labour supply in the country of destination. Off-diagonal, on the contrary, no movement is observed but for different reasons: job-seekers would be ready to move and also to work in the country where protection and wages are lower than in their home country (*a fortiori* in the country where wages and protections are higher);

Worker *M* / Country *K*	**Worker *N* / Country *J*:** *High wages High protection*		*Low wages Low protection*	
High wages High protection	*M* (positive supply, null demand) no movement	*N* (positive supply, null demand) no movement	*M* (positive supply, null demand) no movement	*N* (positive supply, null demand) no movement
Low wages Low protection	*M* (positive supply, null demand) no movement	*N* (positive supply, null demand) no movement	*M* (positive supply, null demand) no movement	*N* (positive supply, null demand) no movement

Figure 5.1 Labour demand and supply and labour mobility under the host-state principle (current situation)

		Worker *N* Country *J*			
		High wages High protection		*Low wages Low protection*	
Worker *M* Country *K*	*High wages High protection*	*M* (positive supply, null demand) no movement	*N* (positive supply, null demand) no movement	*M* (positive supply, null demand) no movement	*N* (positive supply, positive demand) movement
	Low wages Low protection	*M* (positive supply, positive demand) movement	*N* (positive supply, null demand) no movement	*M* (positive supply, null demand) no movement	*N* (positive supply, null demand) no movement

Figure 5.2 Labour demand and supply and labour mobility under the home-State principle (potential mutual recognition situation)

however, given that, once they move, they are treated as national workers of the host country (where by assumption there already exists some classical unemployment), there is no labour demand for them as there is no demand for the unemployed national labour force. Thus, under these hypotheses, the host-State principle never helps job-seekers to find a job through mobility, and consequently mobility is not observed.

If, however, the principle of mutual recognition were applied, the demand and supply game would be the one indicated by Figure 5.2.

In this event, too, along the main diagonal (top left–bottom right) there are situations of non-mobility for reasons similar to those listed before: the worker brings all his/her characteristics with him/her, which coincide with those of the host State. But now there is a difference on some of the off-diagonal cases: if the job-seeker of a low-wage/low-protection country moves to look for a job in the country where wage and regulatory rigidities are higher, by carrying along the labour-market conditions of his/her home state, he/she would get a job, because the receiving country's employers would find it profitable to hire newcomers at lower wages and protections than those holding in the host State, which is also in classical unemployment. Thus, there would be labour mobility, overall employment would grow, and unemployment would decrease.

Hence, thanks to the principle of mutual recognition, not only would the classical unemployed of a flexible European country be hired elsewhere, but this would take place by raising competition and importing flexibility in rigid Union countries, thus leading to a maximization of employment of people whose home countries are more flexible than the average in Europe.[50] It is very likely that in the medium–long run the adoption of the principle of mutual recognition in European labour markets and welfare states would induce the national (classical) unemployed of the receiving countries to ask to be non-discriminated against, and to be treated as immigrants coming from more flexible Member States. Therefore, under the mutual recognition assumption, initially the Irish unemployed would be hired in Italy under Irish conditions, while later the Italian unemployed would look for and find an employment opportunity in Italy under Irish conditions. In the end, classical unemployment would tend to decline and possibly to disappear. Thus, one might say that 'initially, workers of different nationality with different labor contract and social security provision would be found within the same firm. Soon, however, each worker, regardless of nationality and residence, would be likely to begin to shop around for the best labor contract and social security provision.'[51] The principle of mutual recognition in European labour markets and welfare states, therefore, would imply a positive-sum game, whereby losers could be subsidized by winners. This contrasts with the outcome of the host-State approach, where no advantage emerges in labour mobility, and no possibility exists of decreasing classical unemployment through migration.

Policy conclusions

We have carried out a law and economics analysis of the impact of the potential (and sometimes factual) introduction of the principle of mutual recognition in the European labour markets and welfare states.

Up to now, the principle of mutual recognition has been fully or partially adopted in Europe in three of the four areas of the fundamental freedoms envisaged by the Treaty, with relevant implications for the elimination of trade barriers and for the circulation of goods, services and capital. Since the 1979 *Cassis de Dijon* judgment and its aftermath, competition between similar but not identical commodities has been spreading and this has caused various effects which, from the viewpoint of an economist, are perfectly expected – namely, price-reduction, quality-improvement and quantity-enhancement. Perhaps this has damaged some producers, but it certainly has increased efficiency together with equity, definitely to the advantage of consumers' well-being. Admittedly, what is interesting is that all these excellent results have been obtained without asking different countries to give up their revealed preferences expressed in their regulations and laws. Each country may keep its own rules, but it cannot refuse to allow – according to the principle of mutual recognition – not only different rules enforced elsewhere, but also that those same rules have to be accepted for imported products and services, provided the latter are not harmful to health, to the natural and artistic environment and the like, the only possible derogations being 'emergency reasons'. Therefore, if one proves that *Cassis de Dijon* does not damage French consumers' health, German consumers may have their way in determining the alcohol percentage of a beverage, but they cannot hamper the import of French alcoholic beverages to Germany, as what does not harm French drinkers will not damage German drinkers either.

This conclusion, once generalized, shows two elements: first, in the transfer of commodities and services within Europe, mutual recognition makes the home-State rules more important than those of the host-State, while a Single Market practically exists already for capital; second, mutual recognition – that is the mutual acceptance of one's diversity – is based on a minimum threshold of common laws and principles which, in the case of *Cassis de Dijon,* concern the safeguard of people's health, assumed to be a shared value in equivalent if not identical ways everywhere in the Union.

On the contrary, in one of the four sectors of the European fundamental freedoms (namely, in the labour market) mutual recognition is not only ignored, but it is banned as 'social dumping', while the opposite principle – so-called 'equal treatment' – is adopted in spite of the fact that mutual recognition might give rise to much fairer treatment. Nowadays, European workers moving to a different Member State are granted the right to be fully assimilated with host state nationals, while they are not entitled to maintain their identities created in their home State. They have no right to diversity in the receiving country, assimilation being their only option: indeed, on the basis of the current interpretation of the European Treaty, any form of employment, remuneration or protection condition different for workers residing in the same Member State on grounds of different nationalities is considered discriminatory. Hence, equality of treatment is set not for all those who are born in the same Member State, but for all those who are working in the same country, with full identity in terms of labour and social protection, between law and localization. It is as if the old alternative between *ius loci* and *ius sanguinis* has emerged again in a new way, with a systematic prevalence of the former. ECJ rulings have always corroborated this stand, repressing any competition in European labour markets due, for example, to different wages or different welfare instruments (and the two are clearly interconnected), as if it were unfair.

In our opinion, this approach is out of keeping with Delors' White Paper on the internal market[52] when it states that free movement cannot be limited in any sector within the European Union, while 'the immediate and full recognition of different quality standards, of different legislations ... must be the rule'. If this holds true for goods, services and capital, it must hold true for human capital as well, particularly in a European area where fundamental social rights are similar everywhere, as they represent a solid standard network where nobody falls short of the minimum threshold. Indeed, there are some fields of human capital where mutual recognition has already been adopted or at least has already been proposed by European institutions (for example, in the equivalence of professional qualifications of the self-employed, or in some complementary pension and healthcare rules) because these fields are considered parts of the service or capital markets. But the contiguity between the status of the self-employed and those employed, or between complementary and mandatory pensions, is so big that it appears impossible to avoid at least asking what would be the potential effect of using the principle of mutual recognition more generally in European labour markets and welfare states.

What would be the correspondent of the minimum threshold, were the principle of mutual recognition applied to the labour market and social protection in Europe? The minimum 'core' should regard labour incomes and pensions, working time, holidays, maternity and sickness leaves, besides other fundamental benefits and social rights. There are many ways to define the minimum threshold, for instance one might let the market reach the standards of the most flexible European country through competitive pressures, or one might use already existing common rules belonging to the wider set of the *acquis communautaire*, or one could adopt a system of limited negotiations between countries, just as is happening after the Lisbon Summit through open coordination in labour and welfare matters.

There should be a package of rights guaranteed everywhere in Europe, beyond which each country should be left free to rule its own employment and social protection strategies, while respecting those of others, thanks to mutual recognition. Accepting standards beyond the minimum package means that, if the principle of mutual recognition were enforced, a country could employ a worker from another European member state under other than its own conditions, but honouring the sending country's rules and regulations.

A very simple theoretical model was set up with two countries and two conditions for the labour market and welfare state (one with high wages–high regulatory rigidity, the other with low wages–high regulatory flexibility). The model shows the effects obtained in terms of labour mobility and employment by turning from the present system – based on 'equal treatment' (the host-country principle) – to an opposite one – based on mutual recognition (the home-country system) – under the assumption that in all European countries there exist some unemployed of a classical type (due to excessive rigidities) and that job-seekers of a Member State are ready to move to another Member State provided they get a job. One finds that labour mobility in Europe would rise, as would employment. There would be no unequal treatment, because the present concept of 'equal treatment' states that 'all workers living in one country are equal', while the principle of mutual recognition would mean that 'all workers coming from one country are equal'.

In particular, the model illustrates why an unemployed person living in a low-wage and low-protection state nowadays does not move elsewhere in Europe, the reason being that he/she would not find a job. Under the host-country principle there are no reasons for employers in a high-wage and high-protection country to hire foreign workers coming from the rest of Europe, because once they have moved, they become absolutely identical to national workers. For example, Italian employers would never hire Irish job-seekers (though coming from a flexible and low-wage country) under Italian conditions, but they would like to hire them under Irish conditions; namely, under the hypothesis of mutual recognition. Italians would maintain their own rigidities because mutual recognition enables that, but after a while they would possibly change their attitude, particularly under the pressure of the weakest components of the Italian labour force (women, youngsters, southern): indeed, after some time the Italian unemployed also would not accept being 'discriminated' against, compared to Irish job-seekers, and would demand to be treated as any other European unemployed. This should be allowed out of social justice. The principle of mutual recognition would then trigger the paradoxical, and yet hopeful result of stopping the treatment of an active Irish person in Italy as an Italian worker, and eventually treat an active Italian person as an Irish worker (if he/she wishes). Such a system would in the end reduce (perhaps eliminate) European classical unemployment, that is particularly strong in highly rigid countries like Italy.

What is important is that beyond the minimum threshold there would exist in the European labour markets and welfare states a mutual recognition system which would no longer be labelled as 'social dumping' or unfair competition just because it is not welcome by some powerful insiders who are *de facto* rent-seekers. All these people advocating rigidities – irrespective of their intentions to protect the weak brackets of the labour force, but certainly protecting the strong brackets of it; namely, themselves – would oppose the adoption of mutual recognition because this would increase competition in the labour market. This would imply enhancing the well-being of the society as a whole, particularly for the unemployed and first job-seekers, but certainly worsening it for those who already have a job highly protected and well-paid.

Should the principle of mutual recognition be adopted – at least as a worker's right, not as a duty – one would observe that in the same firm of a given European country heterogeneous wage and welfare conditions would be applied to similar workers. This should not raise fears, because it would bring about the exercise of a right and the benefit of being no longer unemployed, at least if the labour force were ready to accept wage and regulatory flexibility.

Orthodox thinkers would pretend that all that is unfair, because living costs are different in different countries, so that in each of them wages should be proportional to prices and social security contributions to benefits. However, if competition fully pervaded the European labour markets and welfare states – as is not the case nowadays, but as would happen as a consequence of mutual recognition – there would be a fall in rigid countries' prices and labour costs, probably a rise in flexible countries' prices and wages, so that this problem would gradually disappear. In any case, in order to reduce the inevitable opposition of conventional wisdom, and especially of insiders of the most rigid countries, one could envisage that mutual recognition might be initially introduced in the European labour markets and welfare states only of a limited number of countries (in strengthened cooperation) and only for some categories of workers and sectors. Indeed, the latter process is already underway for self-employed workers with skills certified by law (doctors or lawyers) and for some components of healthcare and pensions. That formula might initially be extended to employees with qualifications comparable to those of the recalled self-employed (for example to University professors and the like), according to a method of variable geometry.

To conclude, the socio-economic differences one may observe between various European labour markets and welfare states depend on disparities which are not only unavoidable, but which have to be exploited in order to create those opportunities for exchange and competition which are necessary to reduce production costs, raise efficiency, eliminate artificial obstacles to the free movement of workers, increase employment and hence equity, and improve quality of life and well-being particularly for consumers and for the weakest components of the labour force. In the long run, the final result would be an *a posteriori* harmonization of the European labour markets and welfare states reached in a bottom-up process, not in a top-down process as is usually the case with harmonization. Were the principle of mutual recognition applied 'to all sectors', as proposed by the European Commission Communication (1999b), each European citizen might use both the *ius loci* and the *ius sanguinis*, without being always compelled to opt for the former.[53]

Notes

1 Nicolaïdis, K., 'Managed Mutual Recognition: The New Approach to the Liberalization of Professional Services', 2000, available on the website www.ksg.harvard.edu/prg/nicolaidis/managemr.htm#I

2 This wording is traditionally accepted, as stressed for example by Mattera. However, Weiler prefers the term 'functional parallelism', because for imports-exports the existing standards of one Member State have to functionally correspond to those of the others. According to Weiler, this explains 'the practical failure of the principle of mutual recognition. In many cases, there are lines of products created on the basis of regulatory regimes with substantial differences, among which there does not exist a functional parallelism. In this situation, only standard harmonization may solve the question and it cannot be reached through the jurisdictional instruments; moreover, in some cases, the very nature of the product requires one standard for the whole of Europe'. Admittedly, the implicit assumption of the present chapter is different from Weiler's position. See Weiler, J.H.H., 'La costituzione del mercato comune', in M. Cartabia and J.H.H. Weiler (eds), *L'Italia in Europa. Profili istituzionali e costituzionali*, Bologna, Il Mulino, 1997.

3 Court of Justice, *Judgment Rewe-Zentral* (C-120/78), 1979, available on the website http://curia.eu.int/

4 The legal fundaments of the principle of mutual recognition in the commodity and service markets derive from Arts 28–30 (ex Arts 30 and 36) within Part Three – Title I (*Free movement of goods*), Chapter 2 (*Prohibition of quantitative restrictions between Member States*) of the Treaty, which prohibit any restriction on imports and exports or any 'measure having equivalent effect'. Upon initiative of the Commission, in 1983 an agreement between European countries was reached, as set in Directive no. 83/189/EEC, now replaced by the wider Directive no. 98/34/EC of the European Parliament and Council. This started a mutual information and consulting procedure between member states putting the Commission at the centre of the system and having the objective to prevent – upon adoption of technical ruling on the part of Member States – the emerging of any trade barrier undermining Single Market development. In practice, Member States have to notify to Brussels and to

their partners any product which is not mutually recognized, which assumes that renouncing objections on a given product is a signal of readiness to let it be marketed in one's territory.

5 It was not necessary to officially introduce the principle of mutual recognition in capital movements, because capital mobility is almost perfect: its globalization – and the fact that *pecunia non olet* – make it difficult to understand the origin and destination of capital flows and therefore imply that this area is an effective Single Market. On the basis of Arts 56–60 of the Treaty (ex Art. 73 B-73 G), great progress was made to fully attain free capital movement. In particular, Art. 56 prohibits any restriction to capital movements. To this end, for example in the banking sector, Directive no. 89/646/EEC of the Council states the mutual recognition of authorizations. The exceptions to free capital movement are mainly limited to movements with third countries and are subject to Community decisions. Member states – in keeping with Art. 58 letter b of the Treaty (ex Art. 73 D) – maintain the faculty to take all required measures, which are justified on grounds of public policy to prevent infringements of national laws and regulations, in particular in the field of taxation and prudential supervision of financial institutions.

6 Derogations to the principle of mutual recognition and to the consequent free movement of goods depend on justified reasons of public morality, public policy or public security.

7 Some authors, including Pelkmans, identify within the structure of the Treaty of Rome mutual recognition as a negative complementary form of integration rather than as a substitute to harmonization.

8 Commission of the European Communities, *Completing the Internal Market: White Paper from the Commission to the European Council*, COM(85)310 final, 1985.

9 European Council, *Conclusions on Standardization Approved by the Council*, 16 July 1984.

10 Commission of the European Communities, Directorate-General on the Internal Market, *Mutual Recognition in the Context of the Follow-up to the Action Plan for the Single Market*, 16 June 1999, available on the website http://europa.eu.int/comm/internal_market/en/update/general/index. htm

11 The Treaty (Art. 39, ex Art. 48, par. 3) states that Member States may refuse to a Community citizen the right to enter and stay in their territory exclusively on grounds of public policy, public security or public health. With Directive no. 64/221/EEC of February 25 1964 of the Council, and in particular through a number of Court of Justice cases, those limits are strict and well-identified.

12 See Gorce, G. (ed.), *Rapport d'Information Déposé par la Délégation de l'Assemblée Nationale pour l'Union Européenne sur le Dumping Social en Europe*, Paris, Assemblée Nationale, no. 243, 2000, and Marini, P. (ed.), *Rapport d'Information au Nom de la Commission des Finances, du Contrôle Budgétaire et des Comptes Économiques de la Nation sur la Concurrence Fiscale en Europe*, Paris, Sénat, no. 483, 1999.

13 The German Law on Posted Workers envisages that even employers residing outside the area of competence of bargaining agreements must respect statutory minimum standards on minimum wage, minimum length of holidays,

minimum holiday bonuses and on any system of holiday funds (*Urlaubskassen*) for payments of holiday bonuses. This holds true provided those collective bargainings have obtained the so-called *erga omnes* effectiveness. At present, this prerequisite applies to German collective bargaining in the sectors of construction and other construction-related services (electric, fitting, installation, etc.). Any breach of the provisions is punishable as an administrative offence and implies a fine up to 1,000,000 euros. The minimum wage for construction, determined through a Decree law, amount on 1 September 2000 to approximately 37 euros per hour in old Federal *Länder* and to 33 euros per hour in new Federal *Länder*. Since September 2001, it has grown. In 1999, according to the *Bundesanstalt für Arbeit* (Federal Institute of Labour), more than 19,000 proceedings were started for violations to the *Arbeitnehmer-Entsendergesetz*. Fines and penalties amounted to about 152,000,000 euros. Data prove to what extent this law is binding.

14 It would be misleading to face these questions only in terms of wage and job conditions. One should go beyond and tackle problems such as healthcare and pensions at the same time: it is for this very reason that labour-market problems should be dealt with together with social protection issues.

15 This is part of the European employment strategy, initially launched by the European Council during its Luxembourg summit of November 1997. The European Union identified four areas of action (four pillars): improve employability; develop entrepreneurship; encourage firms' and employees' adaptability; strengthen policies for equal opportunities. In 2000, the debate on common social policies became more demanding: responses were the European Councils in Lisbon (March), in Santa Maria de Feira (June) and in Nice (December). In this phase, indicators and benchmarks were fixed to evaluate the situation reached and progress made in each Member State. The Commission's Document drawn up for the European Council in Lisbon proposes quantity objectives not only for employment, but also for social exclusion. In June 2001 all Member States submitted their National Action Plans on Social Inclusion in response to the common objectives on poverty and social exclusion agreed by the European Union at Nice. See European Council, *Community Action Program to Combat Social Exclusion 2002–2006*, Nice, 2000, available on the website http://europa.eu.int/comm/employment_social/soc-prot/soc-incl/ex_prog_en.htm. The Lisbon strategy – which embodies the Koln and Luxembourg processes – represents an important reference point for the innovations in European labour markets and social policies. It is carried out through the 'small-step method' suggested by Jean Monnet at the very beginning of the European creation. But it would be wrong to think that those steps have already triggered a change, as Pelkmans says: 'The Luxembourg process does not really face the legal overprotection of insiders on the labor relevant market and other rigidities, but only identifies the answers to structural unemployment in the development of competencies, employability and active policies'. See Pelkmans, J., *European Integration, Methods and Economic Analysis*, 2nd edn, London, Pearson Education, 2001.

16 Admittedly, since that European Council (March 2000) a series of objectives and priority actions have been fixed for labour and social protection. In

particular, three areas of actions were identified: the development of a competitive and dynamic economy, based on knowledge; the modernization of the European social model, through interventions to enhance human capital quality and to construct an active welfare state (the first objective being to bring the European employment rate from the present figure of 61% to 70%, and the female employment rate from 51% to 60% by 2010); the coordination of macroeconomic policies with the goal of consolidating the public finance equilibrium, guaranteeing its sustainability and improving its quality. See European Council, *Presidency Conclusions*, Lisbon, 2000.

17 The main legal acts to which the *acquis communautaire* may be traced back with reference to employment and social protection policies are the Treaty of Rome (1957); the first Social Action Programme (1974); the Treaty on European Union (1986); the second Social Action Programme and the Community Charter of the Fundamental Workers' Social Rights (European Council, 1989, Community Charter of Fundamental Social Rights for Workers, Strasbourg, 9 December, available on the website www.etuc.org/fundrights/en/resource/ccfsr_.cfm); the Treaty of Maastricht 'Protocol on Social Policy' (1992); the third Social Action Program (1994); the Treaty of Amsterdam (1997).

18 European Parliament, Council and European Commission, *Charter of Fundamental Rights of the European Union*, 2000.

19 European Council, *Community Charter of Fundamental Social Rights for Workers*, Strasbourg, 9 December 1989.

20 Council of Europe, *European Social Charter*, Turin, 18 October 1961.

21 Two opposite fiscal approaches are proposed in Europe, namely the competition-based and the harmonization-based approaches. On the one hand, tax competition *à-la-Tiebout* favours factor mobility and is closer to the mutual recognition viewpoint (See Tiebout, C.M., 'A Pure Theory of Local Expenditures', *Journal of Political Economy*, no. 5, October 1956, available on the website http://www.courses.rochester.edu/caucutt/ECO54/tiebout.pdf); on the other hand, tax harmonization provides Member States 'more effective instruments to fight against erosion' (Commission of the European Communities, *Taxation in the European Union*, SEC(96) 487 final, 1996), though tax coordination at the European level is no easy goal. With regard to corporate taxation, the Stockholm Group – 'The Taxation of the European Company', *mimeo*, 18 May 1999 – outlines that mutual recognition applied to it could be a useful instrument to avoid double taxation, reduce transaction and administrative costs, favour foreign direct investments and growth.

22 An updated version of all the modifications of these Council Regulations can be read in the *Official Journal of the European Commission* no. 28 of 30 January 1997. A simplified description of these provisions is provided in Commission of the European Communities, *The Community Provisions on Social Security – Your Rights when Moving Within the European Union*, Directorate-General for Employment and Social Affairs, 2000.

23 An exception to this rule occurs when the working period abroad lasts less than 12 months and for particular categories of workers: public employees who continue to be covered by their reference administration; people employed on board vessels insured in the state which the ship belongs to;

persons serving in the armed forces; and persons employed by diplomatic missions and consular posts. People usually working in more than one member state are insured with (and thus subject to the legislation of) the member state of residence, if he/she carries out part of his/her work in that country. For workers employed in one state and self-employed in another state, the rules of the state of employment prevail.

24 All contribution periods are considered: those envisaging at least one year of contribution are afferent to the country where they were paid, those with shorter length are afferent to the country where the worker became eligible to pension.

25 A posted employee is a person employed in the territory of a Member State by an undertaking to which he/she is normally attached, whose main location is in the territory of another Member State, to perform work for a maximum period of 12 months; the latter may be prolonged to 24 months in exceptional cases.

26 What is stated here only concerns social protection of posted employees. As for the labour legislation regarding them, the central document is Directive no. 96/71/EC of the European Parliament and of the Council, which gives binding rules on the minimum working conditions which an employer in the host Member State must guarantee to posted temporary employees. The Directive states that the latter have to receive the same employment conditions offered to others in the Member State where the work is carried out (maximum work periods, minimum paid annual holidays, minimum wage, safety and hygiene at work, equality of treatment between men and women etc.); obviously there are no obstacles to supplying even more favourable terms.

27 See European Court of Justice, *Judgment Kohll* (C-158/96), 1998, available on the website http://curia.eu.int/; Court of Justice, *Judgment Decker* (C-120/95), 1998, available on the website http://curia.eu.int/ and Court of Justice, *Judgment Smits-Peerbooms* (C-157/99), 2001, available on the website http://curia.eu.int/

28 In the past there were no European-level initiatives aimed at developing a specific legislation on the distribution of healthcare services for all the population of the Union. Notice that, on the basis of Regulations 1408/71 and 574/72 – except for emergency situations or for situations where a prior authorization was required (and *de facto* this authorization was limited and was under the full discretion of the competent institution of the member country concerned) – the right to access to medical treatment in another Member State derived from the working status of the individual more than from the European citizenship.

29 To enhance the opportunity to receive medical treatment abroad and to overcome the problems stemming from the interpretation of Regulation 1408/71, bilateral agreements were concluded between the Netherlands and Belgium, between Luxembourg and its neighbours and between the United Kingdom and Ireland. The European Union programme INTERREG aims at prompting the economic development of border regions and foresees measures and initiatives to promote cooperation in medical treatment between those regions.

30 A fundamental reform proposal of the 1971 and 1972 Regulations is found in the Commission's Draft COM(98)779, which envisages, among other things, the possibility to extend the Union rules on social security to all persons rather than to all active people and to all sectors defined by the BIT Convention no. 102, including pre-retirement pensions.

31 An example is the extension of the Community legislation on the coordination of social security schemes for general government employees.

32 This means that, if a person has worked in a Member State where the pension age is 67 and later is working in another State where the pension age is 60, he/she retires at 60 by receiving the pension benefits acquired in the latter State and will wait till he/she is 67 to receive the pension benefit share acquired in the former State (see Commission of the European Communities, *The Community Provisions on Social Security – Your Rights when Moving Within the European Union*, Directorate-General for Employment and Social Affairs, 2000).

33 'Totalization' also affects the pension benefit in other cases; for example, working periods spent elsewhere in Europe are considered if this enables to reach a higher benefit amount (Art. 49 of the Regulation confirmed by many ECJ rulings, among which judgment C-244/97).

34 This does not apply to cases, such as the Italian one, where voluntary insurance is based on closed funds not subject to competitive mechanisms.

35 Commission of the European Communities, *Supplementary Pensions in the Single Market, A Green Paper*, COM(97)283, 1997.

36 The *Green Paper* (see previous note) deals with topics such as the regulation and prudential control on pension funds operating in Europe, in particular minimum obligations on the pension funds pattern of investments; the need to match a good rate of return with stability and risk minimization; the need to allow portability of vested rights for workers withdrawing from a supplementary pension fund because they move to another Member State, at least to the extent guaranteed to those who stop making contributions but remain within the same Member State; the need to guarantee in other Member States the payment of benefits deriving from all contributions paid within all supplementary pension schemes the worker has subscribed to during his/her working life.

37 It is worth noticing that in the *Green Paper*, the European Commission leaves open the discussion on the opportunity to diversify the fiscal treatment of pension funds from those of other forms of life insurance schemes implying life annuities.

38 Apart from those already mentioned, they state the following principles and obligations: the Member States adopt the necessary measures to allow posted workers to maintain a supplementary pension scheme in one Member State during the period of their posting in another Member State (portability of a supplementary pension scheme within the Community); and whenever this is applicable, posted workers and their employers are exempted from any obligation to make contributions to a supplementary pension scheme in the member state where the worker is posted.

39 In 1999, an Action Plan on financial services is also defined: it explicitly sets the objective of defining a consistent European-level legal framework on pension funds.

40 For instance, this may happen if a worker, after working in a TEE (Taxed contributions, Exempt investment income and capital gains of pension funds, Exempt benefits) country, becomes a pensioner and moves to an EET country. Vice versa, cases of total tax exemptions might emerge.

41 For instance, in some Member States tax deductions granted at national level are not extended to contributions paid to pension funds located in another Member State; in others, tax reliefs vary or are subject to requisites different from those adopted for national regimes.

42 The Commission's Communication of 2001 explicitly mentions the *Safir* judgment (C-118/96), whereby a Swedish rule penalizing premiums paid to a life-insurance company established in another Member State created an unjustified obstacle to the free movement of services, and the *Bachmann* judgment (C-204/90), whereby the Court held that the Belgian legislation making the deductibility of pension and life insurance contributions conditional upon the institution being located in Belgium violated the principle of free movement of workers. See Court of Justice *Judgment Safir* (C-118/96), 1998, available on the website http://curia.eu.int/ and Court of Justice *Judgment Bachmann* (C-204/90),1992, available on the website http://curia.eu.int/

43 In the same document, the Commission proposes the creation of pan-European pension institutions (see European Federation for Retirement Provision, *A European Institution for Occupational Retirement Provision – A Single License to Enable Multi-Nationals to Pool their Pension Liabilities and Assets on a Tax Neutral Basis*, July 2000) regarding complementary pensions of multinational companies. Single workers, even after mobility, would continue to be enrolled to the same pension fund, though the enforced legislation would change. However, some might find it smoother to remain in the home country section, which is the principle which sometimes inspires the Commission in the area of complementary pension schemes and is welcome in a mutual recognition perspective.

44 Eleven Member States have the EET system, three have the ETT scheme and two the TEE one, while Germany adopts both the EET and the TEE. Those acronyms are used in the European Commission Communication of 2001.

45 Capuano, R., 'La Direttiva Europea: I punti essenziali dell'accordo politico sul nuovo testo', MEFOP (Sviluppo Mercati Fondi Peusione) vol. 3, no. 10, 2002.

46 Blanchard, O., *Macroeconomics*, Upper Saddle River/New Jersey, Prentice-Hall, 2000.

47 See Padoa Schioppa Kostoris, F. (2000), 'Commentaire' to Freyssinet, J., 'La Réduction du Taux de Chômage: les Enseignements des Expériences Européennes', in Conseil d'Analyse Economique (ed.), *Réduction du chômage: les réussites en Europe*, Paris, 2000, where the author stresses the positive correlation existing in Europe between the unemployment variation in the 1990s and the labour-market degree of overprotection. The paper highlights the positive correlation between the labour-market regulatory rigidities and the unemployment rate in the year 2000.

48 A more general case would be one where each country finds itself in one out of four, rather than out of two possibilities (high wages–low protection, low wages–high protection, high wages–high protection, low wages–low protection): without loss of generality, we treat only the two extreme cases,

because they are sufficient to show that mutual recognition in the labour market enhances mobility, competition and employment. Again, without loss of generality, we only treat the case of two, rather than *n* countries.

49 There is a large literature on this topic: among the most recent papers see, for example, Malinvaud, E., 'Il ruolo delle politiche strutturali a favore dell'occupazione', *Rivista di Politica Economica*, no. 12, 2000, available on the website www.rivistapoliticaeconomica.it

50 In the case of *n* countries, should the principle of mutual recognition be applied, all the unemployed of the countries which are more flexible than the average are likely to find a labour demand in the high–wage/high–protection countries, starting, of course, with the full employment of the least rigid European country. In this case, too, there would be employment growth which would particularly benefit the unemployed of highly flexible countries.

51 Kostoris Padoa Schioppa, F., in collaboration with S. Lubicz, 'State Aid and the Principle of Mutual Recognition', in C.D. Ehlermann and M. Everson (eds), *European Competition Law Annual 1999: State Aid Control in the European Union – Selected Problems*, Oxford, Hart Publishing, 2001.

52 See note 8.

53 Commission of the European Communities, *Commission Communication. Towards a Single Market for Supplementary Pensions. Results of the Consultations on the Green Paper on Supplementary Pensions in the Single Market*, COM(99)134 final, 1999.

6
The Cultural Foundations of Mutual Recognition*

Fiorella Kostoris Padoa Schioppa

From the strain
of binding opposites
comes harmony.

Heraclitus (V b.c.), *Fragments*

From wherever the glance looks up at the sky,
the distance between human and divine is always the same ...
the most beautiful things shall follow us everywhere:
universal nature and one's own virtue.

Seneca (V a.c.), *Consolatio ad Helviam Matrem*

From everywhere it is the same distance to Heaven.

Thomas Moore (1515), *Utopia*

The three forms – *ghettoization, assimilation* (either *closed* or *open*) and *mutual recognition* – discussed in the Preface of this volume have emerged in the course of time and have also been present in the twentieth century. Indeed, there not only exist oscillations in history or

* This text is the English translation of an updated version of a paper published in Italian partly in Padoa Schioppa, F. Kostoris (2001b), 'Riconoscere il diverso: una sfida per l'Europa', *Lettera Internazionale*, no.70, 2001, and partly in Padoa Schioppa, F. Kostoris (2001c), 'Il principio del mutuo riconoscimento e il mercato del lavoro europeo', *Il Mulino*, no.6, December 2001. A French and a Chinese version are also available in Padoa Schioppa, F. Kostoris, 'Reconnaissance Mutuelle', *Transcultura*, Special Edition, 2002, and Padoa Schioppa, F. Kostoris, 'Reconnaissance Mutuelle', *Tractatus*, 2002 respectively. I am grateful to Eloi Laurent, Sascia Lubicz, Nicola Salerno, Grazia Sgarra and particularly to Paolo Reboani for the collaboration given in the writing of chapter 2 of Padoa Schioppa, F. Kostoris (ed.), *ISAE Rapporto sullo stato dell'Unione Europea*, Bologna, Il Mulino, 2001, which includes an old version of this chapter and of the first two sections of Chapter 5 of this volume.

returns to the past, but, as it hopefully will become clear in what follows, there is also a *continuum* for example between philosophies advocating assimilation, those favourable to tolerance, and the principle of mutual recognition. Perhaps only the extremes – represented by mutual recognition and ghettoization – are truly disconnected.

However, in Western societies, the passage from the first to the second and to the third form of the combination of unity with diversity seems to correspond to the transition from a more archaic conception to a more modern form of acceptance of diversity according to the neo-positivist idea (or utopia) of the 'magnificent destinies and progressions'. The thesis is correct but is spoiled by simplistic optimism if it takes the view that movements are irreversible. The Roman Empire was certainly able to assimilate a North African and make him an Emperor, but it could not but ghettoize (before Constantin's Edict of Toleration) the Christians because, as the Jews, they questioned the basic power of the Emperor.

On the one hand, the Old Testament recognizes such a value to diversity as to induce God to destroy the Tower of Babel because, having one single language, that society risked believing itself omnipotent ('Come, let Us go down and there confuse their language, so that they will not understand one another's speech', *Genesis* 11, 7). On the other hand, the Catholic Church after Paul did not know, and did not want to know, how to cultivate that noble idea. Indeed, it rejected as elitist the Hebrew view that 'one must convert no-one' and showed itself disposed to accept everybody by 'generously offering' to each individual – without distinction of race, color, culture, origin – the possibility of salvation through baptism. In substance, it was operating a form of closed assimilation, aimed at saving people irrespective of the implied destruction of previous identities (think of the end of the Aztecs, the Mayas, the Incas), according to an ethics whereby intentions are relevant even though they are profoundly different from results (even 'the road to hell is paved with good intentions').

And, on the one hand, open assimilation, to some extent more respectful of the role of diversity, is fundamentally the daughter of the Renaissance (Marsilio Ficino,[1] 1473, justifies the variety of religions by stating that 'Divine Providence does not permit any part of the world at any time to be completely without religion, although it does allow rites to differ. Perhaps variety of this kind is intended as a beautiful ornament' and Pico della Mirandola, 1486, conceives the idea of a religious syncretism[2]). But, on the other hand, open assimilation also existed in the pre-Christian world, where '*Grecia capta ferum victorem coepit*'. To a certain degree, it was practiced in Cordova and Toledo in the fifteenth century before the arrival of the highly Catholic king and queen Ferdinand of Aragon and Isabella of Castilla (but perhaps even after 1492 there emerged a sort of tolerance towards the *moriscos* and the *marrani*, not always denounced by the Spanish pure blood Arians). It was also practiced outside Europe (for example, in China, which traded with the Western world, adopting some of its rules and exporting some of its own).

As for the logical continuity of the three forms of the unity–diversity combination, it is enough to think of the thread binding the Levinas-styled humanistic monotheism rooted in the Old Testament, with Pauline monotheism, and indeed this last one with the position expressed by Plato and the neo-Platonic movement of the fifteenth century. However, since *c'est le ton qui fait la musique*, one cannot but note a remarkable dissonance between Levinas and the triumphant sense of assimilation 'to one' in neo-Platonic Cardinal Nicholas of Cusa's *coincidentia oppositorum*:

> With a non Jew who leads a moral life – says Levinas (1976) – a Jew can communicate as intimately and religiously as with a Jew. The rabbinical principle whereby the just of all nations participate in the world to come does not only express an eschatological point of view. It affirms the possibility of extreme intimacy beyond the dogma affirmed by one group or another ... This is our universalism ... We have the reputation to think of ourselves as a chosen people and this reputation does much hard to such universalism. The idea of being a chosen people should not be taken as a form of pride. It does not represent the recognition of exceptional rights, but of exceptional duties ... the Hebraic concept of the election of Israel is not anterior to the universalism of a homogenous society where the difference between Jews, Hellenics and Barbarians is abolished. It encompasses this abolition, but remains for a Jew at any moment an indispensable condition for that abolition, a condition which must be recreated in any moment.[3]

Conversely, Plato wrote in his *Parmenide*: 'Again, the like is opposed to the unlike. And the other to the same ... And to be the same with the others is the opposite of being other than the others. And in that it was other it was shown to be like ... Then the one will be both like and unlike the others; like in so far as it is other, and unlike in so far as it is the same'.[4] More than 1,800 years later Cardinal Nicholas of Cusa in his *Apologia doctae ignorantiae* (Cusa, 1440) reiterates the concept of the 'coincidence of opposites' when he affirms that 'there cannot be one maximum of all maxima. Maximum is something that is not opposed by anything else, where maximum and minimum coincide. Thus, the infinite unity is the complication of all things (something embracing all things) and it is called unity because it unifies everything'.[5] The dissonance of Cardinal Nicholas of Cusa becomes in open contrast to Levinas, when in his *The Healing Power of Faith* (1453) recalls that the Jews who reject some Christian beliefs, being 'scarcely numerous ... will not be able to upset the whole world with arms'.[6]

But approximately five hundred years later, thanks to John XXIII first and Paul VI later, the Church position seemed to have completely changed (though it is still unclear whether that change is irreversible or not). Indeed, the *Declaration on the Relation of the Church to non-Christian Religions, Nostra Aetate,* proclaimed by His Holiness Pope Paul VI on 28 October 1965 says:

> Since in the course of centuries not a few quarrels and hostilities have arisen between Christians and Moslems, this sacred Synod urges all to forget the past and to work sincerely for mutual understanding and to preserve as well as to promote together for the benefit of all mankind social justice and moral welfare, as well as peace and freedom ... Since the spiritual patrimony common to Christians and Jews is thus so great, this sacred Synod wants to foster and recommend that mutual understanding and respect which is the fruit, above all, of biblical and theological studies as well as of fraternal dialogues.

And how not to see the continuity–discontinuity dualism in the multiculturalism implicit in the 'separate but equal' doctrine (according to the Supreme Court's landmark *Plessy* v. *Ferguson* ruling of 1896 acknowledging to Blacks the right to accommodations identical to those for Whites, though without the right to share them) and the apartheid emerging in the principle 'equal but separate' (according to the 1954 ruling *Brown* v. *Board of Education* of 1954), both originated by that obscure and yet fascinating concept which is the American *melting pot*?[7]

If we wish to quickly follow the path leading from culture to politics and to economics, it is worth noticing that the principle of the *a priori* coincidence of opposites, characterizing the divine synthesis, is transformed and yet maintains its own nature in the shift from harmony-by-faith to harmony-by-law made by Graziano, the XII-century monk from Bologna and author of the gigantic work *Concordia discordantium canonum*, which has been for centuries the Single Text of the Canonic Law.[8] Once again, the non-contradiction principle is used with the aim of assimilating (namely reducing, if not eliminating) differences.

The elaboration of the political doctrine corresponding to the *Great Inquisitor* culture seems to reach its apex in Hegel's idealism, where the step from unity conquered through a dialectic process of thesis–antithesis–synthesis to the one obtained through the ethical State is more immediate. The nineteenth-century creation and strengthening of National States is its historical-political expression. Indeed, also the aberrations of the twentieth century dictatorships, from the Nazi/Fascist one to that of proletariat, though being neither intrinsically not necessarily correlated to that philosophy, seem to be consistent with that principle (for instance, Hegel, 1821, finds 'the ethical moment of war, which is not to be considered as the absolute evil ... it has its highest meaning inasmuch it maintains the ethical health of peoples').[9]

In economic terms – and that is an aspect worth noticing – those aberrations become assimilation-based policies or approaches favouring apartheid. More precisely, closed assimilation – aiming at including the different provided it stops being different and converts himself/herself, which is the only way to safety – has been characterizing real socialism up to 1989. Stalin's USSR exported its own economic-planning model by imposing it on Central and Eastern Europe with the aim of prompting the regeneration of the 'Socialist man'. Apartheid emerges in the Fascist autarchic regimes (similar to pre-market societies, to agricultural civilizations of self-production and self-consumption): the other remains the other; no form of interchange is even attempted with it; there is no need for it (the regime is absolutely – or thinks itself to be – self-sufficient).

More deeply, on the level of values, the principle of mutual recognition is based on the awareness of the benefits deriving from diversity and is deeply rooted in a basic – though minoritarian – stand of the European cultural tradition. It runs over a 2,000-year span, which is temporal, geographic, ideal and linguistic at the same time. It ranges from Horace's *Epistolae* (around 20 BC) wondering '*quid velit et possit rerum concordia discors*' ('what the discordant harmony of circumstances would and could do')[10] to Nietzsche's *Gay Science* (1882), where he is grateful 'to stand in the midst of this *rerum concordia discors* and of this whole marvelous uncertainty and rich ambiguity of existence'.[11]

Humanism and liberalism both contribute to the idea of harmony *a posteriori*, meant as a way to meet the other through love, understanding or even conflict, in a balance of powers. Major contributions come from Galilei's scientific spirit (1632, 'for my part I consider the earth very noble and admirable precisely because of the diverse alterations, changes, generations, etc. that occur in it incessantly'),[12] with the consequent modern evolutionism, and from Montesquieu's spirit of law

(1748), with his idea of the separation and independence of the executive, legislative and judiciary powers.[13] The ethics of results of protestant origin and the one inspired by Machiavelli's *The Prince* (1513, 'he who neglects what is done for what ought to be done, sooner effects his ruin than his preservation');[14] Vico's heterogenesis of ends (1725, 'this world without doubt has issued from a mind often diverse, at times quite contrary, and always superior to the particular ends that men had proposed to themselves'),[15] but also Adam Smith's 'invisible hand' (1776)[16] and the whole English-American empirism, show that heterogeneous interests and the darwinian fight for survival provoke in general the best social results. Levinas' *Humanism of the Other* (1972) puts together the ancient and modern humanist heritage, from the Old Testament to the Italian Renaissance to French Enlightenment.[17]

Nobody seems better than Todorov (1992)[18] – or Braudel in his *Grammaire des civilizations*(1993)[19] – to describe this patrimony in his European historic path:

> Western Europe has sought to assimilate what is alien, to force the disappearance of the exterior being and, for the most part, it has succeeded. Its way of life and its values have been spread around the world. As Columbus wanted, those who have been colonized have adopted out customs and clothes ... I think that this period of European history is disappearing today.
>
> The representatives of Western society no longer believe so ingenuously in their own superiority and the assimilation movement is coming to an end ... We are seeking to bring together what we feel are the best terms of the alternative, that is we want equality without it meaning identity, but we also want difference without it to become superiority/inferiority ... we want to resume the sense of a society without loosing the sense of individual.

The recognition of what is alien and diverse, Todorov recalls (1989), is but the result of the awareness that 'each human being is multi-fold and any attempt to unify him/her ends in mutilation'.[20]

Thus, the principle of mutual recognition is, in some aspects, as old as the Tower of Babel, but, for other aspects, is a new discovery of the twentieth century and is an ongoing social and political conquest. This is because globalization has brought about daily contact with diversity, and only now is the idea of belonging to heterogeneous civilizations labelled as a richness, which would be absurd to throw away, though we all are (and want to be) part and parcel of a single society. Mutual recognition is the privileged instrument transforming each individual into a citizen of the world, an *n*-component vector which cannot be found identical in any other human being. Like DNA, these components belong to one single individual who – despite all this – is also part of the surrounding society.[21] If one looks at ghettoization or assimilation, each single member of a group must be (and preferably is) represented by an *n*-component vector (almost) identical to the one characterizing any other individual of that same group. Today the real challenge – for example, in our continent – is making European citizens of Italian language, of Serb-Orthodox religion, of French culture, living in England, residing in a country Dutch-styled manor, live in harmony.

Only mutual recognition can do that, as it separates rights (duties) and geographical location: the law enforced in a Member State is enforceable in another Member State thanks to the circulation of goods, services and capital, or even mobile workers (if our proposals are accepted). Should mutual recognition enter the labour market or social protection schemes, whenever an individual moves within Europe, he/she bears with him/herself also a *social* capital consisting of the whole economic-judicial aspects of his/her home State. Rights would no longer be contingent on geography, as each worker would bear them with themselves when moving within Europe, thus embodying the motto '*omnia mea mecum porto*'.

The intention of mutual recognition in Europe is therefore clear, but it remains unclear how we will get there, how to permanently reconcile individual diversities with a cohesive society, how to identify that minimum common framework possessing the various *n*-component vectors to arrive at a point where each can live with the other in civility and harmony. Perhaps the solution is a wise, pragmatic mixture of logic and experimentation, of deduction and induction, of small steps subject to trials and errors.

To find a theoretical, and yet operative response to those questions means to go towards the future in a vision that, if not historical-theological, is at least evolutionary-innovating. European society is asking for this response ever-more pressingly, as recently indicated by the Eurobarometer survey (SORA, 2001), where 'the number of those considering immigrants as people able to enrich the life of one's own country has grown from 33% in 1997 to 48% in 2000'. But, even more, Europe needs that – in spite of what we have just stated – because only 39 percent of the population is ready 'to accept immigrants coming from other Member States in one's own country of residence without restrictions'. We therefore have the duty to learn and teach'.[22]

Notes

1 Ficino M. [1473], *Della religione cristiana*, in Sancipriano M (ed.) *Opera omnia*, Turin, Botteghe d'Erasmo, 1962.
2 Pico della Mirandola G. [1486], *Oration on the Dignity of Man*, Washington D.C., Regnery Publishing, 1996.
3 Levinas, E., *Difficile liberté*, Paris, Albin Michel, 1976.
4 Plato [about 370 BC], 'Parmenide', in *Oeuvres Completes Thetete/Parmenide/Critias/Les Lois/etc.*, vol. 2, French and European Publications, 1999.
5 Cusa, Nicholas of [1440], 'On Learned Ignorance', in *Selected Spiritual Writings*, Mahwah, Paulist Press, 1997.
6 Cusa, Nicholas of [1453], 'The Healing Power of Faith', in *Selected Spiritual Writings*, Mahwah, Paulist Press, 1997.
7 See Supreme Court of the United States, *Judgment Hammer Plessy* v. *Ferguson*, 1896, and Supreme Court of the United States *Judgment Brown* v. *Board of Education*, 1954.
8 Graziano [about 1140], 'Concordia discordantium canonum', in *The Treatise on Law (Decretum DD 1–20) with the Ordinary Gloss*, Chicago, The Catholic University of America Press, 1993.
9 Hegel, G.F.W. [1821], *Elements of the Philosophy of Right*, Cambridge, Cambridge University Press, 1991.
10 Horace [about 20 BC], *Horace's Satires and Epistles*, New York, W.W. Norton & Co., 1977.
11 Nietzsche, F. [1882], *The Gay Science*, Vancouver WA, Vintage Books, 1974.
12 Galilei, G. [1632], *Dialogue Concerning the Two Chief World Systems: Ptolemaic and Copernican*, Berkeley, University of California Press, 1967.
13 Montesquieu, Ch. De [1748], *Spirit of the Laws*, New York, Free Press, 1970.
14 Machiavelli, N. [1513], *The Prince*, New York, Bantam Classics, 1984.
15 Vico, G.B. [1725], *New Science*, New York, Penguin USA, 2000.
16 Smith, A. [1776], *The Wealth of Nations*, Bungay, Suffolk, Penguin, 1982.
17 Levinas, E., *Humanisme de l'Autre Homme*, Saint Clement la Rivière, Fata Morgana, 1972.
18 Todorov, T. [1992], *The Conquest of America*, Norman, University of Oklahoma Press, 1999.
19 Braudel, F., *Grammaire des Civilizations*, Paris, Flammarion, 1993.
20 Todorov, T., *Nous et les Autres*, Paris, Éditions du Seuil, 1989.
21 The exhibition *'Tous parents tous différents'* organised at the Musée de l'Homme in Paris illustrates the idea that race distinctions are pointless, and not because races do not exist, but because there are too many races, as they are not five, but more than 5 billions, that is as many as our DNAs.
22 SORA (Institute for Social Research and Analysis), *Attitudes towards Minority Groups in the European Union*, European Monitoring Centre on Racism and Xenophobia, 2001, available on the website www.eumc.eu.int/publications/eurobarometer/EB2001.pdf

Index